T0275130

Safe Gun Ownership

by Greg Lickenbrock

A Wiley Brand

Safe Gun Ownership For Dummies®

Published by: **John Wiley & Sons, Inc.,** 111 River Street, Hoboken, NJ 07030-5774, www.wiley.com

Copyright © 2022 by John Wiley & Sons, Inc., Hoboken, New Jersey

Media and software compilation copyright © 2022 by John Wiley & Sons, Inc. All rights reserved.

Published simultaneously in Canada

For general information on our other products and services, please contact our Customer Care Department within the U.S. at 877-762-2974, outside the U.S. at 317-572-3993, or fax 317-572-4002. For technical support, please visit https://hub.wiley.com/community/support/dummies.

Wiley publishes in a variety of print and electronic formats and by print-on-demand. Some material included with standard print versions of this book may not be included in e-books or in print-on-demand. If this book refers to media such as a CD or DVD that is not included in the version you purchased, you may download this material at http://booksupport.wiley.com. For more information about Wiley products, visit www.wiley.com.

Library of Congress Control Number: 2022941234

ISBN: 978-1-119-89484-1 (pbk); ISBN 978-1-119-89485-8 (epdf); ISBN 978-1-119-89486-5 (epub)

SKY10035280_071422

Contents at a Glance

Table of Contents

Introduction

Americans own an estimated 400 million firearms. They're deeply engrained in U.S. culture — and they're deeply polarizing. Think of all the history and politics wrapped around guns. But regardless of whether you love them or hate them, or whether you grew up around guns or didn't, I bet that if you take a step back from those experiences and perspectives, you'll agree that the United States has a serious problem.

In 2020 alone, more than 45,000 Americans died from firearms. That sobering figure includes homicides, suicides, and accidental shootings, many of which were probably preventable.

Call me an idealist, but I believe gun owners ultimately have the biggest role to play in bringing that number down to zero. It's up to us to practice gun safety, preach gun safety to others, and hold each other accountable. That's why I've written this book, and I'm glad you're joining me on this journey.

About This Book

Safe Gun Ownership For Dummies is dedicated to helping you become a safe, responsible gun owner, whether you're brand new to firearms, considering owning one, or already have a few. It covers gun safety rules, the laws and regulations surrounding gun ownership, secure storage requirements, shooting tips, and much more.

Want to learn how guns and ammunition work? This is the book for you. I also take you through the buying process, help you sign up for a high-quality firearms training course near you, and explain how to handle guns in the safest way possible. This book can also give you a leg up in sifting through some of the misinformation about firearms perpetuated in news stories, movies, TV shows, and every corner of the internet.

I guarantee that everyone can learn something from this book — even old pros who could use some refreshers when it comes to safe gun handling.

Finally, because the gun world uses a lot of jargon that developed centuries ago — including quite a few misnomers — as you read, pay attention to any words that appear in *italics*. These are gun-centric terms that I define along the way to make your life easier. (Don't worry, there won't be a vocabulary quiz at the end. Or will there?!)

Foolish Assumptions

You know what happens when you assume . . . But for this book, I had to make some assumptions about you without even knowing you. Sorry!

The first assumption is that you don't have much experience with firearms. This is a way to reach as many readers as possible; the book would look very different — and be its own special kind of boring — if I were only writing for retired military or law enforcement personnel, for example, or those who have extensive firearms experience.

However, if you do know your way around guns, my next assumption is that you're willing to listen. You might learn a few things in the pages ahead.

My last assumption is that you're a thoughtful, caring person who can legally own a firearm and will do whatever is necessary to safely handle that firearm, secure it when it isn't being used, and won't let it fall into the wrong hands. I'm assuming that you're a good, responsible person and don't ever want to see anyone hurt. Prove me right.

Icons Used in This Book

As you read this book, you'll encounter a few special icons in the margins.

TIP

Tips are little nuggets of information that will hopefully save you time and effort in some way, shape, or form. The tips in this book could be shortcuts, noteworthy gun-handling techniques, or links to proven resources that will expand your firearms knowledge.

WARNING

The Warning icons throughout this book will help you steer clear of some of the lethal and legal dangers that go along with firearms. I don't want you to get hurt or hurt someone else, nor do I want you to end up on the wrong side of the law, so please pay extra-special attention to these cautionary notes.

That said, nothing in this book should be construed as legal advice. I'm not a lawyer, so if you have any questions about any firearm-related laws and regulations where you live, please consult a lawyer.

TECHNICAL STUFF

This icon helps signify more advanced gun knowledge, including specialized tips and techniques as well as discussions of the science behind certain phenomena. If you're brand new to firearms, feel free to skip these passages. I won't be mad.

REMEMBER

The Reminder icon is paired with essential information that you really need to memorize within each chapter. Most of this material centers around keeping you and your family safe as well as other shooters or hunters, depending on the situation at hand.

Beyond the Book

This book is really just the beginning when it comes to learning about guns and gun safety. Not only should you sign up for a firearms training course after you read through it, but you should also check out the Cheat Sheet prepared specifically for this book, which you can view by visiting www.dummies.com and entering *Safe Gun Ownership For Dummies* in the Search box.

This Cheat Sheet is a quick-reference guide that offers several gun safety rules to live by as well as a checklist to help you secure your firearm at home and prevent unauthorized access. On top of that, the Cheat Sheet includes a short glossary of gun-centric terms in case you need a reminder.

Bookmark the Cheat Sheet and return to it often!

Where to Go from Here

To get the most out of this book, I recommend reading it from front to back, beginning to end, in order like the good, voracious reader that you are. The material is arranged in the same order I'd offer it in during an in-person firearms training course.

However, I know that you're busy — never too busy for safety, I hope! — or you might know a few of these topics already, so feel free to skip around. Just know that you might miss some lifesaving advice, cringey jokes, and detailed illustrations along the way.

1

Getting Started with Gun Safety

Chapter **1**

The Basics of Safe Gun Ownership

What makes a safe, responsible gun owner, and what differentiates them from someone who simply bought a firearm without a second thought?

Therein lies the answer. It all comes down to *thinking.*

A responsible gun owner always thinks about safety and the risks of owning a gun. They think about their family members, their friends and neighbors, other gun owners, and people who don't own guns. They consider every angle, including the example they're setting for everyone else, and they aren't afraid to call other gun owners out for unsafe or irresponsible behaviors.

They think before they shoot, before they ever reach for a firearm. They think about how they will maintain control over their weapon in every situation — handling it safely at the range, for example, and securing it when it isn't being used — to ensure that it's never misused or falls into the wrong hands.

As you can see, a responsible gun owner has a lot to consider, and throughout this book, I try to help you inhabit that role and turn those thoughts into actions, turn that mindset into a way of living.

To kick things off in this chapter, I explore the most common reasons people own firearms and help you *think about* some truly important aspects of owning a gun before you hit your local gun shop or sporting goods store. (See what I did there? You're already getting responsible!)

Also in this chapter, you discover the four lifesaving rules of gun safety and how to safely check to see whether a gun is loaded.

Common Reasons to Own a Firearm

If you want to learn more about firearms or are thinking about purchasing one, it might help to understand why other people choose to own them. There are several legitimate reasons or justifications for owning a gun, including self-defense, hunting, competitive shooting, and more.

The emphasis here is on *legitimate* uses. Some people seem to own guns just to brag about them or advertise them in social media posts, but those reasons don't make the cut in my book because they aren't very responsible. Sorry! #nohardfeelings.

REMEMBER

As a responsible gun owner, you should only ever use guns safely, secure them when they aren't being used, and make sure they don't end up in the wrong hands. Showing off your guns on social media could intimidate others, for example, or tell someone you have firearms worth stealing.

Gaining a sense of security

According to a Pew Research poll conducted in 2017, 67 percent of gun owners in the U.S. claim that they own a firearm for "protection." That's a lot of people. For reference, the 2021 National Firearms Survey estimates that 81.4 million Americans currently own a gun.

Maybe you want to protect your home or have a little extra peace of mind as you walk to your car in a poorly lit parking lot. I get it. There's no denying the fact that firearms, as lethal instruments, can indeed help you ward off those intent on harming you and your loved ones.

However, as I stress throughout this book, possessing a firearm does not by itself automatically make you safer. To be a responsible gun owner, you have to take a few additional steps, like talking to your family about owning a firearm and teaching them the safety rules (as I discuss in Chapter 5), securing the gun when you aren't using it (Chapter 6), and obtaining training from a certified firearms instructor (Chapter 12), to name just a few examples.

REMEMBER

You also need to remember that a firearm is only ever a *last resort* when it comes to personal and home defense. To learn more about that particular aspect of gun ownership, head to Chapter 16.

Hunting and recreational shooting

For hundreds of years, people have used firearms to hunt animals and quite literally "bring home the bacon." (I have so many more jokes for you in the pages ahead. Just you wait.)

Today, along with harvesting meat, people take to the hunting fields to enjoy the Great Outdoors and make memories with friends and family. Done correctly, hunting is actually a way to preserve the land and wildlife for future generations, too, through the fees collected from permits and licenses, as I explain in Chapter 15.

Hunting also gives people a chance to hone their shooting skills, or *marksmanship* — just like recreational shooting, which includes casual trips to the firing range to hit targets as well as more formal shooting competitions. I believe that you should try to learn from every shot you take to develop your accuracy, whether you're plinking steel targets with a .22-caliber rifle in your free time or testing your skills on the clock against other competitors. In this way, you're always growing as a shooter and gun owner.

Hunting and target shooting have spawned entire categories of firearms built specifically for those tasks, and both pursuits have specific rules and regulations to ensure that everyone stays safe and has a good time.

TIP

If you're interested in hunting or competitive shooting, turn to Chapter 15.

Taking part in history

As I discuss in Chapter 3, firearms have played a significant role in shaping human history. Think of all the conflicts and wars waged around the world with guns large and small. Museum collections also showcase guns owned and used by famous and infamous people alike, or those given to royal figures with silver and gold embellishments and delicate engraving as symbols of power and wealth.

Learning about guns is one way to learn about history.

Some people own firearms — either authentic models from a certain period or modern replicas designed to look and operate like their historic forebears — to reenact major battles from the Revolutionary War or Civil War, for example, to relive history and give onlookers a greater sense of how things happened so long ago.

Other people may prefer to collect notable models — maybe guns from a certain time period, or a whole series from one manufacturer or another — as a way of preserving history and passing it on to future generations.

Gun collections can be very personal, too. I've lost count of the number of gun owners I've met over the years who still have the shotguns or rifles their grand-parents used for hunting, or fought with in World War II. In this way, they're holding onto pieces of history and their families.

REMEMBER

If you ever inherit such a collection, you'll need a sturdy safe that'll withstand the test of time and keep out moisture. To learn more about secure storage and humidity's effect on firearms, turn to Chapter 6.

Things to Consider Before Purchasing a Firearm

The decision to purchase a gun should never be taken lightly. Firearms are inher-ently dangerous. More than 45,000 people were killed by guns in the U.S. in 2020 alone, and a study published in the *Annals of Internal Medicine* in 2014 shows that owning a gun doubles your chances of being murdered and triples your chances of dying by suicide. In fact, those heightened risks apply to anyone who lives under the same roof as you. So if you're thinking about purchasing one, you have some serious questions to ask yourself, and some serious safety rules to implement, in the hope that you and your family do not add to those heartbreaking statistics.

By the way, if you already own a gun but haven't thought through these same questions before, it's never too late to start!

How will you secure it?

This is easily the most important question to ask yourself if you're thinking of buying a firearm. In a perfect world, the employees at your local gun shop or sporting goods store would show you some of the gun safes they have for sale *before* you start looking at firearms to give you a better idea of all the options available on the market.

If you aren't taking your gun to the range or out hunting, for example, it needs to be locked up in a safe in your home so that no unauthorized users can get ahold of it and do bad things with it.

As I discuss in Chapter 6, brand-new guns typically come with cable locks, but they're easily picked and defeated. So how about a small, steel handgun "vault" that pops open in microseconds after reading your fingerprint? Or a larger safe that requires a keycode for entry and can hold a few rifles and handguns? You can find a gun safe at any price point, from $25 to $10,000 and beyond, with a wide range of security features.

You'll need ammunition for that gun, and other accessories, so why not add a safe to the shopping list, too?

Who will have access to it?

This question goes hand in hand with the last one. When you secure your gun in a safe, you're making it harder for unauthorized individuals — including thieves, children, and other people you wouldn't want handling a firearm — from getting their hands on the thing you may have purchased to protect yourself or your family. You don't want it causing irreparable damage instead.

It isn't enough to hide the gun, and you can't assume that the firearm is too complicated to fire, or that the trigger is too heavy, for example. Sadly, curious children prove these statements wrong every single day.

I also want to point out that several states and Washington, D.C., have "child access prevention" (CAP) laws in place that, although they vary in some ways, penalize those who negligently store their firearms around children.

On the other hand, if you have a spouse or significant other, will they be able to open the safe and grab the gun if, say, someone breaks into your home? More importantly, do they know the four rules of gun safety? Have they taken a firearms training course? Which leads to the next question . . .

When will you attend a training course?

Imagine that you've never driven a car before. You've never taken a driver's ed course; family and friends never taught you how to drive. It would be irresponsible for you to then get behind the wheel of a Lamborghini — a supercar that costs well over $200,000 and can travel faster than 200 miles per hour — right? No right-minded salesperson is going to allow that test drive.

Now think about a 9mm handgun, which can launch bullets that travel well over 700 miles per hour. Would you buy one without taking a "shooter's ed" course?

I can't overstate the value of firearms training. In fact, go ahead and add it to your gun-purchasing checklist. Got a safe? Excellent! Enroll in a training course? Even better. You're on the path to becoming a responsible gun owner.

I know you're going to read every page of this book twice and recommend it to everyone you see on the streets. Obviously. But as much as I hate to admit it, I can only take you so far. A training course will give you invaluable hands-on experience with firearms and allow you to build muscle memory in a safe, controlled environment under the watchful eye of a certified instructor.

A good trainer can teach you how to handle a gun safely, shoot accurately, build your situational awareness and decision-making skills, and troubleshoot malfunctions. No, watching movies and playing video games won't cut it, and some states even require that you attend a training course before you can purchase a firearm or obtain a concealed-carry permit.

TIP

For more advice on training courses and how to find the right one near you, turn to Chapter 12.

The Four Rules of Gun Safety

Firearms are lethal tools that don't offer second chances. I can't stress that point enough. If you aren't careful when you handle a gun, you could kill or seriously injure yourself or another person, or even multiple people, in a split second that can't be taken back. There's no "undo" button here.

REMEMBER

To prevent such a tragedy from occurring, *you must always follow the four rules of gun safety.* Created several decades ago and found throughout the gun world, they're often called the four "universal" rules because they apply in any context or situation, whether you're at home or at a gun shop, at a shooting range, deep in the woods on a hunting excursion, or anywhere in between.

Anytime you're in the presence of a firearm, these four rules should govern your every action. I want you to swear by them, teach them to everyone you can, and call out anyone who breaks these rules. Because if you don't, that person could hurt others.

These four safety rules are the foundation of responsible gun ownership. I bring them up and repeat them throughout this book, but you should consider book-marking or dog-earing these pages and regularly returning to them until you've memorized the rules.

Rule 1: Treat all guns as if they are loaded

Whenever you encounter or handle a firearm, you should assume that it's loaded with ammunition and capable of firing — even if someone has told you otherwise. If you're handed a gun, it's up to you to verify that the gun is empty. Accidents happen when people assume that a firearm is unloaded and don't check its status. So, depending on the model, you must remove the magazine, retract the slide or bolt, and inspect the chamber to ensure that no ammunition is present.

I dive into that process in greater detail at the end of this chapter, but you should feel free to ask for help if you need it. No one will judge you.

This "all guns are always loaded" mindset is part of being a safe gun owner, and inspecting a firearm to ensure that it's empty goes a long way toward showing others that you're knowledgeable about firearms and respect them.

Rule 2: Never let your muzzle cover anything you aren't willing to destroy

The phrasing here is heavy, but rightfully so. Firearms are capable of destroying things, so you must always be aware of your surroundings and keep the gun pointed in a safe direction. In many situations, including inside your home, that means keeping the muzzle, or front end of the barrel, pointing straight down toward the ground. That way if the gun does fire for whatever reason, the bullet will hopefully strike the ground without injury.

If you're at a shooting range, that safe direction will always be downrange, or toward the target. Following this rule to a T means that you keep the firearm pointing toward the target as you take the gun out of its case, load it, shoot it, unload it, set it down, and put it back in its case when you're done. If you have any questions, ask the range safety officer.

If you're out hunting, you might carry the gun with the barrel pointing toward the ground or straight up toward the sky. This is especially important because you might have other hunters walking in front of you.

Even if your firearm is unloaded, etiquette dictates that you still keep it pointing in a safe direction. Doing so shows other gun owners that you care about their safety as well as your own.

Rule 3: Keep your finger off the trigger until you're on target and ready to shoot

Whenever you handle a firearm, you must have good "trigger discipline," which means keeping your index finger away from the trigger and outside the trigger-guard, the plastic or metal loop that surrounds the trigger. Instead, you should keep your index finger fully extended and resting against the side of the gun, just above the triggerguard. This is known as "indexing" your trigger finger.

You may place your finger on the trigger only when you're on target, your weapon's sights are aligned, you know what is beyond your target (as I explain in a moment), and you've been authorized to shoot and can safely do so. If any of those conditions haven't been met, your finger must stay away from the trigger.

In other words, 99.9 percent of the time that you're holding a gun, including when you first pick it up, reload it, unload it, fix a malfunction, and so on, your finger should be indexed alongside the gun's frame or receiver.

Rule 4: Be sure of your target and what is behind it

You are responsible for every round that leaves your gun — and whatever it comes into contact with. This is why it is vitally important that you take the time to identify both your target and what's beyond it before you even think about pulling the trigger.

To put it simply, bullets travel at blistering speeds, which is what allows them to penetrate through multiple surfaces before eventually slowing down and coming to a stop.

Many people own guns to protect their homes, but as I mention in Chapter 5, if you attempt to shoot a deadly home invader, for example, that bullet can easily pass through an interior or exterior wall, or several, and hit a family member or another innocent bystander. It could also ricochet off a hard surface and cause more damage.

REMEMBER

Because of a bullet's capabilities, you must always be keenly aware of your surroundings, and if you don't know what's behind your target, *don't take the shot.* If there's a chance that you might not hit what you're aiming at, or that the bullet could stray or ricochet and hit someone else, again, *don't take the shot.*

Knowing other important rules to follow

Although the four rules of gun safety are the most widely accepted and publicized rules, they aren't the only ones you have to follow. I've already mentioned a few in this chapter alone, and I cover more in the pages ahead, including these:

>> Never touch a firearm after you've had any drugs or alcohol.

>> Secure your firearm in a safe when it isn't being used to keep it away from unauthorized users.

>> Wear eye and ear protection when operating a firearm.

>> Use only the correct ammunition in your gun.

>> Ensure that the gun is safe to operate, and if you have any doubts, unload it completely and let a professional inspect it.

>> Always listen to and obey authorities when it comes to using firearms, including police officers, game wardens, and range staff.

Again, these are just a few examples. Certain activities and locations require additional safety precautions and regulations, which you'll discover as you read this book — such as in Chapter 12, where I discuss some of the most common rules posted at shooting ranges.

Checking Whether a Gun is Loaded

Remember that first safety rule: If you encounter a gun, regardless of context, assume that it's loaded. Even if someone says a gun is empty and then hands it to you, you still need to verify that the gun is actually unloaded. Skipping that step can lead to tragedy — and it happens every single day.

TIP

In Chapter 3, I cover all the different types of firearms you might come across today so that you can identify them and learn how they work, and in Chapter 7, I discuss in further detail the steps to safely unload a gun.

Whether you can identify the type of gun or not, you need to 1) keep the gun pointed in a safe direction and 2) keep your fingers away from the trigger.

The next steps change depending on the firearm at hand. If you have access to the gun's user manual, great — that'll tell you exactly how to determine whether the gun is unloaded. If you don't have that manual handy, however, I can help.

Checking semi-automatic pistols

To determine whether a semi-automatic pistol is loaded, follow these steps to remove the magazine *and* check the *chamber*, the rear portion of the barrel (far too many people skip that second part):

1. **Look for the magazine release, which is a small button or lever usually to the rear of the trigger and just below it.**

2. **Engage the button or lever to make the magazine drop free from the gun's grip.**

   If the magazine doesn't drop free, you might need to tug on the base of it to help free it.

3. **Set the magazine aside.**

4. **Retract the slide by holding the gun's grip in your strong, or dominant, hand, and then use your nondominant hand to grab the slide by the rear serrations and pull it back toward you.**

   Pointing the gun straight up as you pull rearward on the slide can help a round fall out of the chamber as well.

   Pulling the slide back far enough should make it lock back on its own. If it doesn't, you might need to engage a small button called the slide release. Otherwise, a heavy-duty spring inside the gun will keep trying to return the slide to its forwardmost position.

REMEMBER

5. **Look inside the gun to see if the chamber is empty — and then check it again.**

   If you've locked the slide back, you might even want to stick a finger into the rear of the barrel to ensure that it's clear. (If you can't fully lock the slide back for whatever reason, avoid using your finger because it'll get caught in the slide. Ouch!)

Checking revolvers

To determine whether a revolver is loaded, follow these steps:

1. **Locate the cylinder release.**

   This release is a textured button usually on the left side of the gun and just behind the cylinder, which is the round or cylindrical component that holds all the ammunition.

2. **Use your thumb to activate the cylinder release, which could mean pushing it forward or pulling it rearward.**

3. **Pivot the cylinder to the side so that it sticks out of the frame.**

4. **Carefully check every single chamber, or hole, within the cylinder to make sure no ammunition is loaded.**

   You should see daylight through each chamber.

5. **Empty the cylinder quickly by either pointing the gun straight up and letting the rounds or empty casings fall out, or by pushing on the ejector (the rod protruding from the front of the cylinder).**

   Either technique should clear every chamber in one motion.

Checking rifles or shotguns with detachable magazines

To determine whether this type of rifle or shotgun is loaded, follow these steps:

1. **Look for the magazine release, a button or lever located somewhere near the magazine.**

2. **Press the release to make the magazine drop away from the gun.**

3. **Locate the bolt, a cylindrical component of the gun that is partially exposed through the ejection port.**

   Your gun's user manual can show you where the bolt and bolt/charging handle are positioned.

4. **Retract the bolt by pulling the bolt handle or charging handle rearward until the bolt locks back.**

5. **Inspect the gun's chamber to ensure that it's empty.**

Checking rifles or shotguns with internal magazines

To find out whether a rifle or shotgun with an internal or nondetachable magazine is loaded, follow these steps:

1. **Keep your finger away from the trigger.**

2. **Retract the bolt to the rear. Depending on the model, this might mean:**

   - Pulling a bolt or charging handle back as far as you can

   - Pivoting a lever below the gun's receiver

   - Retracting a pump underneath the barrel

   You might have to disengage a safety button or lever as well.

3. **Check the firearm's chamber for ammunition.**

4. **To empty any ammunition that's inside the magazine, run the bolt forward and rearward repeatedly — keeping your fingers away from the trigger — until every cartridge or shotgun shell has been ejected from the gun.**

   For some rifles, you might also be able to pivot open a bottom floorplate and remove all the ammunition simultaneously.

To learn more about various types of firearms and the differences between, say, internal and detachable magazines, head to Chapter 3.

REMEMBER

Chapter **2**

Legally Speaking

When it comes to guns laws in the United States, the Second Amendment gets all the attention. Honestly, I can't think of another amendment in the Bill of Rights with as much fervent support. Gun enthusiasts like to don "Shall not be infringed!" T-shirts and remind each other to "exercise their 2A rights." But you don't exactly hear people chanting, "No quartering of soldiers!"

Where's the 3A love?!

In all seriousness, the Second Amendment is a key aspect to understanding gun ownership in America, but since it was ratified over 230 years ago, a number of firearm regulations have been enacted on the federal, state, and local levels, and the Supreme Court has played a major role, too. A lot has changed in those intervening centuries!

Luckily, I designed this chapter to help you navigate the maze of federal regulations, Supreme Court decisions, and state and local ordinances related to firearms. I want you to stay on the right side of the law, whether you're brand new to guns or are considering buying another one.

WARNING

Although I'm well versed in America's gun laws, I'm also not a lawyer. (My friends and family would never hear the end of it if I passed the bar.) So if you have any questions concerning the legalities of owning a firearm, consult a lawyer in your area.

Understanding U.S. Federal Gun Regulations

Every year, tens of thousands of Americans die in car accidents. To counter the dangers posed by motor vehicles, the U.S. government mandates that cars come with turn signals, seatbelts, airbags, backup cameras, and other safety equipment, and that they meet or exceed certain crash-testing standards, to name a few examples of safety measures. State governments also have laws concerning licenses, registration, speed limits, drunk driving, and much more.

So far, these safeguards have worked in reducing the traffic fatality rate. Although the country experienced more than 50,000 traffic fatalities per year in the 1960s, before many of these regulations were put in place, that number was down to just over 32,000 by 2014, according to the National Highway Traffic Safety Administration (NHTSA).

Similarly, federal, state, and local authorities have created certain guard rails or "rules of the road," if you will, for firearms because they are inherently dangerous. To understand the federal regulations, we have to go back to 1791.

The Second Amendment and its interpretations

Of all the amendments to the U.S. Constitution, the Second Amendment is perhaps the most controversial. Ratified on December 15, 1791, along with nine other amendments that later became known as the Bill of Rights, the Second Amendment states, "A well regulated Militia, being necessary to the security of a free State, the right of the people to keep and bear Arms, shall not be infringed."

It's a short sentence that leaves a frustrating amount of room for interpretation. For example, some people take the second half — "the right of the people to keep and bear Arms" — to mean that every individual has a constitutionally protected right to "keep and bear Arms." This is known as the "individual rights theory," and some believe it prohibits, or at least restricts, the federal government from regulating the ownership of weapons.

Others point to the beginning of the sentence — the "well regulated Militia" clause — to argue that the Framers of the Constitution only intended to restrict Congress from infringing on a *state*'s ability to raise a militia from civilians if needed, and that federal, state, and local authorities can still regulate firearms without impacting constitutionally protected rights. This is known as the "collective rights theory."

What does history say? James Madison, who proposed the Second Amendment, originally wrote about the topic in *Federalist No. 46*, in a time when people feared that a strong centralized federal government could potentially become too powerful like the British monarchy and rule over the states. Madison argued that state militias "would be able to repel the danger" of a federal army in that situation.

Moreover, the Bill of Rights limited the *federal* government's powers, not the states' powers. The Fourteenth Amendment, ratified in 1868, says that "No state shall make or enforce any law which shall abridge the privileges or immunities of citizens of the United States; nor shall any state deprive any person of life, liberty, or property, without due process of law; nor deny to any person within its jurisdiction the equal protection of the laws." The Supreme Court has interpreted this amendment to extend most of the constraints in the Bill of Rights to the states.

Finally, throughout American history, the federal government, as well as state and local governments, have regulated the ownership and use of firearms, as I discuss in the pages ahead.

The National Firearms Act of 1934

To fight the gangland crime of the Prohibition era, with incidents like the St. Valentine's Day Massacre of 1929 capturing headlines across the country, Congress enacted the first major federal regulations on firearms.

The National Firearms Act (NFA) of 1934 requires the registration of certain weapons considered too dangerous to own among civilians, including:

>> **Machine guns,** or weapons that automatically fire more than one shot per trigger pull

>> **Silencers,** or sound suppressors, that muffle the sound of gunfire and make it difficult to identify where a shot came from

>> **Short-barreled rifles,** or shoulder-fired weapons with rifled barrels shorter than 16 inches

>> **Short-barreled shotguns,** or shoulder-fired weapons with smoothbore barrels shorter than 18 inches

>> **Other easily concealable weapons** that fall into an "any other weapon" (AOW) category

I know those last three are a little confusing. Why do rifle and shotgun barrels have to be at least 16 and 18 inches long, respectively?

The original intent of the NFA was to restrict *handguns* — which, to this day, account for most gun deaths in the U.S. — as well as any other firearm that someone could hide on their person, say, under a trench coat or in a small bag. Think of the Tommy guns (shown in Figure 2-1) and sawed-off shotguns that gangsters unleashed on unsuspecting victims. But somewhere along the way, Congress dropped the handgun provision and kept the rest.

FIGURE 2-1:
The NFA placed restrictions on fully automatic weapons like Tommy guns.

REMEMBER

If you need help distinguishing among handguns, rifles, and shotguns, I've got you covered in Chapter 3.

To own an NFA-regulated item, such as a silencer or short-barreled rifle, you must submit an application to the Bureau of Alcohol, Tobacco, Firearms and Explosives (ATF) with a copy of your fingerprints, a passport-style photo, and a $200 payment known as a "tax stamp." Applicants then undergo a strict background check that can take several months to make sure they're eligible to own one of these items.

If you're approved, you may take possession of the NFA weapon, but because of the registration requirements, if you ever want to sell it or transfer ownership to another individual, they must submit their own application, pay the $200 tax stamp, and so on.

According to the ATF, the paperwork and $200 tax stamp — equivalent to $4,224 in today's dollars — were meant to "discourage or eliminate transactions in these firearms," but the $200 tax has not changed since 1934.

That said, the system appears to work. Crimes are rarely committed with properly registered NFA firearms, and federal regulations impose stiff penalties on those who possess *unregistered* NFA firearms. For example, if you alter your gun's internal components so that it can fire more than one shot per trigger pull, you're facing up to 10 years in prison, a $250,000 fine, or both.

The Federal Firearms Act of 1938

In 1938, Congress enacted the Federal Firearms Act (FFA), which required that gun makers, importers, and dealers obtain a Federal Firearms License (FFL), and that gun dealers keep records for every firearm sold. It also prohibited certain people, including fugitives and those convicted of a violent crime, from purchasing guns. By 1961, the prohibition applied to all felons.

The Gun Control Act of 1968

Following the assassinations of President John F. Kennedy in November 1963, Martin Luther King Jr. in April 1968, and Robert F. Kennedy in June of that same year, Congress enacted the Gun Control Act (GCA) of 1968, which revised and replaced some provisions of the earlier Federal Firearms Act while adding new regulations.

In particular, the GCA required that all weapons manufactured after October 22, 1968, feature serial numbers that could be logged by gun dealers for every sale, and if someone tried to remove, or deface, that serial number, they could face up to five years in prison.

The act also banned the importation of certain weapons not designed for "sporting purposes" (that is, hunting or target shooting) and the sale of mail-order guns because Lee Harvey Oswald ordered the Italian rifle he used to kill President Kennedy from an ad in the NRA's *American Rifleman* magazine.

Finally, the GCA implemented Form 4473, which is used to record all gun sales between licensed gun dealers and unlicensed individuals, and it prohibited specific classes of individuals from owning firearms, including felons, minors, fugitives, and more.

TIP

To learn more about the gun-buying process and Form 4473, read Chapter 4.

The Firearm Owners Protection Act of 1986

Unlike the previous acts, the Firearm Owners Protection Act (FOPA) of 1986 loosened several regulations related to firearms. Notably, it prohibited the ATF from creating a registry of sales records and inspecting gun dealers more than once per year unless the agency uncovered serious infractions. The act also made it easier for people to sell guns at gun shows and ammunition across state lines.

However, the act also prohibited civilians from owning any machine gun made after May 19, 1986. You can still obtain one that was manufactured before that date, but it'll cost you tens of thousands of dollars — and you still have to go through the NFA approval process. Only military and law enforcement personnel can obtain automatic weapons made after 1986.

The Brady Handgun Violence Prevention Act of 1993

Known simply as the Brady Bill, this act updated the GCA to require background checks for any gun sale between a licensed dealer, manufacturer, or importer and an unlicensed individual. The act also established the National Instant Criminal Background Check System (NICS), which officially came online in 1998 and is maintained by the FBI. Between 1993 and 1998, before NICS launched as a way to provide instant background checks, every handgun sale required a five-day waiting period.

In short, if you go to a gun shop or large sporting goods retailer to buy a firearm, you have to fill out Form 4473 and undergo a background check to make sure you're eligible to own said firearm. (Again, to learn more about that process, turn to Chapter 4.)

REMEMBER

However, the Brady Bill has some holes. For example, nothing in the act requires background checks for sales between unlicensed individuals as long as the seller is not "engaged in the business" of selling firearms to make a profit.

The federal assault weapons ban of 1994

Although the Violent Crime Control and Law Enforcement Act of 1994 (or simply the "1994 Crime Bill") covered a range of topics, one of the most notable was the Public Safety and Recreational Firearms Use Protection Act, which became known as the "federal assault weapons ban."

Remember, the NFA already regulates *fully automatic* weapons that will keep firing as long as you depress the trigger and the gun has ammunition. But this section of the 1994 Crime Bill was crafted after a series of high-profile mass shootings in California and Texas involving *semi-automatic* weapons that — as I discuss in Chapter 3 — load subsequent rounds for you, though you still have to pull the trigger for each shot.

Specifically, the ban outlawed the manufacture, sale, and possession of:

>> Eighteen different semi-automatic weapons based on, or sharing characteristics with, military weapons, including the Colt AR-15, AK-47 variants, and the Intratec TEC-9 (shown in Figure 2-2)

>> Any semi-automatic pistol, rifle, or shotgun that 1) accepted detachable magazines holding 10 or more rounds of ammunition, and 2) had two or more features derived from military weapons, including pistol grips, collapsible stocks, barrel shrouds, and more

>> Magazines that could hold more than 10 rounds of ammunition

FIGURE 2-2:
The federal assault weapons ban explicitly outlawed guns like the TEC-9.

Courtesy of Robert Basile/Shutterstock

However, weapons that fit within those parameters but made before September 13, 1994, were grandfathered in, and manufacturers could simply change a semi-auto firearm's external features to sidestep the ban. Thus, you could still purchase a "post-ban" AR-15 with a fixed stock instead of a collapsible one, for example.

Finally, because of a sunset provision, the ban expired in 2004 after 10 years, and Congress did not renew it.

REMEMBER

Assault weapons aren't exactly *assault rifles.* To learn more about these and other commonly confused terms, turn to Chapter 18.

The Protection of Lawful Commerce in Arms Act of 2005

This one marks the last major piece of firearms legislation passed by Congress. The Protection of Lawful Commerce in Arms Act (PLCAA, or the lovely sounding "placka") prevents most lawsuits against gun manufacturers and dealers when guns are used in the commission of a crime. However, PLCAA contains narrow exceptions, including when a member of the gun industry knowingly violates federal gun laws.

The act also includes the Child Safety Lock Act (CSLA), which makes it illegal for a licensed gun maker, importer, or dealer to sell a handgun without including a locking device. This is why your gun will probably come with a small cable lock, as I mention in Chapter 6.

Breaking Down Landmark Supreme Court Decisions

Along with federal laws, the Supreme Court, with its nine justices, has also played a major role in shaping the rules surrounding gun ownership in the United States.

However, the court has only heard a few significant cases involving firearms in its long history, so this section won't feel like a law school seminar — big sigh of relief!

United States v. Miller

Decided in 1939, *United States v. Miller* upheld the National Firearms Act as constitutional after two men were convicted for possessing and crossing state lines with an unregistered short-barreled shotgun.

The court also stated that the Second Amendment's "obvious purpose" was to "assure the continuation and render possible the effectiveness of" the state militia, and that the Amendment "must be interpreted and applied with the end in view." In plain English, that means the Second Amendment protected the rights of states to form militias — not an individual's rights.

So the federal government could regulate weapons like short-barreled shotguns that had no "reasonable relationship to the preservation or efficiency of a well-regulated militia."

District of Columbia v. Heller

In 2008's *District of Columbia v. Heller,* the Supreme Court struck down Washington, D.C.'s ban on handguns in a 5-4 ruling and held that the Second Amendment gives individuals a right to keep firearms in their homes for self-defense.

REMEMBER

However, the court also made it clear that Second Amendment rights were "not unlimited." The majority opinion stated that the decision should not "be taken to cast doubt on longstanding prohibitions on the possession of firearms by felons and the mentally ill, or laws forbidding the carrying of firearms in sensitive places such as schools and government buildings, or laws imposing conditions and qualifications on the commercial sale of arms." It also stated that precedent supports prohibitions on "dangerous and unusual" weapons.

McDonald v. Chicago

Two years later, in *McDonald v. Chicago,* the Supreme Court ruled that the right to keep arms in the home — as it had upheld in *Heller* — applied to all 50 states, not just Washington, D.C. Once again, the court also recognized that other laws regulating the possession, carry, and sale of firearms were still constitutional.

New York State Rifle & Pistol Association v. Bruen

In this 6-3 decision, the Supreme Court struck down New York's over-100-year-old requirement for residents to demonstrate "proper cause," or a special need, to obtain a permit to carry firearms outside the home. The decision, announced just before this book was published, could affect at least five other states with similar carry permit requirements.

Navigating State and Local Laws

Federal laws are just the beginning when it comes gun regulations. Every state in the Union has its own regulations related to firearms, and many local jurisdictions have additional requirements as well.

Of course, state and local laws change all the time, and I don't want this chapter to be at least 50 times longer than it already is. Instead, this section offers some examples of gun laws that you might run into around the country and points you to helpful resources so that you can learn what rules and regulations are in place wherever you live.

Recognizing significant laws

Some states prohibit their residents from purchasing certain weapons, ammunition types, or accessories, as follows:

» California, Connecticut, Delaware, Hawaii, Maryland, Massachusetts, New Jersey, New York, and Washington, D.C., have their own assault weapons bans that resemble the federal ban that lapsed in 2004. There are some differences between how these laws define "assault weapons" and handle legacy weapons that residents owned before the bans were enacted.

» Those same states also prohibit large-capacity magazines (LCMs) that hold more than 10 rounds of ammunition (though Hawaii's rules apply only to handguns). Adding to that list, Colorado restricts all gun magazines to 15 rounds, Vermont limits handgun magazines to 15 rounds and shotgun and rifle magazines to 10 rounds, and Rhode Island and Washington restrict magazines that hold 10 rounds. These states also have different rules governing LCMs that were owned before their bans were enacted.

» Several states, including California, Massachusetts, and New York, prohibit the sale of "unsafe handguns," or those lacking specified safety features, including magazine disconnects and loaded-chamber indicators. (For more on those features, turn to Chapter 7.) These states also test handguns to certify that they are safe before they are sold to residents.

» California, Maryland, Massachusetts, and Washington, D.C., maintain "rosters" of handguns approved for sale. If a gun isn't on the roster, a licensed dealer can't sell the gun in the state.

» Currently, 20 states and Washington, D.C., ban the sale and possession of ammunition that can penetrate body armor — you know, the protective gear that police wear.

Of course, there are other ammunition regulations to heed as well. A handful of states require background checks to purchase ammo, and many more require that hunters use lead-free ammo to protect people and the environment. Finally, New Jersey is the only state that regulates hollow-point rounds.

Then there are purchasing requirements. For example:

» Twenty-one states and Washington, D.C., close gaps in the Brady Bill by requiring background checks on *all* handgun sales, including private sales between unlicensed individuals. Seventeen of these states and Washington, D.C., also require background checks on all rifle and shotgun sales. In 11 states, background checks happen at the point of sale and are generally processed by licensed dealers. In five states, the laws require that residents first pass a background check and obtain a license or permit before they can make a purchase, and in an additional five states and Washington, D.C., a purchaser must obtain a license or permit *and* pass a point-of-sale background check. As you can imagine, the specifics vary, and residents must attend a formal firearms training course in seven of those states. (In case you can't tell, I'm the world's biggest fan of firearms training.)

>> Nineteen states and Washington, D.C., have extreme-risk protection order (ERPO) laws, or "red flag laws," that, depending on the state, allow family members, law enforcement, and/or mental health providers to petition the court to temporarily keep guns away from someone who is at risk of harming themselves or others. In many of these states, it's also a crime to file a petition under false pretenses or as a way to harass someone.

>> Some states back up the federal Child Safety Lock Act of 2005 by requiring that unlicensed individuals include locking devices with every private sale. (To learn more, turn to Chapter 6.)

>> Although the Gun Control Act specifies certain classes of people who are ineligible to purchase or possess firearms, states can add their own prohibitions and minimum-age requirements. For example, whereas you must be 18 to purchase a rifle or shotgun or 21 to buy a handgun from a licensed dealer on the federal level, you have to be 21 to purchase *any* firearm in states like Florida.

>> Many states also have their own mandatory waiting periods. So, to use Florida again as an example, if you purchase a gun from a licensed dealer in sunny Miami or Orlando, you'll have to wait either three days or however long it takes for the background check to be completed — whichever takes longer — to take possession of the gun.

The idea is to stop people from getting a gun when they're angry or upset and making an irrevocable mistake that very same day.

TIP

Chapter 4 can help you learn more about the laws regarding gun purchases.

Finally, other state laws focus on how guns can be kept, carried, or transported.

>> As I detail in Chapter 6, Massachusetts and Oregon require you to secure your firearm, either with a lock or by placing it in a locked container, when it is not in use.

>> Similarly, six states and Washington, D.C., have laws that require gun owners to secure their firearms if a child is likely to access a gun stored unsecured, and 15 states have laws that hold gun owners accountable if a child *does* access an unsecured firearm.

>> States have their own laws regarding how firearms may be carried, whether out in the open or concealed. Many states require that you first obtain a permit before you can carry a gun concealed, for example, but 25 have "permitless carry," which requires no paperwork or background checks beforehand. To learn more, turn to Chapter 11.

>> On a related note, every state has its own laws when it comes to how you transport a firearm in a vehicle, which I also cover in Chapter 11.

>> Although federal regulations prohibit firearms on federal property, including post offices and the U.S. Capitol building, and K–12 schools, the law leaves an exception for those with concealed-carry permits in schools.

Many states and municipalities supplement the federal statutes by banning *all* guns in schools and defining other "gun-free zones," which might mean state government buildings, police departments, churches, or restaurants and bars where alcohol is served, depending on the location.

Finding helpful sites and resources

Hopefully the past few pages have made it painfully obvious that you need to know your local and state gun regulations. You can't claim ignorance if you find yourself on the other side of the law.

REMEMBER

Thankfully, states and counties are typically pretty good about posting their gun laws on their websites for residents.

You should also check the websites of local and state law enforcement agencies because they're usually the ones in charge of processing firearms-related permits, for example. You can always talk to a police officer or lawyer, too.

TIP

I also recommend visiting the Everytown Gun Law Navigator (www.maps. everytown.org/navigator), which can help you learn more about your state's gun laws and how they've changed over the years around the country — going all the way back to 1991. You should also visit Everytown's Gun Law Rankings website (www.everytownresearch.org/rankings) to see how your state's gun laws stack up against other states.

WEBSITES TO AVOID

If you use Google or another search engine to find out more about the gun laws in your state, you'll probably receive dozens of results. But you should be skeptical of some of these websites.

First, state laws change all the time, so you need to make sure that the website you're looking at is still current. This is why I generally stick with those that end in .gov and will keep an eye out for the "last updated" dates on websites.

Never trust an old website. That's like using a MapQuest printout from 1999 for driving directions today.

Second, some gun groups and concealed-carry associations offer information regarding gun laws in the hopes that you'll join them. Many of these websites actively advertise guns and ammunition as well, and some even ask for your email address with the aim of marketing to you after you click away. So be wary. You don't need any more spam in your inbox.

Looking at Gun Laws Outside the United States

Aside from the United States, Guatemala, and Mexico are the only other countries that have constitutions allowing their citizens to own guns, but those countries also have many more gun regulations.

Other countries, including Bolivia, Costa Rica, Colombia, Honduras, Nicaragua, and Liberia, *had* their own versions of the Second Amendment at one point or another but have since rescinded those provisions.

In other words, the U.S. is uniquely positioned in the world when it comes to gun laws. To help drive that point home, the next sections describe how some other countries regulate firearms.

Canada

At the northern end of North America, firearms are widely owned, but federal restrictions apply. For example, in Canada, you must undergo 15 hours of firearms training and an extensive background check to obtain a license allowing you to own a firearm.

On top of that, all currently owned handguns have to be registered, and the country recently banned the sale, importation, and transfer of handguns. And if you want to carry one outside your house — either openly or concealed — you need another license that is typically reserved for guards or others who need guns for work. You also have to keep your guns locked up and unloaded if you aren't using them, and you can't own magazines that hold more than 10 rounds of ammunition.

Canada also banned fully automatic weapons in 1977, and in May 2020, following a mass shooting in Novia Scotia, the country banned about 1,500 different semi-automatic rifles.

Switzerland

Switzerland has a proud history of gun ownership. Since the 1600s, the country has held annual target-shooting competitions for kids ages 13 to 17, and Swiss men are encouraged to keep their service weapons after completing their mandatory military service.

The country also has one of the highest rates of gun ownership in the world, with more than 2 million privately owned firearms among 8.7 million citizens. Yet in 2017, the country had only 217 total firearms-related deaths, whereas the U.S. approaches 40,000 every year.

Moreover, local Swiss authorities can decide whether you deserve a gun permit — sometimes after consulting a prospective owner's psychiatrist — and keep a record of everyone who owns a gun in the region. Guns are mostly kept at home as well, but if you want to carry a firearm for defensive purposes, you have to pass a shooting test to obtain a license.

United Kingdom

The United Kingdom is known for having some of the most restrictive gun laws among developed countries. Unless you're in the military or law enforcement, you can't own a handgun or military-style weapon.

A strict licensing process governs rifles and shotguns as well as their ammunition. Only those with a "good reason" — including hunting and sport shooting, but *not* protection — can receive a license. Local police chiefs will then verify that your reason for owning a gun is legitimate as you undergo a background check.

Firearms licenses have to be renewed every five years, but the police can also revoke your license if they suspect you're a danger to others.

Australia

In April 1996, a gunman killed 35 people with semi-automatic weapons in Tasmania. Less than two weeks later, all six Australian states enacted the same gun laws banning semi-auto rifles and shotguns.

They also instituted 28-day waiting periods and background checks for other firearms, and like the United Kingdom, citizens must present a "justifiable reason" for owning a gun. Self-defense (or should I say "self-defence"?) isn't considered one of those reasons.

In the 21 years since the laws were passed, Australians sold about a million semi-auto firearms back to the government as part of buyback programs, cutting the number of gun-owning households in Australia in half. And although the country experienced 11 mass shootings in the decade before 1996, it's only had one since then.

New Zealand

Less than a month after a mass shooting occurred in Christchurch, New Zealand, in March 2019, the country's leaders took a page out of Australia's playbook and banned most semi-auto weapons while implementing buyback programs.

In addition, New Zealanders must pass rigorous background checks and obtain licenses from the police to own those weapons that weren't banned, such as hunting rifles and sporting shotguns. Since that time, the country hasn't experienced another mass shooting.

Chapter **3**

The Three Main Types of Firearms

As a kid, I loved taking things apart to understand how they worked. I'd sneak off to my room with whatever gadget or electronic I could find, disassemble it, and hopefully put it back together before anyone noticed it was gone. I voided countless warranties in my day.

As an adult, I've taken all sorts of firearms apart to learn how they operate, including those built by Old World artisans that required three hands and a healthy dose of French to be reassembled. In this way, I was able to take some of the mystery out of guns, and I hope to do the same for you.

It turns out that they aren't nearly as complicated as you might think. A firearm or gun — the terms are interchangeable — is simply a weapon that fires a projectile via gunpowder. I would argue that today's firearms, despite all their clever advances and technology, aren't all that different from the cannons that inspired them. In the end, they still use gunpowder to launch projectiles. My goal here is to help you understand *how* they do this.

Of course, this being a book, I can't exactly fire up a PowerPoint or give you a one-on-one demonstration at the range. So, instead, I crafted this chapter as a "Firearms 101" crash course to give you a solid foundation of gun knowledge. Here you can learn how guns operate along with common terms and phrases and the main differences among rifles, shotguns, and handguns. (However, I won't be helping you disassemble or modify a weapon's key components here — doing so may lead to dangerous malfunctions or void the manufacturer's warranty.)

TIP

The gun world also has a lot of confusing jargon that developed over hundreds of years. To help you navigate this terrain, this chapter includes a running glossary of gun-centric terms. Just pay attention to italicized words.

I also discuss a little history in this chapter to ground your understanding and provide some helpful context. However, in condensing over 1,200 years into a few dozen pages, I know I have left out a few odd guns and developments (that were never really mainstream to begin with) along the way for the sake of simplicity. This isn't a textbook. So go easy on me, gun scholars.

I can already hear the furious keyboard typing.

Taking a Quick Trip through History: Cannons, Muskets, and More

Gunpowder, or *black powder*, was first invented during China's Tang Dynasty in AD 808, when an alchemist mixed sulfur, charcoal, and potassium nitrate in the hopes of finding the secret to eternal life. Obviously, that didn't work out as planned.

After people learned of gunpowder's explosive nature, they began packing it into paper and bamboo shoots, creating the first fireworks, and by AD 904, gunpowder explosives were already being used for warfare.

By the late 1200s, China had built the first cannons that launched projectiles using gunpowder. Over time, the technology traveled west, where it was perfected in Europe.

Understanding early naming conventions

European cannons were much larger than early Chinese cannons, but the firing process remained the same. You packed gunpowder, cloth or rope wadding, and a cannon ball down the *barrel* — essentially a launching tube — and then ignited the gunpowder through the touch hole (or priming vent) at the top-rear of the cannon. The resulting explosion launched the cannon ball out of the barrel.

I'm sure you've seen the cannon firing process hundreds of times in cartoons and pirate movies. The longer the barrel, or the greater the powder charge, the farther the cannon ball traveled — up to a point, at least. Figure 3-1 labels the important parts of a traditional cannon.

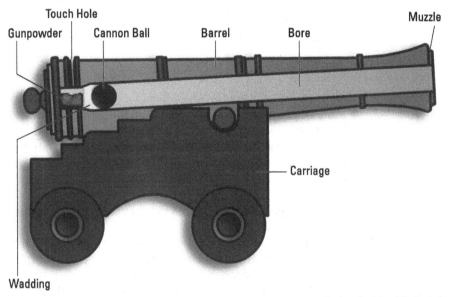

FIGURE 3-1: Many of the names for cannon components carried over to small arms.

As you can see in the figure, the names for major cannon components carried over to man-portable weapons, like the barrel; the *muzzle*, or the front of the barrel; and the *chamber*, or where the ammunition ignites. To build cannons, armorers, or gun builders, would also drill out the center of the cast-iron barrel, which is why this area is called the *bore.*

The bore diameter — otherwise known as the *caliber* or *gauge*, which were interchangeable at this point — dictated the size of the cannon balls.

Sizing down for individual soldiers

Cannons were heavy and required teams of soldiers or sailors to operate in battle. But what if you scaled things down?

Muskets arrived in the 1400s. Think of these as smaller, handheld cannons (see Figure 3-2 for an example). Although a few different methods of ignition, or lock types, were developed, every musket was loaded from the muzzle end with gunpowder, wadding, and then a single ball or several smaller balls, known as *shot*. Flintlocks became the most popular lock types.

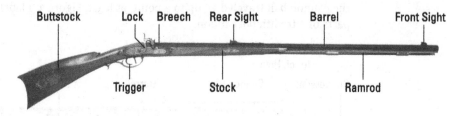

Buttstock   Lock   Breech   Rear Sight   Barrel   Front Sight

Trigger   Stock   Ramrod

FIGURE 3-2: Muskets were known for their long barrels and wooden stocks.

Courtesy of JanSommer/Shutterstock

Many musket parts were also named after cannon components, like the muzzle, barrel, and *breech,* or the rear of the barrel. But new names were coined, too, like the *stock,* a wooden component that supports the barrel; the *buttstock,* or the rear portion of the stock that rests against your shoulder; and the *trigger,* which causes the lock to ignite the gunpowder and fire the gun.

Over time, *sights* were also added to help marksmen line up their shots.

Muskets eventually gave way to smaller and more accurate rifles, which I explain later. Then there's the *blunderbuss* (Dutch for "thunder pipe"), which is essentially the original shotgun. As you can see in Figure 3-3, the barrel is wider than a musket's, and the muzzle is flared. You could load these firearms with one big ball, a handful of smaller shot, or even rocks for hunting and self-defense at relatively short distances. The shot scattered outward, which is why these guns were also known as *scatterguns.*

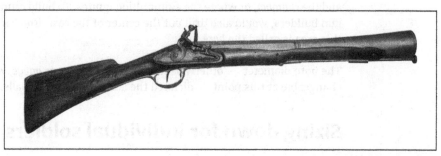

FIGURES 3-3: *Blunderbusses* could be loaded with a variety of ammunition.

Courtesy of Denis Rozhnovsky/Adobe Stock

Finally, there were pistol versions designed for one-handed firing, as Figure 3-4 shows. Just remember that muskets, *blunderbusses*, and pistols were still *smoothbore muzzleloaders* at this point, meaning their bores were smooth and they were loaded from the muzzle.

FIGURE 3-4: Pistols were designed to be used with just one hand.

These are the guns that were around when the Founding Fathers wrote the U.S. Constitution, and they were popular well into the 1800s.

Tracing 1800s innovations to today's guns

The 1800s saw several technological advances that got us much closer to what you see in contemporary weapons. The Industrial Revolution brought easier steel manufacturing and precise engineering, and the American Civil War created a massive demand for firearms. For the first time, people saw the mainstream use of:

» **Breechloaders,** or firearms that could be loaded at the breech, or rear of the barrel, which sped up the entire firing cycle. To reload, a soldier no longer had to lower their gun and ram ammunition down the barrel before picking the gun up again, reshouldering it, and aiming.

» **Rifling,** which consists of the spiral grooves formed into barrels that impart spin on projectiles (see Figure 3-5). Think of the opening credits for James Bond movies. (I mistook that image for a camera shutter when I was an innocent angel of a kid.) This spin allows the projectiles to travel much farther than before without as much of an arc. Thus, the bullet flies straighter.

FIGURE 3-5:
Rifling is what
makes a
projectile spin as
it travels down
the barrel.

Courtesy of rami_hakala/Adobe Stock

Long guns with rifled barrels became known as "rifles." Pistols were also given rifled barrels, but scatterguns like the *blunderbuss* were left alone. Their smooth-bores were desirable because they allowed you to fire shot, rocks, or whatever. Of course, a round ball would not travel as well through rifling, leading to . . .

>> **Improved ammunition.** Over the course of the 1800s, musket balls eventually morphed into conical lead projectiles known as *bullets.* These have a more aerodynamic shape (meaning they're less affected by air resistance, or drag), allowing them to travel faster and farther.

Instead of loading loose powder and then a projectile, soldiers eventually began using paper cartridges that combined the two components. Again, this innovation sped up the loading process, and the paper gave way to copper and finally brass casings to create *self-contained metallic cartridges.*

Even the gunpowder evolved, too. The world transitioned from black powder to *smokeless powder,* which is a bit of a misnomer because it still produced *some* smoke — just not as much as a blackpowder shot, which would engulf soldiers and ruin their visibility.

>> **Repeaters.** After breechloaders, barrel rifling, and improved ammunition, the next biggest advancement was creating a weapon that could load and fire more than one shot before needing to be reloaded.

For centuries, armorers had tried and failed to create repeating firearms, as they're called, but in the 1800s, inventors like Samuel Colt cracked the code and created viable multishot weapons, including revolvers and lever-action rifles, as I discuss later in this chapter, that became popular in the latter half of the 19th century.

Today, virtually every gun — except for a few single-shot firearms — is considered a "repeater." The rest of this chapter focuses on *how* today's guns repeat, or load and fire consecutive rounds.

RIFLE AND HANDGUN AMMO MADE EASY

Self-contained metallic cartridges for rifles and handguns might seem complicated at first, but I promise they aren't that hard when you understand the names for various components. I cover just the basics right here, but look for a more advanced discussion in Chapter 9.

The following figure shows a pistol *cartridge,* or *round.* The *case* is what holds the primer, gunpowder, and bullet together. When you fire a round, the gun's hammer or firing pin strikes the *primer,* which causes the gunpowder to ignite. This sends the projectile, the *bullet,* screaming down the barrel toward your target. The *rim* holds the cartridge in the chamber and helps with extraction, or ejecting the case after the bullet has been fired.

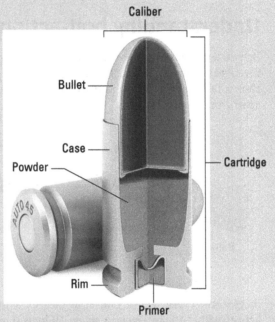

Courtesy of natatravel/Adobe Stock

The term *caliber* simply means the diameter of the bullet. In America, caliber is typically expressed in inches. So a .45-caliber round uses a 0.45-inch-diameter bullet. Europeans use millimeters to denote the same thing, so a 9mm bullet has a diameter of 9 millimeters.

Rifles and handguns originally used similar-looking ammo, but rifle cartridges eventually received longer, more aerodynamic bullets that flew farther and larger cases that provided room for more powder, thus offering more power. Pistol rounds remained the same relative size.

Going the Distance with Rifles

Okay, so I had to fast-forward through a lot of history in the previous section to give you an overview of how firearms developed, but now I can start breaking down the various types of weapons within each major category.

Rifles are a great place to start because they are easy to learn on paper and at the firing range. They also excel at medium- to long-distance shooting. And I mean *long*. I've hit targets more than a mile away with bolt-action rifles, and I've seen shooters much more skilled than I hit targets as far as two miles away. There's nothing quite like fighting gravity and wind to successfully *ping* a steel target at such distances.

Understanding bolt-action basics

Bolt-action rifles are relatively simple and haven't changed much since they were invented in the late 1800s. You have a few new parts to learn, but the *bolt handle*, shown in Figure 3-6, is the distinguishing characteristic that sets these rifles apart from all others.

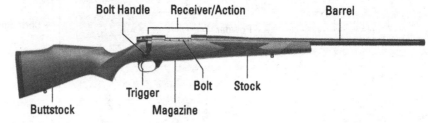

FIGURE 3-6: Note the bolt handle on this traditional bolt-action rifle.

Courtesy of SolidMaks/Getty Images

In essence, every bolt-action rifle utilizes a manually operated, rotating bolt housed within the receiver, or *action*. (Why is it called an action? It's where all the action happens!) The *bolt* is what loads a fresh round into the chamber, the rear portion of the barrel, from the *magazine*, which holds all subsequent ammo. After firing, the bolt also extracts the spent casing.

I know that sounded like word salad, but Figure 3-7 can help. This cutaway illustration shows what it looks like when the magazine is loaded and the shooter slides the bolt forward to lock a round in the chamber. Pulling the trigger releases the *firing pin* held under spring tension within the bolt, which fires the bullet.

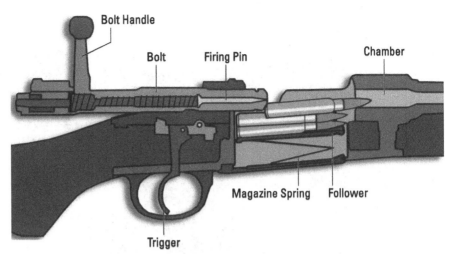

Bolt Handle

Bolt   Firing Pin   Chamber

Magazine Spring   Follower

Trigger

FIGURE 3-7: The bolt chambers a new round as it moves forward.

When the user unlocks the bolt handle and retracts the bolt, the spent casing is ejected from the action. Pushing the bolt forward again loads another round from the magazine. The *magazine spring* pushes upward against the *follower*, which holds the next rounds, so they are ready to be chambered.

These days, all bolt-action rifles still have obvious bolt handles. That's your dead giveaway. But today's models come in a wide range of calibers, and they feature stocks made of wood, aluminum, or even synthetic materials, like plastic or carbon fiber. Many of the stocks are also designed for adjustability — allowing shooters to customize the rifle to fit their frames, for example — and the addition of accessories like scopes and bipods. (To learn more about these add-ons, turn to Chapter 10.)

SORTING OUT MAGAZINES AND CLIPS

This is the perfect opportunity to discuss the differences between magazines and clips, and why the terms are not interchangeable. *Magazines* are simply the parts of guns that hold ammunition. Early bolt-action rifles used integral magazines built into their stocks, as do many current models. You simply push rounds down into the magazine while the bolt is locked back.

To speed up that process, some older weapons, like those used in World War I and World War II, use *clips,* which hold rounds in a stack so they can easily be pushed downward into an integral magazine. The following figure shows a man using a clip to load five rounds into a Mosin-Nagant bolt-action rifle.

(continued)

(continued)

Courtesy of Gabriel Cassan/Adobe Stock

Over time, bolt-action rifles — and most other repeaters — began using detachable magazines that insert into the bottom of the action. Detachable magazines speed up the reloading process and allow the weapon to hold more ammunition.

For more help with commonly confused gun terms and phrases, turn to Chapter 18.

People use bolt-action rifles primarily for hunting, competitive and recreational shooting, and sniping in military and law enforcement situations — virtually any task that requires shooting from very far away.

Dozens of calibers are available, and more seem to come out every year, but the most common are the .17 HMR, .22 LR, .223 Remington, .308 Winchester, .30-06 Springfield, .338 Lapua Magnum, and 6.5 Creedmoor.

Leveling up with lever actions

The next step up in terms of complexity, lever-action rifles were first developed in the 1860s. Like bolt-action rifles, lever actions utilize bolts and are manually operated. But instead of loading the next round with a bolt handle, users instead pivot a *lever* located under the receiver (see Figure 3-8).

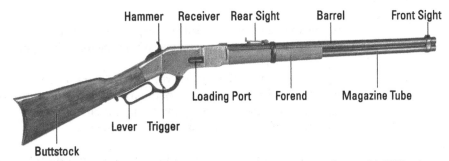

FIGURE 3-8:
A lever-action rifle is easy to identify by the lever underneath its receiver.

Hammer   Receiver   Rear Sight   Barrel   Front Sight

Loading Port   Forend   Magazine Tube

Lever   Trigger

Buttstock

Courtesy of zim286/Getty Images

Along with the lever, pay attention to the *hammer*, which strikes the firing pin within the bolt; the *forend*, or the forward portion of the stock; and the *magazine tube*, which runs parallel to the barrel.

Figure 3-9 is another cutaway illustration that can help you understand how a lever-action rifle operates. As you can see, the magazine tube holds rounds in sequence. Notice how they're all lined up. When the shooter pivots the lever downward and then back up, three things happen: the bolt slides rearward, the *lifter* carries a round from the magazine tube up into the chamber, and the bolt returns forward, ready to fire.

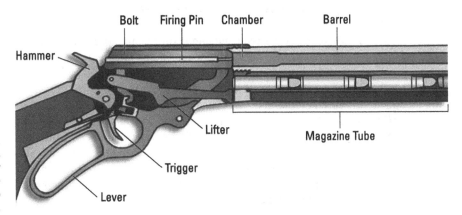

Bolt   Firing Pin   Chamber   Barrel

Hammer

Lifter   Magazine Tube

Trigger

Lever

FIGURE 3-9:
The lever moves the lifter to carry a round from the magazine into the chamber.

Pulling the trigger releases the hammer, which strikes the firing pin within the bolt, launching the bullet. Operating the lever again ejects the spent casing from the last round and loads the next one.

A few different companies have specialized in lever-action rifles over the years, like Winchester, Marlin, and Henry Repeating Arms, but the overall concept has stayed the same. Current models feature wooden or synthetic stocks and various finishes. They're easy to accessorize with slings and scopes, and you can find models that allow you to load the magazine tube from the front or the rear. The latter requires a *loading port* on one side of the receiver (refer to Figure 3-8).

People use lever-action rifles primarily for hunting and recreational shooting, including "Cowboy Action" competitions where attendees cosplay as gunslingers and use Old-West-style weapons to hit various targets. It's hilarious and just authentic enough without exposing you to cholera.

WARNING

Lever-action rifles are available in a few different calibers as well, but note that they can only use ammo with round- or flat-nose bullets, not the more modern pointed (*spitzer*) bullets that fly faster and farther. If you load pointed rounds into a lever-action magazine tube and accidentally drop the gun, the rounds could ignite each other, causing the magazine to explode and possibly resulting in serious injuries. This is why you should always make sure you use the correct ammo in your gun.

Gaining speed with semi-autos

In the late 1800s, inventors began asking themselves, "What if you didn't have to manually operate a bolt handle or lever to load subsequent rounds?" It didn't take long for them to answer that question with semi-automatic and fully automatic repeaters that really took off in the 20th century.

When you fire a *semi-automatic* (or "semi-auto") weapon, the gun will load the next round into the chamber for you as long as the magazine still has ammunition. To fire again, you have to pull the trigger again.

REMEMBER

Semi-automatic doesn't mean *fully automatic* (or "full-auto"), where the gun will continue firing until you release the trigger or run out of ammo. Most full-auto-capable weapons today are in fact *select-fire* models, which means you can toggle between semi- and full-auto modes. Not to get too technical, but full-auto firing requires an "auto sear" that adjusts how the trigger and hammer interact for subsequent shots. Such weapons — and the sears themselves — are federally regulated and difficult to own.

Semi-auto and select-fire rifles fought on both sides of World War II. American soldiers used the semi-auto M1 Garand and the select-fire Browning Automatic Rifle (BAR). The war also spurred the development of the German *Sturmgewehr* of 1944 (StG 44) and Russian SKS, to name more examples. These rifles are all very different from each other, but they all rely on the same method of operation, as I discuss in the next section.

The *Avtomat Kalashnikova* of 1947

In 1947, Mikhail Kalashnikov finalized his select-fire "*Avtomat Kalashnikova*," or AK-47, for the Russian military. It's easy to distinguish by its *top cover* and curved detachable magazines, which hold 30 rounds of 7.62x39mm ammunition. The forend is also broken into upper and lower *handguards*.

Figure 3-10 shows a select-fire AK-47, but semi-auto models were also developed and imported into the U.S.

FIGURE 3-10:
Both semi-auto and select-fire variants of the AK-47 have been developed.

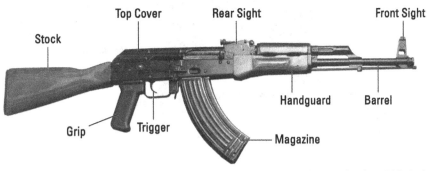

Courtesy of mashurov/Adobe Stock

The rifle is known for its durability and reliability in harsh conditions, but not exactly its accuracy. That said, the design is extremely easy to reproduce. The Soviets spread it to dozens of countries around the world, and according to some estimates, well over 100 million AK-style weapons have been produced.

So how does the AK-47 (and a ton of other semi-auto rifles) work?

When you fire a gun, you're creating a tiny explosion that launches a projectile out of the barrel — just like the cannons of old. That explosion produces gas and recoil. The gas is what designers began tinkering with to power most semi- and fully automatic rifles.

Looking closely at Figure 3-11 should help you follow along with me here. When you pull the trigger, the hammer swings forward and strikes the firing pin within the bolt. The gun fires, and propellant gases push the bullet down the barrel.

The bullet exits the muzzle, but the gases are diverted upward through the gas port, where they impact a *piston*. This piston then pushes against the *bolt carrier*, which reciprocates — meaning that it moves backward and forward in a straight line. As it moves rearward, the bolt carrier ejects the spent casing. Tension from the *recoil spring* then pushes the bolt carrier forward to its original position, and it loads a new round into the chamber along the way. The hammer then resets for the next shot. *Phew*, what a rollercoaster!

Several AK-platform variants, like the AKM and 5.45x39mm AK-74 (no, that's not a typo) were developed over the years, and many countries, including Romania, Bulgaria, and Israel, created their own copies. But they all use the same *gas piston operating system*.

Semi-auto AK rifles and parts kits have been imported into the U.S. from old Soviet Bloc countries for decades (though Russian-made models were banned in 2014, following that country's incursion into Ukraine at that time). More recently, several American companies began producing their own models that accept a wide range of accessories.

Overseas, AKs are common on both sides of the law. You see them in the hands of soldiers and police officers as well as insurgents. Here in the U.S., they're really only used for recreational shooting. Some people keep AKs to defend their homes or trucks, but the 7.62x39mm can penetrate through walls. At the same time, AKs aren't popular for, say, hunting medium to large game because the 7.62x39mm doesn't provide enough power at a distance, and many jurisdictions limit how much ammo you can carry in a hunting rifle.

The birth of the AR platform

This brings me to the most popular, and the most contentious, rifle style, or platform, available in the United States today.

First, some history. Eugene Stoner first developed the AR-10 in 1956 while working for a company called ArmaLite. Firearms at the time were mostly made of wood and steel, but the AR-10 had aluminum *upper and lower receivers* as well as a stock, grip, and handguard made of plastic to save weight. By the way, "AR" stands for "ArmaLite Rifle" — not "Assault Rifle" or "America's Rifle."

The U.S. military originally didn't want the AR-10, which was designed for .308 Winchester/7.62mm NATO ammunition, even though it weighed a pound lighter than comparable weapons at the time. Eventually, ArmaLite scaled the gun down for the smaller .223 Remington/5.56mm NATO rounds to attract military sales, creating the AR-15. Those sales did not materialize quickly enough, however.

In 1959, financial difficulty led the company to sell the AR-15 to Colt, which won military contracts for the select-fire version, the M16 (shown in Figure 3-12), starting in 1964 — first for the U.S. Army, and then the rest of the armed forces. Colt also sold semi-auto versions still dubbed AR-15s.

FIGURE 3-12:
The original M16's stock, grip, and handguard were made of tough plastic.

Courtesy of zim286/Getty Images

The civilian AR-15 and military M16 have evolved substantially since they debuted. For example, the carry handle, with its built-in rear sight, has mostly been replaced by a *Picatinny rail* that allows you to add a wide range of sights and optics, and the fixed stock gave way to collapsible versions. Dozens of gun manufacturers — way too many to keep track of — have made their own AR-style clones in a wide range of configurations, with various barrels, handguards, grips, triggers, and more. You can even mix and match parts, which is what gives the AR platform its "Legos for men" moniker.

Yet the basic operating system is still the same in all the variations. As you can see in Figure 3-13, ARs aren't all that different from AKs on a conceptual level. The big difference is the lack of a gas piston. Instead, the propellant gases created from firing a round travel into a *gas tube* above the barrel and impinge directly on the longer, thinner bolt carrier, forcing it backwards against the *buffer* and *buffer spring* held within the receiver extension, a tube that the stock is attached to.

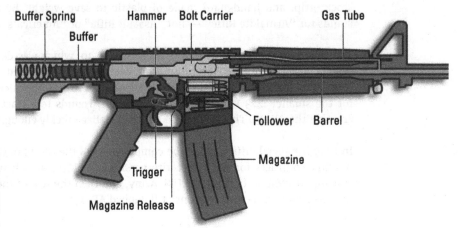

FIGURE 3-13:
Note the long gas tube that rides above the barrel on a typical AR-15.

As it reciprocates, the bolt ejects the spent casing. Then it rides forward, loading a fresh round from the magazine. Pulling the trigger releases the hammer and repeats the cycle.

Virtually every AR, from the M16 and AR-10 to the AR-15, uses this same *direct impingement* operating system. In practice, this system translates to greater accuracy than an AK because less mass reciprocates with each shot, and ARs are generally built to tighter tolerances, but this system also requires more maintenance and lubrication.

Today, the U.S. military still uses an updated version of the M16 as well as the shorter-barreled M4, whereas police departments have access to those guns as well as civilian ARs.

ARs are also used for recreational shooting, and they're popular among competitors. You can hunt smaller game, like varmints, with an AR-15, and larger game with an AR-10 — but semi-autos aren't really necessary for most hunting situations, where your goal is to kill your prey with one shot, and many states regulate how much ammo you can carry in the field. And although a number of people keep AR-15s in their homes and vehicles for protection, the most common calibers will punch through walls.

Those calibers include the .223 Remington, 5.56mm NATO, 300 Blackout, 6.5 Creedmoor, and .308 Winchester, but you can also find ARs built for common handgun calibers, too, such as the 9mm and .45 ACP.

REMEMBER Speaking of AK- and AR-style weapons, the terms "assault rifle" and "assault weapon" are often mixed up in conversation — just like clips and magazines — but they aren't quite interchangeable. To find out more about these and other common gun vocabulary mishaps, flip to Chapter 18.

Sorting Out Various Types of Shotguns

Compared to semi-auto rifles, shotguns are a lot easier to understand. These long guns are also considered the workhorses of the firearm world because they can handle a number of tasks, including hunting and home defense.

Today's shotguns can multitask because, just like their muzzle-loaded forebears, they can accept a wide variety of ammunition to tackle targets from close to medium range. To that end, I think it's important to learn how this ammunition works before I dive into the various types of shotguns.

Simplifying shotgun shells

Like handgun and rifle rounds, shotgun ammunition was also streamlined in the 1860s. For the first time, you had a shotgun *shell*, or shotshell — please don't say "cartridge" for shotgun ammo — made entirely from brass or using a paper casing and a brass case head. Roughly 100 years later, in the 1960s, the paper was replaced with plastic to better withstand moisture and humidity.

Inside the shell, from the top, are several shot *pellets* or a *slug* (basically a large bullet), a wad to hold the projectiles in place, gunpowder, and the primer. The pellets scatter outward as soon as they exit the muzzle. A number of factors affect the amount of spread, or dispersion, like the pellet size and the design of the shell and wad. Here's the rule of thumb for pellets: With a full-choke shotgun, expect the pellets to spread out another inch for every yard they travel.

The *gauge*, or diameter of the shell, dictates the size of the shot pellets or slug. (It might be tempting, but please don't say "caliber" here, either.) The gauge numbering is a little confusing because it comes from old cannon nomenclature, but just know that the lower the gauge, the larger the shell. A 10-gauge shell is larger and generally more powerful than 12- and 20-gauge shells, for example.

As Figure 3-14 shows, the three most common shotgun shells include buckshot and birdshot for deer and bird hunting, respectively, as well as slugs for hunting medium to large game.

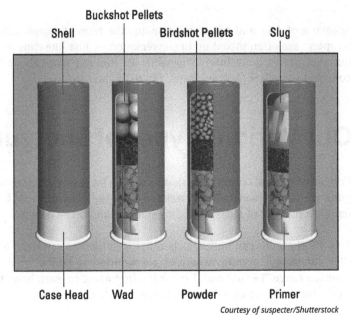

Shell Buckshot Pellets Birdshot Pellets Slug

Case Head Wad Powder Primer

Courtesy of suspecter/Shutterstock

FIGURE 3-14:
Note the different projectiles in each of these shotgun shells.

Breaking down break actions

Break-action shotguns have been around since the 1870s. Simply put, they have one or two smoothbore barrels and an action that pivots (or breaks) open for easy loading and unloading.

Double-barreled shotguns fall into two categories: *over/under* (O/U) models, whose barrels are stacked vertically, and *side-by-side* (SxS) models, whose barrels are positioned horizontally, side by side. Makes sense, right? You can see both of these types in Figure 3-15.

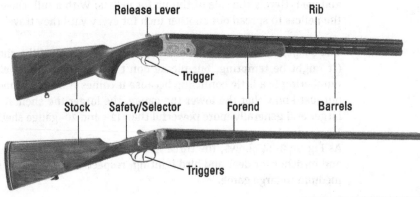

Release Lever Rib

Trigger

Stock Safety/Selector Forend Barrels

Triggers

FIGURE 3-15:
An over/under (top) and a side-by-side (bottom) shotgun.

Courtesy of sergiy1975/Adobe Stock

Unless something has gone horribly awry, a single-barreled shotgun should have only one trigger. But a double-barreled shotgun might feature one or two triggers. If it has two, each trigger is responsible for firing a single barrel. If it has one trigger, there's a good chance that the gun has a *selector* built into the safety that allows you to pick which barrel fires first, and pulling the trigger again will fire the other barrel.

In the rare event that you encounter an older double-barreled shotgun with a single trigger and no selector, the right or bottom barrel should fire first, depending on its configuration. But don't take my word for it. You need to understand how the gun in question operates well before you try to fire it.

In other words, don't be like my grandpa, who let others try out his double-barreled shotgun without first warning them that it was broken and fired both barrels simultaneously.

Some models require you to manually remove spent shells after firing; others eject them for you as soon as you break open the action by hitting the *release lever*. Although most break-action shotguns today are "hammerless," this is actually a misnomer; they still use internal hammers for ignition, as Figure 3-16, a cutaway illustration of an opened over/under, shows.

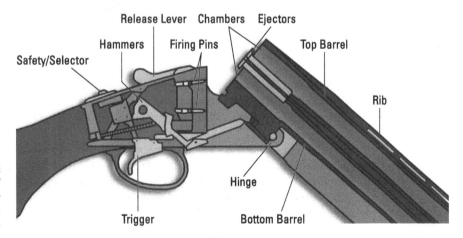

FIGURE 3-16: What an over/under looks like when the action is pivoted open.

As you can see, double-barreled shotguns are relatively simple guns. They're used for home defense, hunting, and recreational shooting. In this realm, the 12 gauge reigns supreme, but 20- and 28-gauge models are also very popular. Over/under shotguns are the top choice for trap and skeet shooting, too.

But don't let their simplicity fool you. The finest handcrafted double-barreled shotguns can cost tens of thousands of dollars. It takes a lot of time and effort to get both barrels to hit the same target.

Moving from levers to pumps

In the 1880s, gun makers like Winchester took the lever-action rifle concept and simply reconfigured it for shotshells. The lever ejected spent shells and loaded fresh ones from the magazine tube under the barrel.

These guns were short-lived, however, because inventors came up with pump-action shotguns (Figure 3-17 shows an example), which operate similarly, but instead of using a lever, the forend performs the same work as it slides along the magazine tube. Some people even call these guns "slide actions."

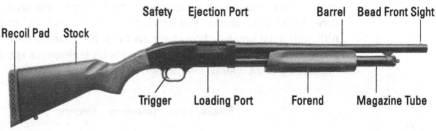

FIGURE 3-17: Pumping the forend ejects a spent shell and loads a new one into the chamber.

Courtesy of SolidMaks/Adobe Stock

If you're familiar with pump actions, you know the infamous sound they make when the forend is racked — a sound movies use all the time, even for guns that are decidedly *not* pump-action shotguns!

Internally, pump-action shotguns are very similar to lever actions. *Action bars* connect the forend to the bolt so that when you slide the forend backward, the bolt travels backward, too, and ejects the spent shell from the chamber. A new shell is also placed on the *shell carrier* (as shown in Figure 3-18), and as you slide the forend forward, the new shell is lifted into position and chambered.

The *loading port* in the bottom of the receiver allows you to load shells into the rear of the magazine tube, and depending on the model, you'll find the safety either just behind the trigger or on the *wrist*, the area just behind or at the rear of the receiver, on top of the stock.

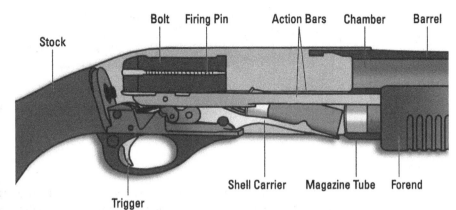

FIGURE 3-18:
As the forend
returns forward,
the carrier lifts a
shell so the bolt
can chamber it.

The most common pump actions are 12-gauge models with wooden or synthetic stocks. These guns are commonly used for military and law enforcement operations because of their close-range power and versatility. They can take doors off their hinges, for example, and fire beanbag rounds as well as rubber pellets to disperse crowds. (Honestly, I winced just typing that.) Among civilians, these guns are popular for home defense, hunting, and clay shooting.

Figures 3-17 and 3-18 depict traditional pump-action shotguns, but a few companies make some very futuristic-looking models that can hold 15 shells at a time in an attempt to overcome the conventional shotgun's weakness: a lack of onboard ammunition. Yet, no matter how sci-fi these guns get, you'll always be able to recognize the telltale sliding forend.

Sizing up semi-auto scatterguns

Finally, there are semi-auto shotguns, which operate like pump actions, except they use either the recoil or the gas from firing a shell to chamber subsequent rounds for you. Their operating systems make them ridiculously fast but also more maintenance intensive. You have to clean semi-auto shotguns regularly.

The operating systems vary a bit too much for a cutaway illustration here, but you have traditional-looking models — like the kind shown in Figure 3-19 — that could easily be confused for pump-action models, but the forend doesn't move. You'll also find a prominent *charging handle* that allows you to retract the bolt and run it forward (like the *bolt release*) to chamber a new shell.

Then you have less traditional semi-auto shotguns, including those based on the AR and AK platforms, as well as *bullpups,* whose action is located behind the grip to create a more compact, maneuverable weapon.

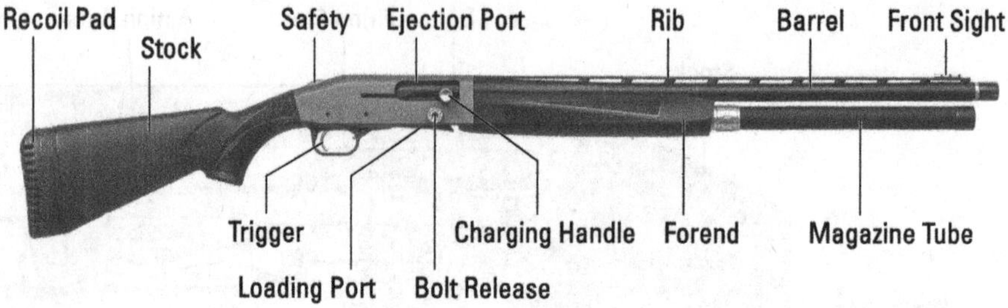

Recoil Pad Stock Safety Ejection Port Rib Barrel Front Sight

Trigger Charging Handle Forend Magazine Tube

Loading Port Bolt Release

FIGURE 3-19: This semi-auto shotgun has a fixed forend and a prominent charging handle.

Courtesy of SolidMaks/Shutterstock

These guns are almost always 12 gauges, and they're primarily used for military and law enforcement operations as well as competitive shooting among civilians.

Getting Hands on with Handguns

Of the three main types of firearms, handguns are the top sellers among Americans, but they're also the most difficult to shoot accurately. Think about it: Unlike long guns, you can't use your shoulder to support a handgun, so you're left with only two points of contact — your hands — to stabilize the weapon before you pull the trigger.

On top of the issue with stability, the distance between the front and rear sights, or the *sight radius,* is a lot shorter on handguns, which makes it significantly harder for you to notice when your aim is off target. With a longer sight radius, you can more easily detect the gun's movement, for example, as you aim and thus correct for it.

But I digress. You can delve more deeply into marksmanship in Chapter 13. To get back on target (pun!), the next section dives into revolvers, the simplest and oldest of contemporary handguns.

Grasping the revolver revolution

Samuel Colt invented the first revolver in 1831. The gun was named after its revolving, or rotating, *cylinder* that held five rounds in five individual chambers. Eventually, Colt settled on six-shot cylinders. It didn't take long, however, for companies like Smith & Wesson and Remington to copy Colt with their own models in various calibers, sizes, and finish options. Oh, you want deluxe engraving and mother-of-pearl grips? You got it! Grab your wallet.

All the early models were *single actions,* meaning you had to cock the hammer before firing a shot. Cocking the hammer also advanced the cylinder — clockwise or counterclockwise, depending on the make — to the next chamber. The trigger performed only one action: dropping the hammer to fire a shot.

Old revolvers were extremely slow to reload, even with *loading gates* that pivoted outward, providing access to one chamber at a time, and spring-loaded *ejector rods* mounted alongside the barrel that, when pushed toward the cylinder, helped shove spent casings back through the loading gate. The Colt Peacemaker (shown in Figure 3-20) had both of these innovations.

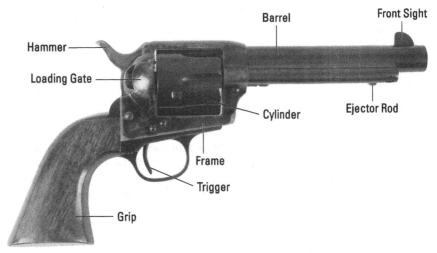

FIGURE 3-20: The most famous revolver of the Old West, the Colt Peacemaker, was a single action.

Courtesy of JackF/Getty Images

In the 1860s and 1870s, companies began developing *double-action* revolvers where the trigger performed two actions — cocking the hammer *and* dropping the hammer — to fire a shot. As the trigger is pulled rearward, the hammer cocks and the cylinder rotates to line up the next chamber for firing. If you keep pulling the trigger rearward, the hammer drops, igniting the cartridge.

The first revolver with a *swing-out cylinder* appeared in 1874, speeding up the reloading process considerably. With this setup, hitting the *cylinder release* allows the cylinder to quite literally swing out to the side of the frame on a *crane* so that you can empty and reload every chamber simultaneously.

Aside from Old West replicas, most revolvers today (like the kind shown in Figure 3-21) are double-action models with swing-out cylinders. This type of firearm is what police relied on for decades, well into the 1980s and 1990s, before departments began switching to semi-auto handguns that held more ammunition and were faster to reload.

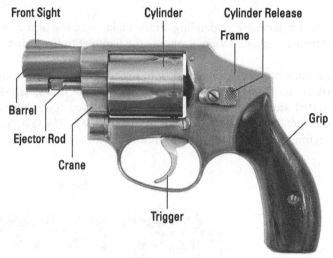

Front Sight Cylinder Cylinder Release
Frame
Barrel
Ejector Rod
Crane
Grip
Trigger

FIGURE 3-21:
"Hammerless"
double actions
actually have
hammers within
their frames.

Revolvers are still popular for concealed carry and, to a lesser extent, recreational shooting and hunting because of their ease of use and reliability. If a round doesn't fire for some reason, you simply pull the trigger and drop the hammer again. (Once again, I want to point out that even if you come across a "hammerless" model for concealed carry, there is still a hammer — it's just hidden inside the frame.)

Common revolver calibers include the .38 Special, .357 Magnum, 9mm, .44 Special, and .44 Magnum. But you can find revolvers in everything from the tiny .22 LR to the powerhouse .454 Casull and .500 S&W Magnum.

Charting the rise of semi-autos

In the 1890s, inventors began creating semi-automatic handguns that were faster to reload than revolvers, held more ammunition, and streamlined the firing cycle.

A few designs were mass produced, like the Borchardt C93 of 1893 and the Mauser C96 of 1896, but the biggest development came in 1911, when the Colt Model 1911 was adopted by the U.S. military.

The 1911 and other hammer-fired pistols

John Moses Browning — a man with more than 120 firearm patents to his name — developed the Model 1911 around a brand-new caliber, the .45 Automatic Colt Pistol, or ACP, that packed quite a punch back in the day. The 1911, and the slightly updated 1911A1 (shown in Figure 3-22), provided the same basic layout for all subsequent semi-auto pistols of the 20th century.

Front Sight   Slide   Slide Release   Rear Sight   Hammer

Thumb Safety

Frame

Grip Safety

Trigger

Magazine Release

Grip

FIGURE 3-22:
By World War II, the 1911 had received a few tweaks to become the M1911A1.

In other words, semi-auto pistols were forever divided into two major halves. The top portion, the *slide,* is a steel component that houses the barrel and firing pin as well as the front and rear sights. The lower half, the *frame,* has everything else, including the trigger, grip, safeties, and other parts.

Note that 1911-style pistols are single actions. (See Figure 3-23.) Racking the slide, or pulling it to the rear and releasing it, chambers a round and cocks the hammer. (You can also cock the hammer with your thumb.) Pulling the trigger then drops the hammer to fire a round. The recoil from firing forces the slide rearward, ejecting the spent casing and re-cocking the hammer. Then, as the slide returns forward — thanks to the recoil spring — a new round is stripped from the top of the magazine and loaded into the chamber. The gun is now ready to fire again.

If you think about it, the reciprocating slide essentially serves as the bolt you'd find in rifles and shotguns. But, although semi-auto rifles are mostly gas operated, and semi-auto shotguns can either be gas or recoil operated, most semi-auto handguns, including the 1911, are recoil operated. The recoil produced from firing a round is used to cycle the action.

As Figure 3-23 shows, the 1911 uses *single-stack magazines,* where all the rounds are positioned in a single vertical column within the detachable magazine. This detachable magazine was a huge upside compared to revolvers at the time, and it's one of the reasons the U.S. military adopted it. It's extremely easy to hit the magazine release, drop the empty magazine from the bottom of the grip, and slide a full magazine into its place.

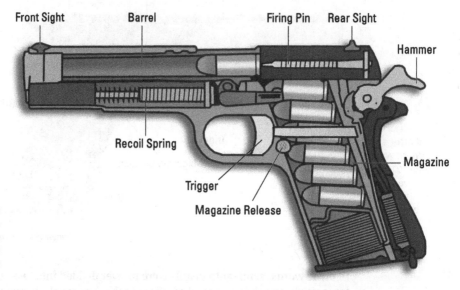

Front Sight   Barrel   Firing Pin   Rear Sight

Hammer

Recoil Spring

Magazine

Trigger

Magazine Release

FIGURE 3-23: When you fire a 1911, the slide reciprocates and re-cocks the hammer.

On the civilian side, a number of Colt competitors developed their own 1911 clones in a range of calibers and sizes that are still popular among enthusiasts. These aren't the easiest guns to use because of their *thumb and grip safeties,* however, which must be deactivated before firing, which is why they never quite took off among police officers.

In terms of capacity, the 1911 originally used seven-round magazines before developers figured out how to fit eight rounds into the same space. Then, in 2011, the competition world brought about the first models — dubbed "2011s" — that use *double-stack magazines* holding anywhere from 14 to 20 rounds. These magazines are much wider, accommodating two staggered columns of ammunition that still feed into the chamber one at a time.

Finally, if you understand how the 1911 operates, you understand how virtually every other hammer-fired semi-auto operates, including the Browning Hi-Power (guess who made that one!), the Beretta 92, CZ 75, and the Smith & Wesson Model 39. Of course, there are some obvious differences between the most popular models, like their single- and double-action triggers and the types of metal used for the frames, for example, but a hammer is still present for ignition.

Striker-fired pistols

The semi-auto handgun world changed with the 9mm Glock 17, which was invented by Gaston Glock in 1982 and hit U.S. shores around 1986. This semi-auto handgun used a frame made of polymer — "plastic" to us commoners — to reduce weight, and instead of using a hammer and firing pin, the Glock 17 combined the two in what's known as a *striker*. Wrapped in a spring, this component greatly simplified the overall design. There's no external hammer that might snag on clothing, or that needs to be cocked before firing.

Every subsequent Glock pistol, including the Glock 19 shown in Figure 3-24, has the same basic design and operating system.

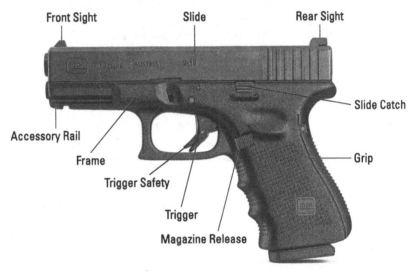

Front Sight   Slide   Rear Sight

Slide Catch

Accessory Rail

Frame

Grip

Trigger Safety

Courtesy of Shutterstock

Trigger

Magazine Release

FIGURE 3-24: The success of the full-size Glock 17 led to the slightly smaller Glock 19.

REMEMBER

For the record, the Glock 17 wasn't the first handgun to use a striker or a polymer frame, but it was the first to popularize these advances. The slide and barrel are still made of heavy-duty steel, by the way, so these guns will still set off metal detectors, despite what *Die Hard 2* might have you believe.

The Glock 17 was also designed to use double-stack magazines holding 17 rounds of 9mm ammunition — an astonishing amount for a pistol at the time. But the gun is actually named the Glock 17 because it was Gaston Glock's 17th patent. (The more you know!)

Along with being lighter, the Glock 17 was easier to use than previous handguns. It's essentially a "point and shoot" proposition. As Figures 3-24 and 3-25 show, the only external safety is the pivoting tab built into the face of the trigger — known as the *trigger safety* — that must be fully depressed for the whole trigger to move backward. Of course, the term "safety" is used a little loosely here. This is not a traditional manual safety that physically prevents the gun from firing unless it is disengaged. If someone attempts to pull the trigger on a Glock, the gun will fire.

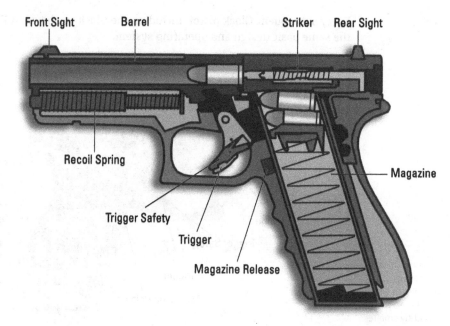

FIGURE 3-25: Glocks are still recoil operated like almost every other semi-auto handgun.

However, Glock pistols became a top choice among law enforcement and civilians alike because of their simplicity and reliability. According to the manufacturer, 65 percent of law enforcement officers currently carry Glock handguns. As a result, the company has steadily debuted new models in various sizes and calibers over the years along with new "generations" with subtle tweaks and updates. So you'll see Glock 19 (or simply "G19") Gen3 pistols, G17 Gen4 models, among others. Glock is currently producing Gen5 pistols, but the company might be well into Gen6 or Gen7 by the time you read this.

As gun owners began to accept so-called "Tupperware" pistols, competitors began producing their own easier-to-manufacture, striker-fired, polymer-framed pistols in a range of calibers, though the 9mm is far and away the most common today. Now, virtually every major gun maker offers a striker-fired pistol of some sort, and the U.S. military adopted its first service pistol of this kind in 2014, replacing the older hammer-fired Beretta 92.

Striker-fired pistols are highly sought-after for personal defense, recreational shooting, and competitions, and they even show up in hunting circles on occasion. Some are expressly designed for concealed carry and are small enough to slip into a pocket, whereas others are built for maximum capacity, holding more than 21 rounds of ammunition.

Chapter **4**

Purchasing Your Firearm

M aybe you're considering owning a firearm but haven't purchased one yet. I know the whole process can be formidable for the uninitiated. I've been in those same shoes.

In a perfect world, I could go with you to your local gun shop. Alas, this isn't a perfect world, and I don't have enough SkyMiles.

But I still think I can help. In this chapter, I do my best to prepare you for that daunting first visit. I discuss what you should expect at a gun shop, provide some dos and don'ts so that you don't get kicked out of the place, and offer advice to help you make a well-informed purchase.

REMEMBER

Guns are inherently dangerous. There's no denying that. But if you're going to purchase one, I'd rather you find the right one that fits you and your needs — and is easier to control, for example — than the wrong gun that creates an unsafe situation. If the firearm doesn't really work for you, so to speak, you might not seek training or learn to use it properly, practice with it, or take care of it the way you should.

In the pages ahead, I also walk you through the buying process and explain things like background checks and waiting periods to give you a little more confidence before you head to a gun shop.

Your First Trip to the Gun Store

After you've Googled all the gun shops in your area and found the one with the best reviews, it's time for that first shopping foray.

TIP

If you're nervous, consider bringing along a friend. There's strength in numbers, and your friend doesn't need to be a "gun expert." If anything, most gun shop employees probably prefer working with novices over know-it-alls.

Gun shops also aren't known for their modern architecture or handsome façades. I don't think I'm offending anyone when I say that most could be confused for dental offices or pawn shops from the outside. A good number of pawn shops do indeed sell used guns, as I discuss later.

So the exterior might not seem that inviting to you — or criminals, which is the point. You, an upstanding citizen and pillar of your community, have nothing to fear. So go on in.

Inside, you should expect glass countertops full of handguns, and the walls behind the counter might be decked with rifles and shotguns. The same goes for the gun section of any large sporting goods stores. The employees will probably have pistols on their hips as yet another security measure. I know this can all be over-whelming, but the next sections can help get you prepared.

What to expect from salespeople

Most of the gun shop employees I've met over the years are kind, genuine, salt-of-the-earth people who love their jobs. They want to help you and share some of their passion for guns.

Only a few were ever gruff or rude. Maybe they were busy that day or had to deal with too many unsafe customers. Maybe they should've retired three years ago. Who knows?

In my experience, you'll have better luck at a gun store, or the gun section of a larger sporting goods store, if you're friendly to the salesperson and communicate with them. Tell them why you're there, what you're looking for, and whether you're new to firearms. Don't be afraid to speak up.

At the same time, the employees expect and respect safe gun handling. So if you ask to see a pistol, for example, they should hand it to you with the barrel pointing down toward the floor and the slide locked back so that you know the gun is unloaded. When you accept the gun, keep the barrel pointing downward, and don't place your finger near the trigger. You never break the four gun safety rules, even if the gun is obviously empty. (Need a refresher on the safety rules? Turn back to Chapter 1.)

Handling a pistol can help you assess its weight, grip, and sights. Is the gun too heavy for you? Does the grip fit your hand well? Can you see the sights easily, or would you prefer a different style?

Further exploration beyond holding and looking at the gun requires more communication. Ask for permission to release the pistol's slide or the pull the trigger before you take these actions. I say this because repeated *dry firing*, where you pull the trigger without a round in the gun, can damage the gun's firing pin, so some retailers prohibit it. So, again, keep an open dialogue with the salesperson and carefully hand the gun back to them when you're ready. Please don't drop the gun on the glass countertop; I've seen it happen and still cringe when I think about it.

WARNING

Conversely, if it's the salesperson who doesn't demonstrate safe gun handling, it might be time to find another shop. Seriously. Every gun shop employee should be setting a good example for everyone else to follow.

Deciding on the type of gun to buy

With so many guns available today, a little preplanning goes a long way.

As I discuss in the previous chapter, there are three main types of firearms — handguns, rifles, and shotguns — and you'll save yourself and the salesperson some time if you narrow down your options before you set foot inside the store. So if you're interested in hunting, talk to the salesperson about hunting rifles. Or maybe you want a shotgun for skeet shooting, or a handgun for personal protection. The point is to have some inkling of what you want beforehand.

The salesperson can show you everything they have in stock within a given category. They won't have to guess, feel you out, or potentially take you down an avenue you're not even interested in.

WARNING

On a related note, I must warn you that some gun shop salespeople are incentivized to steer you toward certain brands over others. To counter this, simply ask if the employee has a relationship with the brand in question.

Here are some questions you should answer before you enter the store:

>> **What is the gun's purpose?** I know this sounds like an existential quandary, but I mean it quite literally. How will the gun be used?

Guns have features that lend themselves to specific purposes. A handgun designed for, say, target shooting and competitions will generally have larger sights, a longer barrel, and more weight than one that you'd carry for self-defense. Larger sights are easier to see; the longer barrel helps in the accuracy department; and the added weight can cancel out some of the recoil from firing, making it easier to get back on target quickly.

That's just one example. A shotgun built for hunting and clay shooting will have a longer barrel than one you'd use in close quarters, like the hallway of a home, and bolt-action rifles generally don't come with integral front and rear sights for aiming unless they're meant for hunting dangerous game up close. Otherwise, manufacturers assume that you're going to add a scope for long-distance shooting.

TIP

To find out more about firearm accessories, including scopes and other must-have equipment, go to Chapter 10.

>> **What's your skill level?** Some guns are more difficult to handle and operate than others. For example, most shooters begin with light-recoiling, .22-caliber firearms before progressing to larger-caliber weapons with more kick, and as I hint in the previous entry, long guns can be difficult to maneuver in tight spaces without training.

The hurdle can also be mechanical. With a 1911-style handgun, the shooter has to deactivate thumb and grip safeties before the gun can fire. This is a big reason why law enforcement agencies have mostly avoided these pistols. In contrast, striker-fired models like Glocks pistols are essentially "point and shoot" affairs.

Obviously, I recommend training for *any* firearm, and some states require it, but certain guns are just easier for beginners to use.

>> **What safety features do you want included?** Most modern firearms have internal safeties that, assuming everything functions properly, prevent unintentional discharges if they're ever dropped. But this is really the bare minimum, and the "difficulty" of the previous question might be a good thing.

For example, although a 1911-style pistol is more difficult to learn than, say, a Glock, it's also inherently safer because it has two external safeties that must be disengaged before it can fire. You can also look for guns with magazine disconnects, loaded-chamber indicators, and other safety features to provide a little extra peace of mind.

>> **Who's going to use the gun?** This is an important question that really speaks to the gun's size and caliber. Because, despite what some gun enthusiasts say, it is possible to have "too much gun."

If you want to teach your son or daughter about marksmanship and safe gun handling, start with a small-caliber rifle that fits them — not some double-barreled, 12-gauge shotgun.

Pay attention to the *length of pull,* or the distance from the trigger to the rear of the stock. If that measurement is too short or too long, it'll be difficult for your kid to control the weapon and shoulder it comfortably.

>> **What's your budget?** Knowing this information will narrow your options down considerably. Today's firearms come in a range of price points. You can find cheap guns in the $200 range and high-end models that cost thousands of dollars. But you don't need to spend $10,000 for an accurate, reliable rifle when many fit the bill for less than $1,200. Also, your budget should have enough room for more than just the gun. You'll need ammo, a training course or two, range gear, hunting equipment, and so on.

>> **How much time will you invest in the gun?** Or, to put it another way, will you keep the gun clean and well maintained?

You probably shouldn't own a gun if, deep down, you know you aren't going to take care of it. However, by virtue of their designs, some guns are more maintenance intensive than others. For instance, semi-auto shotguns must be cleaned regularly — a lot more often than pump-action shotguns — to run reliably. Generally speaking, the more complicated the gun, the more maintenance it requires.

If you have some or all of these questions answered in your mind by the time you interact with a salesperson, you'll be in great shape. They can then use their experience and expertise to steer you in the right direction.

Trying before you buy

You can learn a lot about a firearm before you ever get to the store. Check any gun manufacturer's website and you'll find all the specifications you could ever want, including a model's:

>> **Caliber**, which tells you the ammunition the gun is designed to accept

>> **Barrel length**, an important indicator for that ammunition's velocity potential as well as the gun's portability

>> **Overall length**, another piece of information that can tell you how easy the gun is to handle, store or transport

>> **Unloaded weight**, which can play a big part in determining a gun's handling characteristics and portability

>> **Grip or stock material**, which refers to whether the gun has a polymer grip frame, interchangeable grip panels, an aluminum stock, and more

>> **Sights** for aiming, including three-dot, tritium, or fiber-optic sights for handguns, an "optics rail" so you can add sights to a long gun, and more

>> **Action**, which describes the gun's operating system

>> **Finish**, which can denote how the metal components were treated, or the color of other parts

>> **Capacity**, which indicates how many rounds of ammo the gun can hold

All this information is useful, especially when it comes to differentiating between two similar models. But these details can only tell you so much about a gun. You need to try it before you buy it.

TIP

To test a gun before purchasing it, you need to visit a gun shop with an attached shooting range and a good rental policy, as opposed to a big-box retail store. For a small fee — as well as the cost of ammo, targets, and eye and ear protection if you didn't bring your own — such gun shops will let you rent a gun similar to the one you're interested in. Even if it's not the same make and model, it can be one close enough to it for you to get an idea of how it shoots.

WARNING

Many states allow you to purchase a gun from an online retailer and pick it up at a brick-and-mortar gun shop, where you'll undergo a background check. But I really don't recommend this route if you haven't tested the gun, or a similar model, in person beforehand. You don't want to be at the mercy of the online retailer's return policy.

Testing a handgun allows you to assess a few characteristics, like its sights, trigger, grip ergonomics, ease of reloading, and *felt recoil,* or how much the gun kicks when you fire it. These are all subjective qualities. You might find the front sight too difficult to pick up, for example, or the trigger too loose or gritty for good accuracy. The grip might not fit your hands well when you're pointing the gun at a target, or it might be too slippery for your tastes. The recoil might feel light, sharp, smooth — it varies for every shooter.

For rifles and shotguns, you'll want to judge those same characteristics as well as the ergonomics of the stock and forend. Is the buttstock comfortable on your shoulder? Can you establish a solid *cheek weld* — the interface between your cheek and the top of the stock — when you're aiming? Is the forend comfortable in your support hand? How easy is it to add accessories?

BUYING NEW VERSUS USED

When you purchase a new firearm, you get to dictate the make, model, caliber, sights — everything you could want. If the exact model you want isn't available, a gun shop can order it for you. On top of that, the gun will usually arrive in a lockable hard case built specifically for it with, at the very least, a user manual, a cable lock, and a spare magazine or two. I've also seen manufacturers include extra grip components, magazine loaders, cleaning tools, fresh recoil springs, and replacement sights.

Finally, most new weapons come with warranties in case something goes wrong and the gun needs to be repaired. Of course, the trade-off for all of these benefits is having to pay full price. (And if you decide to return the gun for whatever reason, even the next day, you might not get a full refund for it. Many gun shops consider new guns "used" as soon as they leave the store.)

To save money, you might be tempted to purchase a used firearm from the secondary market, which includes auctions, gun shows, and online marketplaces. But there are some cons:

- You don't know where the gun has been. With a used car, you can at least order a vehicle history report to see what the car has been through, but no such option exists for firearms. So the original owner might have run over the gun with their used car before repairing and replacing a ton of components, and you'd never know.

- You're the only person responsible for assessing the gun's condition. Unless you're with a gunsmith or someone who really knows firearms, you have to assess the gun's components all on your own. That means the barrel, the safeties that prevent the gun from firing unintentionally, the sights — everything. And if something goes wrong, there might not be a warranty to cover it.

- At the same time, the venue might not give you the opportunity to examine the gun carefully. If you're at a gun show or using an online marketplace, you won't be able to take the gun apart and inspect the barrel and other internal parts for flaws or damage.

- Although gun shop employees can hopefully answer your questions, you might not have that luxury at a crowded gun show where vendors are dealing with multiple customers simultaneously.

- The gun will be sold as is, so it might not come in its original case, and you might not get a user manual, a cable lock, or other accessories. In short, *caveat emptor*.

Knowing the Purchase Requirements

Say you're at your local gun shop. After testing a few different models, you've found the right gun for your needs. Now you just head to the cash register, pay for the firearm, and take it home, right?

Wrong. Federal law requires that licensed gun dealers run background checks whenever they sell or transfer a firearm to an unlicensed individual. This requirement helps to ensure that the buyer isn't legally prohibited from owning a gun.

In other words, according to Title 18, United States Code 922(g) — trust me, I'm a blast at parties — it's illegal for you to purchase a gun if you:

>> Have been convicted of a felony

>> Are a fugitive from justice

>> Are an unlawful user or someone addicted to a controlled substance, including opioids, hallucinogens, or marijuana

>> Have been declared mentally unfit or been institutionalized involuntarily

>> Are an alien, either unlawfully or under a nonimmigrant visa

>> Have been dishonorably discharged from the U.S. military

>> Have renounced your U.S. citizenship

>> Are currently under a final domestic violence protection order, including a restraining order or injunction for protection

>> Have been convicted of a misdemeanor crime of domestic violence

>> Are under indictment for a felony

On the federal level, licensed dealers also cannot sell a rifle or shotgun to anyone under 18 years old, or handguns to anyone under 21 years old, according to the federal Gun Control Act (GCA) of 1968.

WARNING

State and local laws might place their own restrictions on top of those federal requirements. For example, in several states, including California, Florida, and Illinois, you have to be 21 to purchase any firearm, including rifles and shotguns.

Although there are no federal licensing or registration requirements, as Table 4-1 shows, several states require that you obtain a permit to purchase a firearm. Some states require you to have a license to own any firearm. Of course, the requirements for these permits and licenses vary, and some might also come with exams or training requirements. Some also require state or local authorities to keep records of guns or completed gun transfers.

TABLE 4-1

States with Permit or License Requirements

State	Licensed Required To . . .
Connecticut	Acquire any firearm
District of Columbia	Possess any firearm
Hawaii	Acquire any firearm
Illinois	Possess any firearm
Maryland	Acquire a handgun
Massachusetts	Possess any firearm
Michigan	Acquire a handgun
Nebraska	Acquire a handgun
New Jersey	Acquire any firearm
New York	Possess any firearm
North Carolina	Acquire a handgun

REMEMBER

The specifics are different for each state, so it's important for you to understand the laws where you live. This information might be listed on a state or county website, including those run by law enforcement agencies. The employees at a local gun shop will be happy to answer your questions, too.

Filling out the required paperwork

The Bureau of Alcohol, Tobacco, Firearms and Explosives (ATF) is the federal law enforcement agency tasked with overseeing and regulating firearms among all those other responsibilities. As you can imagine, between all the booze, cigarettes, and the estimated 400 million guns owned by Americans, ATF agents are stretched pretty thin.

When you buy a gun from a licensed dealer, you have to fill out the ATF's Form 4473, the "Firearms Transaction Record." Most gun shops these days have a dedicated PC or laptop so you can fill out the form electronically, but older dealers might require good ol' fashioned pen and paper, so print legibly.

WARNING

Currently, no federal regulations prohibit an unlicensed individual from selling firearms without background checks, as long as they aren't "engaged in the business" of selling guns. However, 17 states and Washington, D.C., require background checks for *every* sale, and four more require them for all handgun sales. To learn more, turn to Chapter 17.

The dealer fills in the first part of the form, Section A, where they'll note the firearm's make, model, serial number, type, and caliber or gauge.

Section B is all you. In this section, you enter all your personal information, including your full legal name, address, place of birth, height, weight, sex, birth date, social security number, ethnicity, race, and country of citizenship.

WARNING

You don't have to include your social security number on Form 4473, but I highly recommend it. This is the best way to ensure that you aren't confused for another person with the same name *and* a criminal record or another red flag that will halt the transaction.

Next, you have to answer a series of yes-or-no questions, such as "Are you the actual transferee/buyer of the firearm(s) listed on this form?" This question is meant to ensure that you aren't buying the gun for someone else, which would be considered an illegal *straw purchase.* If someone wants you to buy a gun for them, they're probably prohibited from owning a gun, so be wary.

The rest of the questions get into the other disqualifiers I list early in the "Knowing the Purchase Requirements" section, such as whether you've ever been convicted of a felony, are a fugitive, or have a received a dishonorable discharge, and so on.

WARNING

Answer each question honestly. Lying on Form 4473 is a felony punishable by up to 10 years in prison, and as I discuss in the upcoming "Understanding holds and wait times" section, as soon as the form is submitted, the government will begin combing through your records to verify your answers.

Take your time. No one should rush you. And after you've answered all the questions, you simply sign the form to certify you've read through it, understand it, and have answered every question truthfully. Then you're all done — well, almost.

Understanding holds and wait times

After you complete Form 4473, explained in the preceding section, your part in completing the purchase requirements is done. The dealer then fills in a few more boxes and submits the form, which triggers a background check.

Who performs the background check? It depends on where you live.

States can either conduct their own background checks using their own records and databases as well as those on the federal level, or they can have the Federal Bureau of Investigation (FBI) conduct background checks using the federal National Instant Criminal Background Check System (NICS) database.

Currently, the FBI's NICS staff performs background checks for licensed dealers in 31 states, Washington, D.C., and all five inhabited U.S. territories. Six states receive partial NICS service, and the 13 remaining states perform their own background checks using the NICS database.

I live in one of those 31 states that fully relies on the FBI in this regard and have never encountered a problem during a gun sale or transfer.

How effective is the background check system? Since 1994, it has stopped more than 4 million illegal gun sales, preventing more than 300,000 in 2020 alone. In recent years, Congress has also bolstered the system by ensuring that federal agencies submit records to the FBI that could prohibit purchases and requiring the Department of Justice to notify local law enforcement agencies of NICS denials.

That said, states are not required to provide the FBI with state-level information about their residents, such as mental health records, that might prevent a gun sale from going forward. Whatever states submit is purely voluntary, which obviously creates gaps in the background check system.

In some states, you can bypass the background check after filling out Form 4473 if you've received a concealed-carry permit (which entails its own background check). Again, check your state laws.

After Form 4473 is submitted, the dealer can contact the FBI's NICS staff electronically or over the phone. Ninety percent of the time, the dealer will receive one of three responses in less than two minutes:

>> **Proceed:** The sale is fully authorized and can be completed.

>> **Denied:** The sale cannot be completed because of a disqualification in the buyer's records. If you think this was in error, however, you can appeal the decision.

>> **Delayed:** The FBI needs more time to dig through the buyer's records.

Regarding that last option: Federal regulations give the FBI three business days to continue its investigations to determine whether the sale should proceed or be denied because of a disqualifying factor, like the buyer's past convictions.

If, after three business days, the FBI has not found any red flags in the buyer's records, even if the background check isn't finished, the sale can be completed. This is called a "default proceed." The dealer doesn't necessarily *have* to sell you the gun at that point, but there are no federal laws stopping them.

This three-day time frame does not stop the FBI from completing the background check, however, and if the bureau later finds a red flag (or several) in your records, it can notify the ATF to retrieve your weapon. You don't want to be in that position.

If a prospective rifle or shotgun buyer is 18 to 21 years old, the Bipartisan Safer Communities Act (BSCA) of 2022 also gives the FBI seven additional business days, on top of those previous three, to comb through a state's juvenile records before greenlighting the transaction.

Finally, states can can extend the default proceed period, or dictate their own waiting periods for firearms, as listed in Table 4-2. Waiting periods differ from default proceed periods in that they apply to all purchases — not just those where background check operators need more information to determine if a buyer is indeed prohibited.

TABLE 4-2   ## States with Waiting Periods

State	Type of Firearm	Duration
California	All firearms	10 days
District of Columbia	All firearms	10 days
Florida	All firearms	3 days
Hawaii	All firearms	14 days
Illinois	All firearms	72 hours
Maryland	Handguns	7 days
Minnesota	Handguns, assault weapons	7 days
New Jersey	Handguns	7 days
Rhode Island	All firearms	7 days
Washington	Semi-auto rifles	10 days

BEWARE OF THE GUN SHOW

No, I'm not talking about your favorite kitschy tank top. You can put those biceps away.

I mean the weekend-long event at your local convention center where hundreds of vendors try to sell new and used weapons to anyone who's bought an entry ticket. You'll find tables upon tables covered in guns of every make, model, color and caliber — not to mention knives, holsters, and other related gear. It's pretty wild walking through all of the aisles.

But once again, I want to offer some warnings about this side of the secondary market, as it's known. For example, although many of the sellers at gun shows are indeed federally licensed, some are not. Federal background check laws apply only to the former category. If an unlicensed individual wants to sell an entire arsenal that they've collected over the years, for whatever reason, they can do it all without submitting any Form 4473s or other paperwork. Five guns, 20 guns, 231 — it doesn't matter as long as they aren't selling guns primarily for profit.

You can see the problems with that. The seller has to essentially decide whether the interested party can legally own a firearm all on their own, without the FBI's resources.

On the other side of the table, if you buy a gun from such a seller, you might not be able to carefully inspect the firearm to ensure that it's safe and reliable, as I mention earlier in this chapter. And if you skip the background check, there won't be a paper trail for your purchase. That's another gun that can be difficult to trace if it ever shows up at a crime scene. To me, that's not the route for a safe, responsible gun owner to take.

I have the same warnings for online marketplaces, which have overtaken gun shows in popularity in recent years. Depending on the platform, the sale might not have to go through a licensed dealer and involve a background check, and thus you won't have a paper trail for your purchase. You also won't be able to handle or test the gun beforehand to ensure that it's safe and reliable. That's why I will only ever interact with a licensed dealer at a brick-and-mortar store who does everything by the book. Every single time.

2

Building a Gun Safety Mindset

Chapter **5**

Introducing a Firearm into Your Household

The headlines in every newspaper and media outlet are all too familiar. Someone — usually a parent, but possibly a sibling or neighbor — leaves a loaded gun unsecured and unattended in their home or their car, in their backpack or their purse, just waiting for a curious child's hands. Disaster ensues.

Accidental shootings like these play out again and again, hundreds of times every year, across the U.S., proving that firearms do not necessarily make people's families safer. And yet, many of these tragedies are preventable.

REMEMBER

Children are inquisitive by nature. They're constantly learning through experiences and all five senses. But they won't ever grasp how dangerous firearms are unless they're taught as much.

For millions of adults, the easiest answer is to *not* keep a gun in the home. Why take the risk? Those who do decide to own firearms, however, must act responsibly, which starts with having honest conversations about firearms with family members and securing all weapons.

To help with those conversations, I've included some sobering statistics in Chapter 17 outlining the dangers of owning a gun. I also discuss secure storage options and best practices in Chapter 6. But in this chapter, I focus on the dialogues people must have with their families — especially their children — to ensure that everyone is on the same page regarding firearm safety.

Having "The Talk" with Your Family

As you can imagine, bringing a gun home is very different from bringing home a newborn puppy. Sure, they both require heavy doses of responsibility, but you should never surprise your family with a firearm. In fact, "no surprises" would make a great subtitle for this chapter.

You need to be slow and deliberate here. Start by introducing the topic to your significant other, as I detail below, and then more broadly with your children. That way, you and your partner can present a united front for your kids. And understand that the conversation with your kids must be ongoing, growing and evolving with them. It won't be a one-time thing. You have to regularly check in with your kids and make sure that they still remember the safety rules and what to do if they encounter a gun.

TIP

For best results, try talking to your family members without having the weapon present. This might seem counterintuitive, but the gun could be intimidating or serve as a distraction.

Addressing your partner's concerns

This might seem obvious, but your significant other shouldn't first learn about your firearm when you pull it out of the case. Big mistake.

In a perfect world, you can discuss the *idea* of owning a firearm with your partner ahead of time, well before you head to the gun shop. However, you might already own a gun or two by the time you meet that special someone. In either case, your partner may express some concerns about having a gun in the house, so you need to know how to respond.

The conversation will go a lot smoother if you:

>> Listen to your partner and try to understand where they are coming from. Maybe they didn't grow up around guns, or they've had a bad experience with one. Put yourself in their shoes.

If your significant other mentions a traumatic event in their past involving a gun, do not retraumatize them by digging for details and having them relive the experience, or, worse yet, showing off your firearm. Instead, you might want to reconsider owning a gun if it's that important to your partner. There are other safety solutions.

>> Be honest in describing why you want the firearm. If the gun is meant for hunting, or if it would make you feel safer in your home, say that. "Because I wanted one" isn't a solid justification for buying a gun.

>> Make it obvious that you've taken your significant other and family into consideration. The best way to do this is to buy a gun safe and pick a smart location for it — far away from your children's rooms, for example. Having a plan like this ahead of time, and asking for your partner's input, will go a long way toward showing that you are indeed ready to own a firearm.

>> Offer to take them to the range to learn more about how guns operate. You can even make it a date night. Better yet, sign up for a training course together. (For more on that, turn to Chapter 12.)

Explaining gun safety rules to children

It would be wonderful if everyone in your home already knew the four rules of gun safety that I cover in Chapter 1 *ahead of time*, before they ever encountered a firearm. You need to take your children's ages into account, however. Young kids might not comprehend the complexities of "Be sure of your target and what is beyond it," for example. So, you have to simplify things.

Younger children must know:

>> **Firearms are not toys, even if they look like them.** To drive this rule home, it might help to show your kids photos or illustrations of real firearms. I recommend applying this rule to BB, pellet, and paintball guns as well, because those items can injure others just as easily as real firearms.

>> **Never touch a firearm without an adult present.** This rule is vital, and you'll have an easier time enforcing it if your kids also aren't allowed to touch toy guns unless an adult is present. In fact, I'd keep toy guns that resemble real firearms out of the house if at all possible.

>> **They can always talk to you about firearms.** From a very young age, your kids should feel that they can always come to you with questions or ideas about guns, free of judgment. This approach establishes trust and sets the tone for future conversations.

As your children get older, the previous rules *still apply* — especially the part about not touching a firearm without an adult present — but you can add some nuance to their understanding, like:

>> **Never point a firearm at another person.**

>> **Stay away from the trigger.**

>> **Always assume that guns are loaded.**

In this way, you're reinforcing what they already know while getting a little closer to the four universal rules of gun safety. A few more concerns arise when your kids become teenagers, as I discuss in a moment.

WARNING

This is a great opportunity to mention that, despite what some parents believe, all children, even toddlers, are capable of pulling a gun's trigger. Even if you think your gun has a heavy trigger, a child might be able to fit two of their fingers within the triggerguard for greater leverage. So lock up your gun!

Teaching children what to do if they encounter a firearm

Sadly, even if you're the safest gun owner on the planet, with your firearms locked away and everything — look at you go! — you can't always guarantee that your neighbors, or your kid's friend's parents, are as responsible as you when it comes to owning a firearm. This is why your children need to know what to do if they come across an unsecured weapon.

As established earlier in this chapter, your kids should already know that guns are not toys, and that they should never touch firearms without having an adult present, regardless of the location. Then, it's critical that they learn to:

>> **Stop what they're doing.** We've all seen kids get lost in the moment when they're playing, but if a gun somehow enters the scene, they need to immediately stop and take a beat.

>> **Resist the urge to touch the firearm.** Once again, children must stay away from the weapon at all costs, even if another child eggs them on, and they should never trust that it's unloaded.

>> **Notify an adult.** After they step away from the gun, they need to go tell an adult about it. At the same time, your kids need to understand that they won't get in trouble for reporting the gun — even if it means their friend will get in trouble. This is one reason why it's so important for your children to trust you.

To test their comprehension, walk your children through a few different hypothetical scenarios, like if they spot a gun at a friend's house or in a classmate's book bag. No matter the context, they should stop, stay away from the gun, and notify an adult.

Finally, establish that your kids can always call or text and ask for a ride home if they think they're in a dangerous situation.

Entering those dreaded teen years

Personally, I'd rather not think about high school again. I even try to avoid movies and TV shows set in high school because, well, I already paid my dues. Acne, the SATs, jean shorts — no thanks. I'm good.

Most people would agree that high school is tough on its own. Sadly, no one can ignore the role guns play in this chapter of life because of things like teen suicides, school shootings, and active-shooter drills. I'm sorry; I wish such traumatic events never happened, but we need to address them. Whenever a shooting occurs, whether it's close to home or 2,000 miles away, check on your kids. Ask how they're feeling. Depression is a very real concern at this age, so remind your children that they can always talk to you — and that you really want them to — even if depression makes them feel like they can't reach out to anyone.

TIP

For more help, check out the Everytown Survivor Network's "Resources for Victims and Survivors of Gun Violence" at www.everytownsupportfund.org/everytown-survivor-network/.

This is also a good opportunity to continue your conversation about guns with your kids. What part did the firearm play in this incident? Would the shooting have happened if the weapon had been properly secured? What safety rules were ignored? What impulsive decision did the gun make irreversible?

Regarding that last point, studies show that only 4 percent of suicide attempts result in death if firearms aren't present, but that figure jumps to 90 percent as soon as guns are involved because their lethality leaves little room for second chances. This speaks to the risks of owning a gun, as I discuss in Chapter 17.

Finally, if your children have grown up understanding the safety rules discussed in this chapter, they should be able to report unsafe conditions, such as another student threatening to bring a gun to school, and know that they're doing the right thing. Again, I wish they didn't have to bear this burden, but their responsibility can save lives — especially in the face of someone else's *irresponsibility*.

GUNS AREN'T AT ALL LIKE VIDEO GAMES

Try to name the last movie or TV show you watched, or the last video game you played, that didn't involve a firearm. Pretty difficult, eh?

Now think about your kids. They're going to see guns on the big and small screens at some point. It's just a matter of when. That's why, to me, the real task is helping your children differentiate between fantasy and reality, especially when it comes to firearms and violence.

Action movies and video games — especially first-person shooters — create worlds free of consequences for, say, shooting and killing other characters. Think about it. In movies, no one ever arrests the action star after the big shootout at the end, and in video games, you can die a thousand times and simply keep hitting the reset button. These are make-believe worlds.

But your kids must recognize that in the real world, one bullet can end someone's life. That victim won't "respawn" or get back up. The damage has been done. It is forever.

So, on one hand, you can pour all of your time and energy into preventing your children from ever seeing a second of violent media. Godspeed, I say. Or, you can monitor what your kids consume and check in with them regularly to ensure they remember that the real world has consequences, that guns and violence are never the answer.

Letting Other People Know You Own a Gun

Should you tell people outside your family that you own guns? That depends.

If you have a firearm on your person or in your car when you're stopped or pulled over by the police, you should notify the officer. Many states actually have "duty to inform" laws requiring it, too. I know this is a tense and possibly dangerous situation (and I discuss it further in Chapter 11), but I will always lean toward notifying the officer of the gun's presence ahead of time rather than letting them find out on their own. Every law enforcement officer I've spoken to has said the same thing. Remember: No surprises.

What about your neighbors? There are exceptions to this rule, as I get into in a moment, but in general, I do not believe in broadcasting the fact that you own firearms to others. To me, that's asking for trouble. Put an AR-15 bumper sticker on your truck, and everyone, including would-be thieves, now knows where they can obtain an AR-15.

You also don't want to intimidate others with the fact that you own a gun. This is wildly irresponsible because it could lead to a potentially deadly confrontation — something safe gun owners strive to avoid at all costs.

REMEMBER

On a related note, I want to mention that dozens of experts, including myself, do not recommend "open carry," where you carry a gun out in the open for everyone to see it. Although many states allow the practice, it's just too dangerous for everyone involved. To learn more, check out Chapter 11.

This part is crucial, however: If you have children, their friends' parents absolutely need to know that you keep a gun in your home — unloaded and locked away in a safe location, of course. Why? Well, ask yourself whether you would want to know that information.

Which brings me to my next point: Feel free to ask the parents of your kids' friends whether they keep guns in their homes. I know this might seem strange or awkward, maybe even like you're judging those parents, but the conversation can be quick and easy, especially via text. Some examples include:

>> "Hey, before I drop Mikey off, I wanted to ask if you had any guns in your home, and if they're secure."

>> "We're excited to see you! And I know this is a little awkward, but here goes: If you have any guns there, will they be locked up? Hope you understand."

>> "My kid is super curious, so if there are any guns in your home, I just want to make sure that they're locked away."

Okay, so I'm not going to win any awards for this hypothetical dialogue, but you get the idea. Don't be afraid to ask directly, even if it feels impolite. Every parent should recognize that you're just trying to keep your kids safe.

In this day and age, asking other parents whether they own firearms and keep them secure in their homes should be as common and uneventful as asking about their kids' allergies or sugar intake.

Understanding the Dangers of Overpenetration

Most homes in the U.S. are built with similar materials. Although the exteriors vary, there's a good chance the interior walls are made the same way, with drywall panels sandwiching a framework of 2-by-4-inch wooden beams, or studs, and insulation.

No, that paragraph wasn't mistakenly copied over from *Home Construction For Dummies*. If you decide to introduce a gun into your home, it's extremely important for you to understand how the walls around you are formed, because they play a major part in the fourth safety rule I discuss in Chapter 1: Be sure of your target and what is behind it.

TECHNICAL STUFF

For a moment, I want to talk about external ballistics, or what happens to a bullet when it leaves the barrel of a gun. Depending on the caliber, modern firearm bullets travel anywhere from 600 feet per second to just north of 4,000 feet per second. When you pair that blistering speed with the conical shape of a bullet, you have a projectile that can drive through, or penetrate, a wide range of materials, including drywall, wooden beams, and, despite what every action movie depicts, even car doors.

I think you probably know what I'm getting at. I talk about ammunition more thoroughly in Chapter 9, but a typical 9mm bullet — the most popular choice for handguns today — can travel through several interior walls and even exterior walls. Rifle rounds, which have much higher velocities, can punch through even more walls and barriers. (Or possibly ricochet off of hard surfaces. Bullets travel unpredictably.)

The term *overpenetration* refers to when a bullet passes through the intended target and out the other side with enough residual energy and speed to continue flying and potentially causing more damage. Overpenetration is something to avoid at all costs. The last thing you want is to fire a bullet in your home, even if it's aimed at a deadly intruder, and have it pass through a wall or two and hit your children or your significant other.

So if you're going to keep a gun for home defense, I recommend purchasing ammunition crafted specifically for that purpose. The packaging will mention that the bullets are designed for limited overpenetration, for example. Modern hollow-point bullets are actually designed to expand and "mushroom" after they hit their initial target, dumping all their energy inside it — and slowing down to the point where they're less likely to continue beyond the target.

Then you have *frangible* rounds, which are designed to disintegrate the moment they strike a hard surface. Frangible rounds are mostly used for indoor training in tight spaces like hallways to prevent bullets from ricocheting back at you after striking a target at close range.

Many people rely on shotguns for home defense because the lead pellets contained within shotgun shells don't penetrate as deeply as rifle or handgun bullets. This limitation doesn't mean that a shotgun blast won't blow a hole through a wall, however. Although shotgun ammunition is a little more complicated, a 12-gauge buckshot shell, for example, packs eight or nine lead pellets that fan outward as they fly toward your target. This is why shotguns are also known as *scatterguns*.

The greater the distance to your target, the greater the pellet dispersion, or spread. So you have to worry about any stray pellets that don't hit your initial target. Thankfully, this spread is rather limited with modern shotgun ammunition, and companies produce shotgun shells designed specifically for home defense that control how far the pellets spread within a given distance.

WARNING

Shotguns can also fire slugs, which are like giant bullets that are intended for hunting. They should never be used inside a home or within close quarters because of the risk of overpenetration.

In the end, I'm not here to recommend any specific weapons or ammunition. It's up to you to test your firearm with various ammo types to understand how they will perform in different environments, including your home. No projectile will perform as advertised 100 percent of the time, and you can't bet the lives of your family members on marketing alone.

The fact is, even in the best of circumstances, even if you've done all your research, a round can still travel through a wall and cause irrevocable harm. This is yet another reason why you should only ever use a firearm for protection as a last resort.

Chapter **6**

Safe and Secure Firearm Storage

According to the 2015 National Firearms Survey, roughly a third of all U.S. households have firearms, and an estimated 4.6 million children live in a home where at least one gun is left loaded and unlocked. That's exactly 4.6 million too many.

Worse yet, the same survey found that people who claimed to own at least one gun for "protection" were nearly 10 times more likely to leave a gun loaded and unlocked in their homes than those who kept firearms for recreation. Perhaps because they believe a safe will slow them down in an emergency — except, as I discuss later, today's gun safes can be opened in milliseconds.

So are you thinking of buying one yet?

How about this: Every year, approximately 380,000 guns are stolen from gun owners and end up being trafficked or used to commit violent crimes.

As sobering as these figures are, the solution is quite simple: Lock up your firearms to keep them away from children, thieves, and any other unauthorized users. You absolutely must. Otherwise, you're only adding to the problem.

REMEMBER

Currently, Massachusetts and Oregon are the only states that require you to secure your firearm, either with a lock or by placing it in a locked container, when it is not in use. Other states, such as California and Colorado, have more specific laws regarding when a firearm must be secured or sold with a locking device. Finally, six states and Washington, D.C., have laws in place requiring gun owners to secure their firearms if a child is likely to access an otherwise unsecured firearm, and 15 states have laws that hold gun owners accountable if a child *does* access a firearm that was not properly stored. These laws vary considerably, so make sure to read up on your state's regulations.

Of course, *how* people lock up their guns is different for everyone. You shouldn't buy the first gun safe you come across at the store. Make that mistake and you might not use it. Instead, this chapter tells you about a wide range of gun storage options to help you find the right solution for your needs.

Understanding the Locks (Sometimes) Included with Guns

Most of the time, a brand-new gun comes with a user manual, a spare magazine or two, cleaning tools if you're lucky, and a small cable or trigger lock — everything but the ammo, as they say.

WARNING

Your gun might also come with an internal mechanism or safety that purportedly disables the gun, but nothing is 100-percent foolproof. Please do not rely on these devices alone and just assume that your gun is "secure."

Now, about those locks: I've seen people ignore them completely, discard them immediately, or use them incorrectly, locking the gun *case* and not the gun itself. I'll be the first to admit that cable and trigger locks are not perfect by any stretch of the imagination, as I discuss in a moment. They should only ever be considered the bare minimum when it comes to securing your firearm, but they are a whole lot better than nothing.

Before I get to all that, however, it's important to understand why these locks are usually included in the first place here in the U.S.

The Child Safety Lock Act of 2005

In 2005, Congress passed the Child Safety Lock Act (CSLA), which requires federally licensed firearm manufacturers, importers, and dealers to include a locking device of some sort with any handgun sold or transferred to individuals. The reasoning is simple: Give gun owners at least one method of securing their handguns from children.

Here's what this congressional act means in practical terms. Whether you purchase a handgun from a small gun shop or a big sporting goods outlet, it typically comes with a cable or trigger lock. Many manufacturers also include these locks with other types of firearms, such as rifles and shotguns, but this is not specifically required at the federal level by the CSLA.

The CSLA also does not require that private sales between individuals include a locking device. (That said, some states, like California and Colorado, require locking devices for *all* weapon sales.) So depending on where you live, if you're in the market for a used handgun, it may not come with a lock.

TIP

If you still want a cable lock, ask your local police department. They usually hand out them out for free. Just don't bring your gun along for the journey!

How to use a cable lock — and why it isn't enough

A cable lock is a rather simple device that consists of — you guessed it — a cable attached to a padlock. Turning the included key unlocks a reinforced cable that you pass through the weapon's action, rendering it inoperable, before you reinsert the cable back into the padlock and lock it with the key.

To install a cable lock, you must first unload the firearm completely, so if it uses a detachable magazine, go ahead and remove it. Then you have a few more steps based on the weapon type:

>> **For a semi-auto pistol,** lock the slide back and insert the loose, unlocked end of the cable down into the pistol's ejection port and out through the magazine well before reconnecting it with the padlock. Turn the key and make sure the lock holds the cable tightly. You should end up with something that looks like Figure 6-1.

   You can also slip the free end of the cable through the barrel and out of the ejection port before securing it in the padlock.

>> **For revolvers,** open the cylinder and pivot it to the side. Now pass the free end of the cable through the barrel and reconnect it with the padlock. Again, make sure that the cable is secured in the lock before you turn the key, as shown in Figure 6-2.

Another option is to run the cable through two of the cylinder's chambers — avoiding the barrel altogether — before locking it.

» **For rifles and shotguns,** lock the bolt back and pass the free end of the cable through the ejection port and out of the magazine well or loading port. Then reconnect it with the padlock and turn the key. Figure 6-3 shows how a cable lock should look on a shotgun.

FIGURE 6-1:
One method for using a cable lock on a semi-auto pistol.

Courtesy of joebelanger/Shutterstock

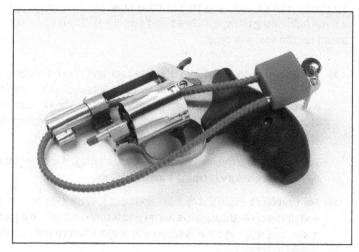

FIGURE 6-2:
Here the cable lock passes through a revolver's barrel.

Courtesy of Atlantist studio/Adobe Stock

FIGURE 6-3:
Shotguns and
rifles are secured
the same way
with a cable lock.

Courtesy of EduardSkorov/Adobe Stock

Cable locks aren't the best storage options, however. On their own, they do nothing to hide or conceal a firearm from a curious child, a would-be thief, or any other unauthorized user.

They also aren't very secure. In 2001, the U.S. Consumer Product Safety Commission recalled a total of 1.2 million cable locks provided by a firearms trade organization and a large gun manufacturer. According to reports, the padlocks could be opened without the supplied key, sometimes just by using brute force or even a paper clip.

Since those 2001 recalls, cable locks have had to pass more tests before being distributed, but those massive recalls highlight some of the dangers associated with these particular locks. These are cheap designs, and with enough time and basic tools, such as a hammer, a screwdriver, or wire cutters, anyone — even a young child — can defeat a cable lock and gain access to the firearm, so you should only consider it a temporary obstruction.

The problems with trigger locks

Your handgun might also come with a trigger lock that is designed to cover the weapon's triggerguard and prevent access to the trigger. Most trigger locks are secured with either a key or a three-digit combination, as you can see in Figure 6-4.

Like cable locks, trigger locks are simple, cheap solutions — and they have many of the same drawbacks. Once again, on its own, a trigger lock won't conceal your firearm, leaving it exposed to children and others who might be tempted to handle it. Trigger locks aren't very strong, either. Your teen just needs the right tools and a handful of minutes to break into one.

Courtesy of thenikonpro/Adobe Stock

FIGURE 6-4: A properly installed trigger lock should completely block off the triggerguard.

Trigger locks are significantly worse than cable locks, however, because they do not interfere with a firearm's action or prevent the gun from being loaded with ammunition. Also, if the trigger lock doesn't fit your gun perfectly, or if it's been installed hastily, an unauthorized user might still be able to access the trigger and, in a worst-case scenario, discharge the weapon.

In short, you should never rely on a cable or trigger lock alone to secure your weapon, and the same goes for any internal mechanisms or safeties that purportedly disable the gun.

Investing in Sturdy Steel with Gun Safes and Vaults

As I mention in Chapter 5, one of the best ways to show that you're a responsible gun owner is to lock up your firearms. But instead of sticking with a temporary solution like a cable or trigger lock, I strongly urge you to invest in a gun safe. (Please? I'm not above begging.) You need an all-steel container that only you and approved users like your significant other can open. Just think of the crimes and crises that *won't* happen because of your diligence.

There's a lot to consider when it comes to buying a safe, but the following sections should help.

Factoring in size, construction, and more

The market is awash in gun safes, which is a good thing in terms of availability, but sifting through all the choices can also be a little daunting. After you figure out the right size for your needs, however, the rest really falls into place, so you can start there:

>> **Size:** Two questions can help you determine the size of the safe you need: How many guns do you need to lock up? And do you want extra room for jewelry, cash, and those ultra-rare baseball cards? Several companies offer small lockboxes — sometimes called "vaults" — designed to fit just one gun. As you can imagine, these are the most affordable and maneuverable options.

If you want to store multiple guns, you're looking at a larger gun safe. Safe manufacturers provide estimates of how many guns fit inside each model they produce, and they typically include photos so that you can see what the safe looks like fully loaded.

Of course, weight is a concern with larger safes. You don't want your safe to fall through a floor. Large safes are much harder to move, too — which is great for thwarting burglars, but quite the headache when it comes to getting the safe into your house in the first place. If the installation isn't included with your purchase, hire movers and tip them well if you can. Don't leave the safe in your garage just because it's too difficult to get it upstairs.

TIP

If you live in a multi-level home and would prefer to keep a larger gun safe upstairs *without having to call movers,* consider a "modular safe" that will arrive in separate pieces. Then you can carry each piece upstairs and assemble the safe in the position of your choosing.

>> **Location:** When you're thinking about buying a safe, you need to figure out where you'll put it. Again, size plays an important role here because it's easier to figure out where to position a smaller pistol vault than a larger safe. The question then becomes, "Where will it fit?"

The goal is to find a place that allows you easy access to the safe but isn't obvious to thieves or children.

A closet in your bedroom is a good starting point. In this location, if your home alarm system goes off in the middle of the night, or if you hear glass breaking, for example, you can simply rush out of bed and into your closet to access your gun safe if needed.

If you have children, your safe needs to be as far away from their bedrooms and play areas as possible. I know that might be asking a lot, especially if you live in a smaller home or apartment, but the more obstacles between your kids and the gun safe, the better.

Garages typically have several strikes working against them: They're relatively easy to break into; they may contain power tools helpful for cutting or drilling into a safe; and they can be far away from your bedroom.

I've also seen people place larger gun safes in their basements, but this is a good idea only if you live where tornados are common and the guns are meant for, say, hunting or clay shooting and not for personal and home protection, when quick access is a priority.

On the other hand, some people might prefer to position their single-pistol vaults in or around their nightstands, or perhaps under their beds, for faster access. But you don't want a burglar to be able to grab the safe — or even the nightstand drawer you've tucked it in — and take off with it. Which brings me to the next aspect to consider.

>> **Anchoring:** Choose a safe that can be securely anchored to the structure of your home, meaning the floor for most safes, but possibly the wall if it's a smaller model. (See Figure 6-5.) Pistol lockboxes and vaults may come with a cable for wall or floor mounting as well.

If you've seen enough heist movies, you know that no safe is impenetrable forever. To counter a thief, however, the idea is to keep the safe in place inside your home. In this way, you're essentially keeping time on your side. If a burglar can successfully flee with the safe in tow, they might have days or weeks to break into it and steal your firearms.

At the same time, as with heavy bookcases and armoires, you need to anchor taller safes that might tip over.

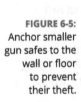

FIGURE 6-5: Anchor smaller gun safes to the wall or floor to prevent their theft.

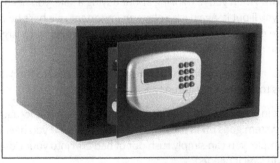

Courtesy of New Africa/Adobe Stock

Never leave a safe "loose," so to speak, or mount it to furniture that's easy to move. Concrete floors are the best anchoring surfaces, but wooden floors will work, too. If you'd prefer to mount a smaller pistol vault to the wall, make sure that you bolt it directly to wall studs or even bricks.

>> **Construction:** You want a gun safe that can withstand whatever someone might throw at it — literally and figuratively. So you need steel, and lots of it.

TECHNICAL STUFF

As with shotguns, steel is measured in *gauges*. The lower the gauge number, the thicker the steel. For larger safes or those designed to hold more than one gun, I recommend at least 10-gauge steel for the body and a heavier, thicker door because it will be the primary target. Single-pistol lockboxes and vaults will be in the 14- to 16-gauge steel range. Anything higher, such as 20-gauge steel, is just too thin and easy to pierce.

How that steel is formed and assembled is just as important as its thickness. You want a gun safe or pistol vault that is "pry resistant," meaning that it doesn't have any edges that will provide a foothold for a crowbar, for example. Safes should also be fully welded, not bolted or spot-welded together, to minimize weak points.

REMEMBER

I keep saying gun *safe* because you want an all-steel container for your guns. You should avoid any gun *cabinet* that is made of wood and has a glass door to display your weapons. Even if the door locks, breaking into it is extremely easy. The same goes for gun *lockers* made of thin aluminum or steel. On their own, lockers are mostly decorative or organizational fixtures.

>> **Fire protection:** According to the National Fire Protection Association (NFPA), more than 350,000 house fires occur every year. At the same time, most home insurance policies won't cover firearms lost due to thefts, fires, or floods. This is why gun safes are usually marketed with fire protection ratings, or estimates of how long a safe can protect its contents from extremely high temperatures over a given duration.

But there isn't a universal standard for safe manufacturers to follow in this regard, and they all use different testing labs to burn their safes and see how long the contents last at various temperatures.

To keep things as simple as possible and avoid a headache, look for a safe that can withstand heat of at least 1,200 degrees Fahrenheit on the outside — while keeping the interior at or below 350 degrees — for at least 30 minutes. If the inside gets hotter than 350 degrees, your guns and valuables might be damaged beyond repair. (Remember, today's firearms use a lot of plastic.)

>> **Extra features:** The best safes come with a few extra features that help them stand out from the pack. In this category I include a nice interior lining so that you won't scratch or damage your firearms; an interior light that turns on automatically when you open the door to the safe, which could be a lifesaver

in the dead of night; waterproofing in case you live in an area prone to flooding; and a dehumidifier. That last one is especially important, as I explain in the pages ahead.

>> **Cost:** Gun safes are available at every price point. Pistol lockboxes and vaults can be had for as low as $20, and larger, high-end safes can cost well over $20,000 before you creep into bank-vault territory. Obviously, find the price that works within your budget, but think about it: You're paying for peace of mind.

TECHNICAL
STUFF
Some safes today are Wi–Fi enabled, which means that if someone tries to move the safe or break into it, you should receive a notification on your phone. Some "smart safes" can even keep track of the combinations, fingerprints, or RFID tags that are used to open the safe.

Breaking down the various lock types

Modern gun safes are available with various lock types that allow you to balance security with ease of access in an emergency. Moreover, many models today can be unlocked using a few different means (that is, safes with electronic locks almost always come with backup systems so they can still be opened using mechanical means if something goes wrong).

You can decide which style is right for you by considering the following options:

>> **Mechanical locks** include those that open with a key, a pin, or a dial. These are considered a bit old school, but they're also known for their reliability and longevity. You don't have to worry about any electronic components failing or a battery dying.

You have a few things to consider with mechanical locks, however. For example, you might have trouble seeing the keyhole or dial if you ever need to open the safe in the dark. And where will you keep the key? Will you have it on you in an emergency, or should you stick to a simple dial?

>> **Keypad locks** are electronic locking mechanisms that use combinations. They're typically a little faster to open than mechanical locks, and most models allow you to program (and reprogram) a few different combinations. The best keypad-equipped safes have backlit numbers so you can see them in the dark, and they will also lock someone out for a set amount of time if they repeatedly enter the wrong code.

With this style, look for a safe that has a mechanical backup option, such as a key, in case the keypad fails. I also recommend a safe that comes with a rechargeable battery or uses as few non-rechargeable batteries as possible (generally no more than four) and allows you to access the battery compartment from the outside.

- » **Biometric locks** are designed to open after scanning a registered fingerprint. No, they aren't as cool or fancy looking as the kind shown in movies, but real biometric locks have come a long way in recent years, and they can be incredibly quick to open in an emergency. The best biometric gun safes also allow you to program multiple fingerprints for a few different users as well.

  You should try out a biometric safe in person before you buy it to test the fingerprint scanner's reliability. You'll also want a backup method for opening the safe, such as a key or keypad. (The safe shown in Figure 6-6 actually has *three* locking mechanisms.) Pay attention to the battery life, too. The manufacturer should give you a rough estimate of how many times the safe can be opened before the batteries die, for example.

- » **RFID locks** open using items like key fobs, watch bands, or decals encoded with a specific radio frequency. These safes are probably the fastest to open, but only if you have the RFID-tagged item nearby or on your person. As with the other electronic safes in this list, you need to consider the safe's battery life, and look for a model that comes with multiple RFID-tagged items as well as a backup mechanism, like a keypad, in case you can't find an RFID-tagged item or the sensor fails.

FIGURE 6-6:
This pistol vault has a fingerprint reader, a keypad, and a mechanical lock.

Courtesy of emholk/Getty Images

REMEMBER

If you're ever locked out of a safe, regardless of its locking mechanism, a lock-smith should be able to help you regain access. You can also check with your safe's manufacturer to see if a technician is available to help.

Avoiding less traditional storage options

If you look online for gun safes, you're likely to come across a few of the newer, more unconventional storage options available today, like safes designed to be mounted *inside* a wall or kept in the bottom drawer of a desk or dresser. These examples just scratch the surface, however.

You'll find grandfather clocks and coffee tables and faux air vents that all secretly hold weapons, not to mention all the devices built for under-bed storage. I've even seen a tissue box designed to expose a small handgun when it's tipped over. If you can think it, someone has probably made it a reality.

WARNING

But I must warn you that, although these items are great for concealing weapons, they are mostly terrible at securing them. Some of these storage options cannot be anchored to the structure of your home, plus they're made of wood just like any other piece of furniture, so they aren't as stationary or durable as a steel safe. Many also lack locks of any sort — presumably to make it easier to draw your firearm — but I have already discussed why this is problematic. Hiding your gun is one thing, but you still need to lock it up.

Finally, although it has become common to see people on social media using magnets to hide handguns under their beds, desks, or wherever, please avoid doing this. In fact, tell your friends not to do it, either. No matter how well the gun is hidden, it will be found by someone. It's just a matter of when, and I don't think you, your family, or your neighbors deserve that uncertainty. Invest in a solid steel safe.

TIP

What about keeping a firearm in your car? To learn more about vehicle storage and everything that entails, including common regulations and best practices, turn to Chapter 11.

NEVER GIVE UP SECURITY FOR SPEED

At the beginning of this chapter, I mention that gun owners who claim their guns are meant for protection, including personal and home defense, are *almost 10 times more likely* to leave a gun loaded and unlocked in their homes than those who keep guns for recreational purposes. Why?

One possible reason is that people believe they need to be able to access their firearms quickly in case an intruder attempts to enter their home — so quickly that they won't have time to fumble with a safe's combination lock, for example. But most gun safes today have locking mechanisms that can help you balance speed with security. It only takes a few nanoseconds to place your thumb on a safe's biometric scanner, or hit its RFID sensor, before you retrieve your firearm. For even greater speed, some safes have gas struts that will pop the door open for you after you gain access.

Statistically speaking, the dangers of leaving your gun unlocked — especially around kids — far outweigh any perceived risks. You can always buy yourself more time in such an emergency by installing an alarm system, for instance, or adopting a dog. These are just a few of the home-defense ideas I discuss in Chapter 16.

Grasping the Importance of Storing Ammunition Separately

Research from a wide range of sources — including the U.S. Government Account-ability Office, medical associations, and groups on both sides of the political debate surrounding guns — all indicates the same thing: Families are exponentially safer when the firearms and ammunition in a household are secured *separately* from each other. Not only that, but a few states, like California and New York, actually have laws requiring you to store your guns and ammo separately.

The idea is pretty simple: If a child is able to gain access to your firearm, through whatever means, you don't want them to be able to fire it and cause irreparable damage. So, on top of locking up your firearm in the first place, you also want to take ammunition out of the equation.

Right off the bat, your firearm should be completely unloaded whenever you're not using it. You should've emptied your gun at the range, before you got home, for example. Or before you got back into your vehicle if you spent all day hunting. But check again. If your gun uses a detachable magazine, go ahead and remove it, and make sure there isn't a round in the chamber as well. Tragedy strikes when people assume that the chamber is empty.

The next step is to lock the firearm in your safe and move the magazines and ammunition to another hidden and secure location. You don't necessarily need another heavy-duty safe for your ammunition — you might just lock the ammo in a closet or cabinet, for example, especially if you're worried about ease of access in an emergency — but be smart about it. You obviously know your situation bet-ter than I do. (I barely know you!)

Find the best setup for your needs, bearing in mind that kids are extremely curi-ous by nature. Always err on the side of caution.

TIP

If you have children and want to learn more about safe gun storage practices, be sure to check out www.besmartforkids.org, which has a number of resources, including helpful guides and videos, all backed by well-documented research.

HUMIDITY'S EFFECT ON FIREARMS

If you live in the Deep South like me, you're used to muggy summer days that bring out the sweat and swear words. Along with making you uncomfortable, that mugginess — "humidity" for the rest of the country — can also damage your firearms. Excess moisture in the air can lead to rust and corrosion forming on the gun's metal components. As someone who has restored vintage firearms that weren't stored properly for decades, I've seen the damage firsthand.

Sadly, gun safes are not immune to humidity. So what can you do?

If you live somewhere that is naturally humid, invest in a dehumidifier. There are generally two types for this purpose:

- **Electric dehumidifiers** are simple devices that slowly heat up the air inside the safe, allowing warm, dry air to circulate. The most popular in this category would be the rod-style dehumidifiers that have protected guns and museum collections for decades, but other compact designs abound. The catch here is that these dehumidifiers have to be plugged in. Larger safes sometimes come with power outlets built into their interiors, but if you don't see one, you might have to drill a hole for the plug.

- **Desiccant dehumidifiers** are great for smaller safes and pistol vaults, or those who live in less humid environments, and they don't need to be plugged in. Instead, they typically use silica gel to absorb moisture from the air. Of course, these dehumidifiers lose their effectiveness after a few months and need to be either replaced or reactivated, usually by reheating the silica gel in the oven.

  Silica gel might sound familiar. If you've ever purchased shoes or luggage, or anything that might be damaged by excess moisture, you've likely come across little packets of silica gel tucked into a nook or cranny of the packaging. Well, it's time to stop throwing those packets away! Instead, throw them into your gun safe (anywhere from one to four depending on the size of your safe), and they'll help pull the moisture out of the air. After a few months, simply replace the packets as needed.

The ideal humidity for storing your guns is 50 percent, with the temperature right around 70 degrees Fahrenheit. In reality, keeping the humidity between 40 and 60 percent will suffice in moderate temperatures. How can you be sure? For a little over $10, you can buy a small digital thermometer with a built-in *hygrometer* (say that five times fast) that measures the humidity in enclosed spaces. Welcome to the 21st century!

Chapter **7**

Manual Labor

I know it's easy to ignore some of the owner's or user manuals that come with certain products these days. We live in a "plug and play" world. I should be able to unbox a brand-new TV set, plug it into an outlet, and turn it on without much hassle. (Hear that, cable companies?)

But you, a reasonable person, also wouldn't try to assemble an IKEA dresser without the instructions. In that same vein, you can't learn every single thing there is to know about your car at the dealership — unless you plan to camp there overnight. That's why the manufacturer has stuffed a hefty owner's manual in the glove compartment, which you should read well before you end up stranded on the side of the road.

The same goes for firearms. If you don't read the manual that comes with your gun, you're driving blind, putting yourself and others at risk. Being a responsible gun owner means knowing everything you can about your specific weapon, including how to safely store it, use it, and care for it. In fact, some gun manufacturers call these little booklets "safety and instruction manuals." Thus, by definition, if you don't read yours, you're being unsafe.

My goal in this chapter is to take some of the chore out of reading your gun's user manual. I walk you through the biggest sections and provide as much background information as I can to get you started on the road to mastering your weapon and all its idiosyncrasies.

REMEMBER
If your gun is brand new, you should find a manual tucked into the case. (You might have to look under the foam inserts.) If you purchased a used gun and can't find a manual, visit the manufacturer's website to download a PDF of it.

Looking Inside Your Firearm's Manual

When you first flip through the user manual for your gun, you'll probably notice all the warnings and legalese littered throughout. I've even read through some manuals with several pages of cautionary text in bold red type. These notes are required because firearms are inherently dangerous, and as the owner, you are always responsible for safely keeping and operating your gun.

TECHNICAL
STUFF
For the record, the Protection of Lawful Commerce in Arms Act (PLCAA, or as some fun lawyers pronounce it, "placka") of 2005 prevents most lawsuits against gun manufacturers and dealers when guns are used in the commission of a crime. However, they can still be held liable for defective products, negligent marketing and sales, and other specific instances where they have violated federal gun laws. To learn more, turn back to Chapter 2.

Thankfully, the manual is a great way for manufacturers to lay out all their recommendations for using and maintaining your firearm in one place, and it's vitally important for you to read every single page, including the one early on that features a diagram of the weapon with all its components labeled — just like the figures in Chapter 3 of this book. Consider the manual to be a map to understanding your gun. But it's just the beginning.

Using the safety

After providing a list of safety rules to follow — including the four universal ones I talk about in Chapter 1 — the user manual should detail all your firearm's *safeties*, or mechanisms that physically prevent the gun from firing unintentionally. These include internal features like *drop safeties* that, as you can guess, stop the gun from firing if it's ever accidentally dropped, for example. These safeties work automatically, so you don't have to worry about them if the gun was built correctly in the first place.

Then there are external, or manual, safeties that you have to manipulate to either secure the gun or ready it for firing. Older handguns typically have *grip or thumb safeties* that you must deactivate for the gun to fire.

With a newer striker-fired pistol like a Glock, you can expect a *trigger safety* — a little tab built into the face of the trigger that you must fully depress for the trigger to move rearward. Rifles and shotguns have their own safeties, too.

Your firearm might also come with a *magazine disconnect* that renders the gun inoperable if the magazine has been removed, as well as a *loaded-chamber indicator* that tells you whether a round is in the chamber or not. For example, the extractor might stick out a little bit if a cartridge is chambered.

Although safety mechanisms are helpful, they can also break or fail just like any other mechanical device, so they should never be considered a substitute for following the four rules of gun safety. Safe gun handling starts with you.

Even if you've handled a thousand weapons, it's important to read up on how the safeties operate for your specific firearm. (And please, please don't be that person who says "My safety's between my ears!") External safeties can vary drastically between guns in terms of size, style, and even their direction of movement, especially across brands. So knowing how to activate and deactivate one does not necessarily mean you've got the hang of them all.

Loading and unloading the gun

The manual will also tell you how to safely load and unload the firearm. Depending on the weapon, the manual could also include instructions on loading the detachable magazine that is then loaded into the gun. Of course, the gun should remain *unloaded* until you're at the range or out hunting, for example.

First off, double-check that you're using the correction ammunition. I dive into this topic a bit further in the next few pages, but loading the wrong caliber into your gun can lead to a catastrophic failure that permanently damages your gun, yourself, or even bystanders. For example, if you get an incorrect round stuck in the barrel and then try to fire another round behind it, the firearm will explode.

To avoid such disasters, you need to match the caliber markings on the gun's barrel, the label of the ammo box, and the bottom of each cartridge. If you see "9mm" or "9x19" on all three, you can probably use 9mm ammunition. Most of the time, a mismatched round won't chamber in your gun, but please don't wing it.

You must also be careful not to mix your ammunition types, and I recommend examining each and every round to ensure that it can be safely used. If you have any doubts or questions, ask a professional.

When you insert the magazine into the firearm, you also have to make sure that it seats properly. You should hear it *click* into position; if you don't, tug on the bottom of the magazine a bit to make sure that it doesn't move.

REMEMBER

And for the 1,000th time, you can't ever ignore the safety rules. So even as you load and unload your gun, keep the muzzle pointed in a safe direction and your finger away from the trigger.

The manual will then show you the manufacturer's recommended steps for chambering a round — also known as *charging* the gun. Depending on the design, you might have to manipulate a bolt, lever, or slide. Each of these parts requires a different *manual of arms*, or operating technique, but the gist is the same: getting a round into the barrel so that it can be fired. (To learn more about the mechanics of various firearms, turn back to Chapter 3.)

To unload the weapon, the manual will explain how to use the *magazine release*, a button or switch that allows the detachable magazine to drop free from the frame or receiver. Some firearms have ambidextrous magazine releases with buttons or paddles on both sides of the weapon so it's easier for righties and lefties to drop the magazine.

More guns have reversible magazine releases. With the latter, the manual will show you how to switch the release from the left side of the gun to the right side, or vice versa, for easier reloading depending on which hand you favor.

REMEMBER

After you've removed the magazine, you must retract the weapon's slide or bolt to ensure that a round isn't in the chamber, or rear portion of the barrel. Too many people forget this crucial step, and tragedy ensues. To learn more about this process, turn back to Chapter 1.

Disassembly made easy

Firing a gun is a dirty process. Remember, you're creating a little explosion that produces all sorts of fouling and residue that builds up inside the weapon over time, so you'll have to take the gun apart at some point to clean it. Otherwise, the moving parts inside the gun will get sticky and eventually jam.

The manual will probably recommend taking the gun apart and cleaning it after each visit to the range. I know this might seem excessive — and some gun enthusiasts love boasting about how long they go between cleaning sessions — but you don't want to risk having an unreliable gun.

Along with cleaning the gun, it's important to keep those moving parts lubricated, and after firing thousands of rounds, you'll eventually need to replace some components that have worn out. I dig into these topics further in Chapters 8 and 10, but for now, here are the two levels of disassembly:

>> **Field stripping** your gun means taking it down to its major components to clean or replace parts *without tools*. So, on a semi-auto handgun, for instance, you're taking the slide off the frame and removing the barrel and recoil spring assembly. That's about it.

>> **Detail stripping** your gun means taking it completely apart — all the way down to the nuts and bolts — which will require tools.

WARNING

Before you begin the disassembly process, you need to be absolutely sure that the gun is completely unloaded. Remove the magazine and double-check that there isn't a round in the chamber. Now check again. This verification is crucial because, as much as I hate it, some firearms actually require you to pull the trigger to take them apart.

The manual will teach you how to field strip your gun for routine cleaning and maintenance (and put it back together, of course), but it probably won't go into detail stripping. In fact, it might even warn against it because the manufacturer doesn't want you tinkering with some of the smaller components and breaking them, or, worse yet, reinstalling them improperly, which could create a dangerous situation. Your gun could become unsafe and you might not even know it.

Instead, the manual will suggest taking the weapon to a qualified gunsmith if you want to replace any smaller parts or modify the gun in some way. Go too far and you could void the gun's warranty, which brings me to . . .

Learning the warranty information

If your gun came with a warranty, the manual will probably describe what is covered or not covered. You should also check with the manufacturer directly if you don't see this information in the booklet.

As you can imagine, the warranties differ between makers. Some companies offer one-year warranties that cover any manufacturing defects that arise within that time frame. Others provide "lifetime" warranties that last as long as the product is still supported by the company and available on the market. It might also be limited to the original owner. But it almost never means that the warranty lasts for *your* entire lifetime. (May it be long and prosperous!)

It's important to read the warranty's fine print for terms and conditions. In most cases, if a manufacturing defect becomes apparent, the maker will repair your gun, or replace it entirely, free of charge. These companies have massive assembly lines, and mistakes happen. Recalls are rather common, too.

You might have to pay for shipping, but again, I recommend contacting the manufacturer to see how its process works.

On the other hand, warranties generally don't cover any repairs your gun might need because of mishandling on your part. If, say, you accidentally back your truck over your hunting rifle or get the wrong ammunition stuck in the barrel — I won't name names, but I've heard many horror stories — the manufacturer will probably tell you to contact a local gunsmith.

WARNING

You can also void your gun's warranty by modifying the weapon in some way, whether that's altering or replacing any of its components, adding a custom finish, adjusting the trigger, or anything like that.

Watching Out for Other Warnings

While you're reading through your firearm's manual, you might come across a few warnings that could honestly use a little bit more background information. As someone who has studied dozens of these manuals over the years, I know that manufacturers can sometimes tell you not to do something without taking the time to give you the *why* behind it. So let me help.

Avoiding the wrong ammunition

Although the manual will remind you to use the correct caliber with your weapon, you might also see some warnings about specific types of ammunition. For example, every manual I've read has recommended that shooters use clean, dry, and commercially produced ammunition, or the kind made by factories with several quality-control measures. What they don't want you to use is *handloaded* ammunition — the DIY stuff that people put together when they want some alone time away from their kids.

TECHNICAL
STUFF

Making your own ammunition is an expert-level endeavor. You have to consult the right guide for the ammo you want to make; find the right bullets, powders, primers, and cases; and use special tools to put everything together correctly so the ammo functions safely and reliably at the range. Get something wrong and your gun could suffer a catastrophic failure, injuring yourself or others.

REMEMBER

To learn more about "squib loads" and other dangerous ammo-related problems, turn to Chapter 14.

Manufacturers also generally recommend against using higher-pressure ammunition, or what are known as "+P" and "+P+" rounds. In the gun world, cartridges loaded to a higher internal pressure level than the standard for the caliber have much more speed and energy when they exit the barrel. But they also put a lot of wear and tear on your firearm's internal components, and some guns are simply not built or rated to handle that extra pressure. So keep an eye out for "+P" warnings or those mentioning specific pressure ratings.

The manual might also contain warnings about certain projectile types or cases. Some guns can be quite finnicky about which bullets will feed properly into their chambers. I've tested a few 1911-style pistols that would jam if you tried to fire hollow-point rounds, for example.

A manufacturer might also tell you to stay away from steel-cased ammo. Although these rounds are cheaper than their brass-cased brethren, they don't seal as well in the chambers of some firearms because steel isn't as malleable as brass, leading to firing and extraction issues.

TIP

Finally, I want to mention that because of how they're made, some guns require a "break-in period" before they can perform at their best. In this situation, the manufacturer will state in the manual how many rounds you should fire through the gun to break it in and loosen up its tolerances. Until you cross that threshold, the gun might repeatedly jam or shoot inaccurately, but stick with it.

Finding the right balance of lubrication

In Chapter 10, I get into the nitty gritty of cleaning and maintaining your gun, and I've dedicated a good bit to lubrication. But you also want to pay attention to the notes about lubrication in your firearm's manual. The manufacturer will tell you how much oil to use, for example, and pinpoint the specific places where it should be applied.

In general, you want to use a light touch with gun oil.

Use too much oil, or put it in the wrong place, and the gun's internal parts can actually attract dirt, unburned gunpowder, and carbon residue from firing, which will gum up the works and lead to jams. The manual will also stress using firearm-specific lubricants and cleaning compounds designed for the environment you live in.

Keeping the Record Straight

For this last section, I want to stress the importance of good recordkeeping. Right off the bat, gun manufacturers are required to stamp serial numbers on their weapons. That way, if the gun is ever stolen, used to commit a crime, and recovered, law enforcement personnel can learn more about the gun and trace it back to its original point of sale. The numbers can tell you when and where the gun was made, too, which can be important for collectors.

You'll find the serial number on the frame or receiver of the weapon, and it might also be printed on a label stuck to the side of the gun case. Write it down, and keep that information separate, away from the gun. Then, if the gun's ever stolen, you can report the loss to law enforcement and give them the serial number in case it ever turns up again.

Similarly, it's a good idea to keep track of your weapon's usage and cleaning schedule. This tracking might seem tedious, but if you record how many rounds you fire each time you visit the range, you'll be in a better position to know when certain parts need to be replaced. Think of it as your gun's odometer.

Your notes can even help you figure out which ammo types, or loads, your gun prefers, too. Bring your paper targets home from the range and measure your groups — or how widely your shots are dispersed — with each load. Over time, you'll see which loads are more accurate in your gun.

TIP

To help you keep track of multiple weapons, visit www.atf.gov to download a free "Personal Firearms Record." This handy chart provides blanks for you to fill in each gun's make, model, serial number, caliber or gauge, and much more.

Chapter **8**

Cleaning and Maintenance

Gun enthusiasts regularly bemoan having to clean their weapons, and online forums are full of people asking questions like "When should I clean my gun?" and "Do I really have to?"

Trust me, I get it. After a lengthy day at the range, it can be tough finding the energy to scrub out the lead, carbon, and unburnt gunpowder that have found their way into every crevice of your firearm. But at the risk of being labeled a weirdo, I actually enjoy the process. There's something Zen about it, and I know that keeping a gun clean and well maintained is yet another cornerstone of being a responsible gun owner. A dirty gun is inaccurate and prone to malfunctioning, which can be dangerous. This is why I clean and lubricate my guns after every trip to the range, and I recommend the same for anyone who asks.

In this chapter, I walk you through the entire process of cleaning and maintenance, from assembling a cleaning kit to replacing worn parts, so that you can keep your gun looking and performing at its best.

WARNING

Before you attempt to disassemble or clean your gun, you must ensure that it's completely unloaded. Remove or unload the magazine, and double-check to make sure there isn't a round in the chamber.

Caring for Your Gun between Trips to the Range

As I mention in Chapter 7, the user manual that comes with your firearm will provide detailed instructions for taking it apart, cleaning it, and lubricating it. (If you purchased a used gun, check the manufacturer's website for a PDF of this important booklet.) The manual might even recommend that you clean and oil the weapon *before* you hit the range with it for the first time because many guns leave the factory with "packing grease," an anti-rusting agent, on their internal parts that should be removed before firing live ammunition.

Obviously, the user manual will be your guide here, but I have a few more tips and tricks to assist you along the way and save you some time. It all begins with collecting the best tools for the job.

Gathering the right tools and supplies

If you're new to this, I recommend a "universal" cleaning kit that can handle multiple weapons (as shown in Figure 8-1) or one designed for your specific weapon type — like a pistol cleaning kit or a shotgun cleaning kit. Each of these options can serve as a great starting point, providing you with an array of tools in a handy bag or box that's easy to tote and store.

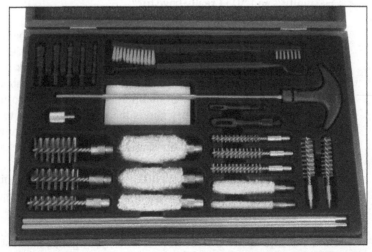

FIGURE 8-1:
Every bore brush in this universal cleaning kit is designed to handle a different caliber or gauge.

Courtesy of Jeffrey B. Banke/Shutterstock

I say "starting point" because the tools in these kits aren't always made for the long haul, so to speak. Over time, you'll have to replace some of them, but then you have a chance to really personalize your cleaning kit.

You might even end up with a dedicated workbench in the garage. Look out!

At the very least, your kit should include:

>> Bore brushes (use one that's the correct caliber for your firearm)

>> Bore cleaning rods or snakes

>> Cloth patches

>> Cotton swabs

>> A toothbrush

>> A dry rag, towel, or microfiber cloth

>> Small screwdrivers and punches

>> A cloth or rubber mat to clean your gun on

>> Latex, nitrile, or rubber gloves

The gloves are important because you're cleaning up toxic substances like lead, and some of the cleaning supplies can be toxic as well, which brings me to my next point. You'll need to clean and lubricate your gun with two separate products or an all-in-one product:

>> **Cleaning solvents** are designed to do just that — clean various surfaces inside and outside your weapon. The classic choice is Hoppe's No. 9, which has a great scent but also contains some toxic chemicals, so look for the company's newer synthetic blend if you go this route.

>> **Lubricants** ensure that critical, high-stress areas within the firearm function smoothly over time. You'll see these products marketed as gun oils or grease.

>> **All-in-one products** are known as "CLPs" because they clean, lubricate, and protect your firearms inside and out. Like the previous options, you can find petroleum-based products as well as synthetic and all-natural, nontoxic formulas. For decades, the U.S. military has been using BreakFree CLP, but Ballistol and FrogLube are also popular choices in this arena.

WARNING

Only use cleaners and lubricants specifically formulated for guns. If you opt for your favorite household cleaner or, say, motor oil, you could damage your firearm's finish or void the warranty.

How do you choose between dedicated products and CLPs? It really comes down to preference and how often you hit the range. If you're only shooting occasionally and need to clean a gun or two, a CLP should do the trick. But if you shoot regularly or have truly dirty guns, you might find that separate products clean and lubricate more effectively.

Taking your gun apart

WARNING

Before you attempt to disassemble or clean your gun, you must ensure that it's completely unloaded. Remove the magazine and verify that the chamber is empty. Then check it again. The safest practice is to remove any and all ammunition from the area, too.

For routine cleaning, you really only need to *field strip* the firearm, or take it down to its major components without tools, as described in the user manual. The process varies by make and model. For a revolver, you just have to pivot the cylinder to the side. *Voilà.* For semi-auto handguns, you need to take the slide off the frame and remove the barrel and recoil spring assembly. You can stop there.

Occasionally, you'll need to *detail strip* the gun, or take it completely apart using tools. This is why I included screwdrivers and punches in the earlier list of supplies. But you must be careful; it's easy to lose small parts like pins and screws, or forget where they belong, and if you aren't careful, any components held under spring pressure could fly across the room when you free them. (Trust me, it's embarrassing.)

TIP

The first time you detail strip your gun, take photos along the way so that you can look back and see how smaller pieces like pins and springs should be oriented when it's time to reassemble the gun. Otherwise, if you, say, reverse a spring during the reinstallation process, you'll run into malfunctions at the range.

Finally, if you're all thumbs or don't want to chase parts around your garage, a gunsmith can take your gun apart and clean it for a fee.

Scrubbing the barrel

After you've gathered your cleaning supplies and disassembled your gun, the first thing you'll want to clean is the barrel to remove any lead fouling or residues that have built up from shooting. To clean the barrel, follow these steps:

1. **Wrap a cloth cleaning patch around the slotted tip at the front of your bore cleaning rod.**

2. **Soak the patch in cleaning solvent or CLP.**

3. **Feed the patch into the bore from the breech end (as shown in Figure 8-2) and push it through the barrel toward the muzzle.**

   Don't start from the muzzle end because doing so could damage the barrel's rifling. The patch should come out covered in soot.

   Alternatively, you can spray solvent or CLP on a bore snake and pull it through the barrel from breech to muzzle.

4. **If the barrel is truly dirty, grab a bore brush of the correct caliber — a 9mm bore brush for a 9mm barrel, for example — and run it through the barrel from breech to muzzle.**

   If you try to use a larger bore brush, it will get stuck in the barrel.

5. **Run a fresh cloth patch through the barrel from breech to muzzle.**

   This step picks up some of the debris dislodged by the bore brush. Repeat this step with fresh patches until you push one through that remains white.

6. **Look down the barrel from the breech end to see whether the bore is bright and shiny. (Good lighting helps here.)**

   If so, you're all done with the barrel.

Note: For a revolver, you'll want to use the bore brush and cloth patches to clean the barrel and each of the chambers within the cylinder. You'll also have to clean the barrel from the muzzle end, so be careful as you go.

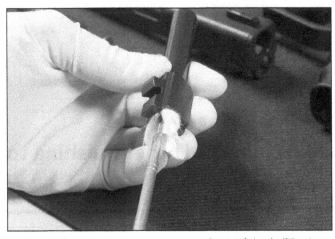

FIGURE 8-2:
Push the cloth cleaning patch into the barrel from the rear, or breech end.

Courtesy of wingedwolf/Getty Images

Inspecting the interior

Although the barrel requires the most attention, gunk can build up in little nooks and crannies inside the slide and frame or receiver of a gun. For these areas, use a dry toothbrush to remove any debris you find.

If the grit and grime seems extra stubborn, dab a cotton swab in cleaning solvent or CLP and wipe in and around the dirtiest areas. You might need a few swabs to remove the fouling.

TIP

Compressed air can also help you clean out hard-to-reach areas, like some of the long, thin grooves cut into slides and frames.

Now take your rag, towel, or microfiber cloth and wipe away any leftover residue or cleaning solvent, as shown in Figure 8-3. If your gun had a quality finish on its metal components to begin with, they should look almost new at this point. You should also keep an eye out for broken or cracked parts that must be replaced.

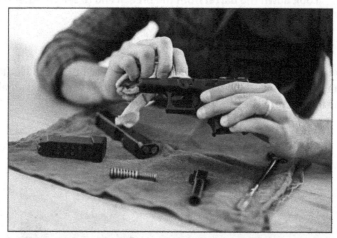

FIGURE 8-3:
Use an old rag or towel to wipe up residues and excess solvent.

Courtesy of Yuri_Arcurs/Getty Images

Adding lube and other finishing touches

Before you reassemble the firearm, you need to lubricate a few critical areas inside it to ensure that it keeps running smoothly. The gun oil or CLP can also protect your gun's internal parts from undue wear and tear.

That said, don't go overboard. You don't want a bone-dry weapon or one dripping with lubricant. Use too much oil or CLP and your gun's internal components will actually attract dirt and fouling, which can then gum up the works, so to speak, and create an unsafe situation.

So binge all the TV you want, grab an extra helping of dessert, go wild. But when it comes to lubricating your firearm, self-restraint is key. A little lube goes a long way.

To help you out, your gun's user manual should tell you exactly where to add gun oil or CLP. A cotton swab can help you apply it precisely, too. Then, when you're satisfied, it's time to reassemble the weapon and work the action a few times — rack the slide, run the bolt, open and close the cylinder — to ensure that everything has been properly reinstalled.

The last step is to wipe the exterior of the gun down one more time with your rag or towel to remove any fingerprints and excess oil. And if "once in a while" finally arrived and you decided to detail strip your entire gun to clean all the small bits, consider cleaning the magazines, too.

TIP

To make sure that you get the most out of your time on the range or out hunting, pack along a small cleaning kit that has all the essentials. That way, if your gun starts jamming, you can address the issue and clean your gun without having to head home first.

Dealing With the Usual Wear and Tear

When you fire a gun, you're essentially harnessing a tiny explosion to launch a bullet toward your target. As you can imagine, that explosion creates immense pressure and heat — along with fouling and debris — that puts a lot of stress on your firearm's internal components.

So, as you fire more rounds through your weapon, you should expect it to exhibit more wear and tear. This is a natural, unavoidable byproduct of repetitive firing. You just have to know what to expect and which parts need to be replaced to keep your gun running smoothly.

WARNING

If you ignore the warning signs and continue using your firearm with worn or damaged parts, the gun may start malfunctioning and could pose a danger to you and others at the range. If you're ever in doubt or have questions about your weapon, talk to a certified gunsmith.

As I mention in Chapter 7, keep a record of how many rounds you fire through your gun at the range. No, you don't need to keep a running tally between shots, but if you have a general idea of the round count, you'll be in a better position to replace parts as needed. Think of it like keeping track of your car's mileage so that you know when to change the oil and rotate the tires.

Identifying common wear points

The exterior of your gun will probably be the first element to show signs of use. Even if you bought a quality firearm with a durable finish sealing the metal components — such as black oxide (more commonly known as bluing), Cerakote, Parkerizing, or any number of marketing catchphrases — and, if applicable, a good stain on the wooden parts, dings and scratches happen.

With enough use, these finishes can wear down, and if moisture enters the equation, the exposed portions of the metal will pit or rust, or the wood will warp. This is why it's important to keep your firearm dry and monitor the humidity in your safe.

You have a gun safe, right? Or you're thinking about it? Check out Chapter 6.

Of course, every firearm is different, and thus wears differently. I can only offer general suggestions here. But if you only take your gun to the range occasionally — and keep it clean and lightly lubricated between outings like a good reader! — the exterior might be your only real concern.

However, if you fire thousands upon thousands of rounds through your gun, you have to examine a few more areas:

>> **The recoil spring** is one of the first parts you'll need to replace on a semi-auto pistol after firing anywhere from 3,000 to 5,000 rounds. After that, the spring can weaken and create cycling issues. Thankfully, these springs are usually pretty cheap and easy to replace. Some guns even come with replacement recoil springs.

>> **Detachable magazines** for semi-auto pistols and rifles will also start failing after heavy use. Specifically, the spring inside the magazine can weaken to the point where it won't push rounds upward and into the chamber properly. The magazine's follower and feed lips can also loosen and give out, causing more failure-to-feed malfunctions. The easiest solution here is to just replace the entire magazine.

To learn more about detachable magazines and how they work, as well as the most common malfunctions, turn to Chapter 14.

>> **The barrel** on any gun will wear out after firing thousands of rounds. Over time, the rifling and *throat* — the portion of the barrel just ahead the chamber but before the start of the rifling — can erode. However, the rate of deterioration depends on several variables, including the gun type, caliber, and ammunition quality.

As I mention in Chapter 9, higher-pressure ammunition (known as "+P" or "+P+" rounds) can shorten the life span of your barrel, as can excessive heat. This is why you should really let your firearm's barrel cool down between strings of fire.

Rifles might need new barrels after firing anywhere from 5,000 to 15,000 rounds, whereas handgun and shotgun barrels should last well beyond 50,000 rounds. Of course, your mileage may vary. A worn-out barrel will be less accurate, so if you aren't quite hitting the bullseye like you used to — assuming that you're still bringing your "A" game when it comes to your shooting skills — the barrel might be the culprit.

>> **The extractor** is another failure point on semi-auto firearms. This small component is responsible for pulling the spent casing out of the chamber and ejecting it from the firearm after you fire a round. When the extractor starts to give out, you'll run into more failures to eject — that is, spent casings won't get out of the way of the bolt (for rifles and shotguns) or slide (for pistols) as it returns forward.

Again, I cover these malfunctions and more in Chapter 14.

>> **Small controls,** including safeties and release buttons or levers, will also wear down with heavy use — I'm talking tens of thousands of activations. Think of a well-worn computer keyboard with keys you can't identify or engage as easily as before. (Try typing out a *For Dummies* book!) The same goes for a firearm's controls, which will need to be replaced.

Replacing parts — and knowing your limits

Hundreds of years ago, firearms were crafted by hand, and if you ever needed a part replaced or repaired, you had to rely on a skilled gunsmith to perform the necessary work, which could be expensive and time consuming.

The concept of interchangeable parts — using machinery to create standardized components of the same dimensions — arrived at the turn of the 18th century, and the Industrial Revolution perfected the technique, allowing factory workers to assemble more guns than ever before from piles of interchangeable parts.

Today's guns are mass-produced using state-of-the-art machinery designed to hold extremely tight tolerances. In other words, the interchangeable parts are more interchangeable than ever before, which means that you won't necessarily need to take your gun to a gunsmith for every repair or upgrade.

For example, if you need to replace your semi-auto pistol's barrel or recoil spring assembly, you should be able to order replacements from the original manufacturer and swap them out with the old ones. This is a great idea for magazines, too. Just make sure to order the right parts for your exact model. When in doubt, give the company a call.

I recommend going to the original manufacturer for the parts you need before you try an aftermarket maker. I say this because the former most likely sells spare barrels made to the same specifications, and perhaps even made using the same machinery and equipment, as your gun's original barrel, for example. The manufacturer should also stand behind its products.

Aftermarket components, however, might not be made to the exact same dimensions, or with similar quality-control measures in place. Also, aftermarket parts can void your gun's warranty.

WARNING

On the other hand, you can only go so far with interchangeable "plug and play" parts. If you need to replace a rifle or revolver barrel, or some important action components, contact a certified gunsmith. Don't risk voiding your gun's warranty or creating a dangerous jam-o-matic simply because you wanted to go the do-it-yourself route.

Here's a good rule of thumb: If the user manual describes how to remove the part, or if you can access the part easily while field stripping your gun, you can probably replace it with a "drop-in" component. Otherwise, go to a gunsmith. Even if you want to change out your gun's front and rear sights, a gunsmith can ensure that the new versions are correctly installed and aligned.

REMEMBER

For more help with customizing or upgrading your firearm, including a breakdown of what you can do at home versus what you should let a gunsmith handle, turn to Chapter 10.

Troubleshooting Two Larger Issues

Replacing worn or defective parts is one thing, but in the course of owning and using a firearm, you might run into a few more problems that are best dealt with sooner rather than later. Remember, you're dealing with machinery, and every machine will fail at some point.

WARNING

If an issue arises, stop what you're doing, lock the bolt or slide back if you can, and unload the gun.

Many complications will require a visit to a reputable gunsmith, especially those that involve the firearm's firing cycle — or your gun's ability to feed ammunition, fire projectiles, and extract casings — but I know of two specific situations that you can hopefully solve on your own, even if you aren't that handy or mechanically inclined.

Clearing bore obstructions

One critical aspect of gun safety is ensuring that nothing ever obstructs your firearm's barrel, be it dirt, debris, or a bullet fragment.

In the course of shooting or hunting, you might end up firing a *squid load* — and hear a softer *poof* sound instead of the usual *bang*. In this situation, a cartridge wasn't loaded with enough gunpowder, so the bullet gets lodged in the barrel. Though rare, this is an extremely dangerous situation because, if you don't notice that a round is stuck in the barrel and you fire another one, the barrel will explode.

I describe squib loads and other ammo-related problems in Chapter 14. But these aren't the only causes of barrel obstructions. As I said, you might get a bullet fragment or a cloth cleaning patch stuck in the bore. So what do you do? Follow these steps:

1. **Lock the slide or bolt back on your firearm.**

2. **Unload the gun completely.**

3. **If you were just shooting at the range, let the barrel cool for a few minutes, and then disassemble the firearm.**

4. **Look through the barrel from the breech end. If you have a flashlight, shine it down the bore to see whether you can spot the obstruction.**

5. **If there's a blockage, take a brass bore cleaning rod or thin wooden dowel and push it down the barrel from the muzzle end.**

   After you hit resistance, keep pushing until you dislodge the obstruction. It might take a few taps.

6. **If the projectile or patch doesn't budge after repeated nudges, you might need to take the weapon to a gunsmith. Sorry!**

7. **If you can remove the blockage, you now need to examine the bore to make sure that the rifling hasn't been damaged.**

   I recommend a brass rod or wooden dowel to avoid damaging the rifling as you remove any obstructions; both materials are softer than steel.

   A bore scope is an excellent tool for examining the interior of the barrel, but you can also tilt the barrel toward a light source while you look through the breech end. Or, if you're in a well-lit area, you can hold a white card about an inch in front of the muzzle and peer through the breech end of the barrel.

   If you see any irregularities or abrasions in the spiral grooves of the rifling, you might need to replace the barrel. Consult a gunsmith for a second opinion.

Removing light rust

As I mention earlier in this chapter, it isn't that hard for rust to develop on your firearm's metal components, especially if you live in a hot, humid environment — or, more specifically, if you forget to monitor the temperature and humidity inside your gun safe. (Buy a hygrometer!)

I've seen every kind of rust on firearms, from the light stuff that forms on guns used in wet conditions, or handled by sweaty dudes, and not wiped down afterward, to the heavy rust that eats away at guns improperly stored long term, including vintage handguns kept inside leather holsters for decades. I was able to restore those damaged firearms and others, but it wasn't easy.

To remove light rust, try these three steps at home:

1. **Use a rag to wipe cleaning solvent or CLP into the rusted portion of the metal surface.**

   Don't be afraid to put a little elbow grease into it — the solvent or CLP won't hurt the metal's finish. If you're lucky, the rust will wipe away immediately, but if it doesn't, go on to the next step.

2. **Purchase a tube of Flitz metal polish and carefully, lightly work a little bit of it into the surface with a rag.**

   Go with the grain of the metal as you wipe to ensure that you don't scratch or abrade the finish.

   When you're done, wipe away the excess polish and lightly clean the area with solvent or CLP once again.

   Still didn't work? You have one more step . . .

3. **Pour a little lubricant or CLP on the affected area and rub it down with 0000-grade steel wool.**

   This is the finest level of steel wool, so it shouldn't scratch the metal as long as it's paired with a lubricant.

   Now wipe away the excess lubricant with a rag and inspect the area. If you still see some rusting or pitting, consider taking the firearm to a professional gunsmith or restoration service.

TIP

For more gun restoration techniques, turn to Chapter 19.

Chapter **9**

Getting to Know Ammunition

The ammo aisle at your local gun shop or sporting goods store can be daunting because of all the different brands and types available — if you're lucky enough to find anything on the shelves, that is. Unprecedented demand has kept ammunition in short supply over the past few years.

That said, you shouldn't jump on the first ammo box that magically appears. The easy route can lead to problems with your gun and even be dangerous. So while you wait for those shelves to be replenished, you might as well learn everything you can about handgun, rifle, and shotgun ammunition. That way, you can make an informed purchase when the time finally comes.

I discuss ammunition briefly in Chapter 3 to give you a better understanding of how firearms work. In this chapter, I get a bit more in depth to help you navigate this crowded landscape. I decode some of the jargon related to this facet of the gun world, explain the differences between today's most common rounds, and give you a peek at what they're used for.

Fair warning: Although I promise to keep things moving along, this is easily the most technical chapter in the book. I also can't possibly go into every single caliber out there. There are just too many — hundreds alive and well, and hundreds more extinct — to describe in this space. Nor am I going to get into debates about which caliber is "the greatest of all time." I have to leave *something* for gun guys to discuss on Reddit!

Making Sense of Rifle and Handgun Ammunition

Choose the wrong ammo, and your gun might not be as accurate as you had hoped. It might jam over and over again. In fact, when I see someone's gun sputter at the range, my first thought is to inspect the ammo they're using. But mismatched ammo can even make your gun hazardous to operate.

My goal is to help you understand all the options available to you so that you're one step closer to finding the right ammunition for your gun and your specific needs, whether that's target practice, competition, hunting, or even self-defense. Starting at square one, it's all about vocabulary.

Getting acquainted with cartridge components and naming conventions

Since the 1800s, handguns and rifles have been designed to fire self-contained metallic cartridges, or *cartridges* for short. You can also call them *rounds*. Figure 9-1 shows what a handgun cartridge would look like if you cut it open. Use it as a guide for the following *bullet*ed list (pun intended).

>> The *case,* or *casing,* is a metal component that holds the primer, gunpowder, and bullet together. Brass has been the material of choice for cases for well over 150 years because of its strength and malleability. It's tough enough to withstand the explosion that goes with firing a bullet, yet it's flexible enough to be reshaped, and thus reloaded with a fresh projectile, after firing. Brass also seals well inside the *chamber,* or the rear portion of the barrel that is designed to fit one cartridge of the correct size and caliber, and won't damage the harder steel components of your firearm.

Steel-cased rounds are also available. They're cheaper than brass-cased rounds but aren't as reliable in some weapon types. Steel cases are also next to impossible to reload with fresh projectiles after they've been fired once, which is why many gun ranges prohibit guests from using them. (They don't want shooters to mix up their brass casings, which can be reused for home-made ammo, and steel casings, which can't be recycled, when they collect them afterward.)

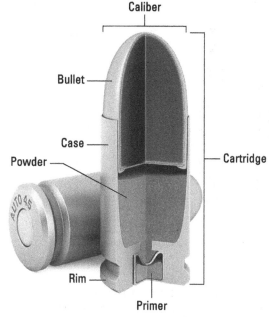

Caliber

Bullet

Case

Powder

Cartridge

Rim

Primer

FIGURE 9-1:
This cutaway
illustration
identifies
the major
components of a
.45 ACP round.

Courtesy of natatravel/Adobe Stock

More recently, companies have begun experimenting with plastic and hybrid cases to create lighter or higher-pressure ammunition for the U.S. military. With the latter, a steel case head is paired with a brass casing.

TECHNICAL STUFF

For some reason, although the top part of the case that accepts the bullet is called the *mouth,* the bottom of the case is known as the *base* or *head.* (I guess "case butt" would be too entertaining.) The case head is normally stamped to identify the maker of the round as well as the caliber (for civilians) or the date of manufacture (for the military). Collectively, this is important information known as the *headstamp.*

REMEMBER

It's always a good idea to check your cartridge headstamps to make sure their caliber markings match the one on your gun's barrel.

The bottom outer edge of the case is known as the *rim.* Some weapons, like revolvers, used *rimmed* cartridges, which has a wider rim than the case to hold the cartridge in the chamber. Semi-automatic weapons use *rimless cartridges,* which is yet another misnomer. There's still a rim, but it's the same width as the case. The rim is paired with a small groove so that the gun can grab onto the case and extract it from the chamber after firing. Figure 9-2 shows both rimmed and rimless cartridges.

Courtesy of Sorathep Manmuang/Shutterstock

» The *primer* is a small, highly explosive chemical compound that erupts when struck by the weapon's hammer or firing pin, igniting the gunpowder inside the case. The location of the primer is important, too.

With *rimfire* rounds, the primer is tucked inside the rim of the case, and the gun's firing pin simply hits the rim to start the ignition process. Many smaller calibers are in fact rimfire rounds, including the .22 Long Rifle (LR), the most popular caliber today for first-time shooters.

Rounds larger than the .22 LR are generally *centerfire* designs that have the primer compound tucked into a small compartment in the center of the cartridge base. This centralized location helps the gunpowder burn more consistently and thus propels bullets with greater velocity and energy.

» The *gunpowder* (or simply "powder") is an explosive that, when ignited, sends the projectile racing down the barrel. The earliest gunpowder was known as black powder, but the 1800s also saw the introduction of smokeless powder. (Yet another misnomer. It still produces smoke, but to a lesser extent.)

Today, almost all ammunition uses smokeless powder, but black powder is still popular among reenactors who use vintage weapons or replicas as well as hunters who prefer to use modern muzzleloaders.

» The final component is the *bullet,* the metal projectile that launches from the barrel and heads toward your target. There are numerous bullet styles today, as I discuss in the coming pages.

The *caliber* is simply the diameter of the bullet. This measurement is typically expressed in inches in the U.S. So for all practical purposes, a .45-caliber round has a 0.45-inch-diameter bullet.

TECHNICAL STUFF

Gun aficionados will remind you that the diameter of a .45 ACP bullet is actually 0.452 inches. This is because every bullet is ever so slightly larger than interior of the barrel to create a tight seal for the propellant gases. The bullet actually squeezes down the barrel as it goes, which is why the barrel will be way too hot to touch after you fire a gun.

Europeans use the metric system, so a 9mm bullet has a diameter of 9 millimeters. You might also see a cartridge described as the "9x19mm," which means that the bullet is 9 millimeters in diameter and the case is 19 millimeters long. (Or should I say milime*tres*?)

Finally, the weight of the bullet is described in *grains*, a prehistoric unit of measurement that has one grain equaling 1/7,000th of a pound. With 9mm rounds, for example, you'll find bullets weighing anywhere from 115 to 147 grains. Larger .45 ACP rounds feature bullets weighing 165 to 230 grains. More on weight in a moment.

As I mention in Chapter 3, handgun and rifle cartridges were originally identical, but over time, rifle cartridges received longer, more aerodynamic bullets that could fly farther as well as larger cases that contained more gunpowder and thus provided more power to propel those bullets. Handgun rounds remained the same relative size, as you can see in Figure 9-3.

FIGURE 9-3: Note how the two rifle cartridges (far left and far right) compare to pistol rounds.

Courtesy of cherylvb/Adobe Stock

Looking at the basics of ballistics and barrel rifling

No, you don't need a PhD in physics to grasp how bullets work and choose the right ammo for your needs, but a little ballistics knowledge won't hurt.

Ballistics is the study of how projectiles move through space. There are three different subfields for the purposes of this chapter:

» *Internal ballistics* deals with how the bullet moves down the barrel after it's fired. For the sake of simplicity, "internal" means inside the gun.

Rifle and handgun barrels are *rifled*, meaning their bores have spiral grooves that impart spin on bullets (as shown in Figure 9-4). This spin is the key to making bullets travel great distances.

Rifling is often described by its *twist rate*, or how far the bullet has to travel within the barrel to complete one full revolution. So if a barrel has a 1-in-7-inch twist rate, the bullet will fully rotate one time as it travels down 7 inches of barrel. If that barrel is 20 inches long, the bullet will rotate roughly 2.85 times before it exits the muzzle.

Why is this important? The goal is to find bullets that are the right caliber, weight, and style for your barrel's twist rate. If you choose bullets that are too light or too heavy for your barrel, they won't stabilize in flight — think of a wobbly football pass — and your accuracy will suffer.

Your firearm's manufacturer might offer recommendations, but you can also test various *loads*, or ammunition types, in your gun at the range.

FIGURE 9-4: Look closely and you can see the rifling inside this gun's barrel.

Courtesy of Guy Sagi/Alamy Images

>> *External ballistics* focuses on how the bullet travels after it leaves the barrel and up to the moment it hits the target.

If you lived in outer space, bullets would travel in a straight line forever after they left the barrel. But here on Earth, bullets move in an arc just like cannonballs, rockets, and arrows because of gravity and drag, or air resistance. Eventually, the velocity and energy run out, and bullets fall to the earth.

In general, lighter bullets travel faster and farther than heavier bullets, but they also don't hit as hard. Conversely, heavy bullets offer more power as well as more recoil.

Table 9-1 compares two popular handgun bullets, the 124-grain 9mm and 230-grain .45 ACP, out to 100 yards. As you can see, the larger, slower .45 ACP drops 18.4 inches and slows down by 60 feet per second (fps) by the time it reaches 100 yards. If you want to hit a target at that distance, you'd have to aim roughly a foot and a half above it before firing. In contrast, the smaller, faster 9mm drops only 11.7 inches at 100 yards, but it loses more energy, often described in foot-pounds. (This is a unit of measurement where 1 foot-pound equals the amount of energy required to raise 1 pound a distance of 1 foot.)

TABLE 9-1

Comparing 9mm and .45 ACP Trajectories

Range (yds)	Drop (in)		Velocity (fps)		Energy (ft-lb)	
	9mm	.45 ACP	9mm	.45 ACP	9mm	.45 ACP
0	−0.1	−0.1	1,120	860	345	378
20	0.1	0.2	1,080	847	321	367
40	−0.8	−1.4	1,045	835	301	356
60	−3.1	−5.0	1,015	823	284	346
80	−6.7	−10.7	988	811	269	336
100	−11.7	−18.4	964	800	256	327

WARNING

While I'm on the subject of trajectories, remember to never fire a gun straight up into the air, even if it's in celebration. Firing straight up is incredibly irresponsible because, thanks to gravity, the bullet will land somewhere, and it could injure or kill someone.

This table also doesn't account for wind, another variable that likes to push bullets off target. Learning to compensate for wind requires practice, but if you're at an outdoor range and shooting out only to, say, 25 yards with a handgun or 100 yards with a rifle, you can mostly ignore it — unless you need an excuse for missing the target, of course.

>> *Terminal ballistics* is the study of the bullet's behavior and effects after it hits the target, which is the topic of the next section.

Understanding today's handgun bullets

If I could predict with 100-percent certainty how a given bullet would behave after it struck a surface, I'd be too busy gambling in Vegas to write this book. Terminal ballistics can seem more like an art than a science, but it helps if you understand the composition of the target as well as the bullet's velocity, energy, and type.

WARNING

Terminal ballistics can be gruesome. Yes, some bullets are meant for target shooting, but most are designed to wound or kill living things. This is the weight that comes with gun ownership. So take care in the pages ahead.

Here are some of the most common bullet types today:

>> **Lead round-nose** (LRN) bullets are easy to describe because they're made entirely of lead and have round noses, or tips. They're the oldest, simplest, and cheapest of the bunch, and they're designed to penetrate a target without expanding, or increasing in diameter. Because the lead is exposed, these bullets also leave a lot of residue in your gun's barrel, so you'll need to clean it more often, and they fragment on impact.

WARNING

More important, lead is toxic, so you need to be careful and make sure you don't ingest any, for example. (Don't take the phrase "bite the bullet" too literally.) Lead's toxicity is why it's a good idea to wash your hands after interacting with firearms and ammunition.

>> **Full-metal-jacket** (FMJ) bullets — also known as *ball* rounds — are essentially LRNs with a thin outer layer, or jacket, made of a harder metal like copper. And like LRNs, these bullets do not expand on impact; instead, they're designed to penetrate deep into a target with limited fragmentation. But they don't perform well against "barriers" like heavy clothing, windshields, or wooden beams. In those situations, the rounds can deflect or stop dead in their tracks.

That said, FMJ rounds (shown in Figure 9-5) are very affordable and are commonly used by militaries around the world as well as for training and range practice among civilians.

FIGURE 9-5:
These cartridges
are all loaded
with full-metal-
jacket (FMJ)
bullets.

Courtesy of Poramet/Adobe Stock

>> **Jacketed hollow points** (JHPs), shown in Figure 9-6, are designed to expand on impact, creating a large wound channel within a target but, in theory, not penetrating beyond it. The cavities cut into the noses of these projectiles allow them to "mushroom" outward as they slow down and dump all their energy into the target. That's why these rounds are popular for personal and home defense as well as law enforcement.

Decades ago, barriers still caused problems for hollow points. For example, denim could fill the hollow cavity in the projectile and prevent it from expanding. But ammo makers have spent years perfecting their designs with computer simulations, Doppler radar, and FBI ballistic testing protocols, creating JHPs that expand (as shown in Figure 9-7) and penetrate better than in the past. Some makers have even added polymer tips to their JHPs to help them expand after passing through heavy clothing or other barriers.

Ammo manufacturers use different names for their trademarked JHPs, and they're always more expensive than FMJs.

REMEMBER

Currently, New Jersey is the only state that restricts the ownership of hollow points. Residents are only allowed to keep them at home or use them for hunting or target practice.

Most NATO militaries have also agreed not to use hollow-point ammunition because of the 1899 Hague Convention, which prohibits expanding ammunition for international warfare because of how difficult it can be to treat the resulting wounds, but the U.S. military recently began using them for its 9mm service pistols.

>> **Frangible rounds** are the least common of the four bullet styles I've outlined here. They might look like FMJs, but they're designed to disintegrate upon impact to prevent penetration. This is why frangible rounds are mostly used for indoor training in close quarters, as I mention in Chapter 12.

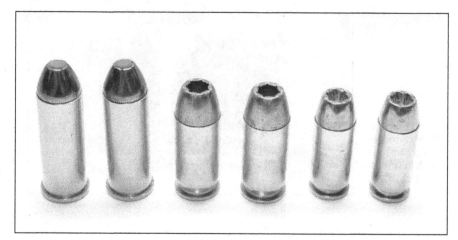

FIGURE 9-6:
Today's hollow points come in a variety of styles, and some have polymer tips.

Courtesy of woodsnorth/Adobe Stock

FIGURE 9-7:
Hollow points "mushroom" outward upon impact.

Courtesy of Guy Sagi/Adobe Stock

Peruse a fully (and miraculously) stocked ammo aisle, and you might find rounds that utilize wadcutter, semi-wadcutter, or fluted bullets, among others. These oddly named examples are designed for specific tasks like target shooting. My space is limited, however, so make sure you read up on their pros and cons. Entire guides are dedicated to handgun ammunition.

Recognizing various rifle bullets

Once again, rifle rounds are typically larger than handgun rounds, and when you pair the former with a longer rifle barrel, you're looking at blistering speeds. A .223 Remington bullet leaves the muzzle of a rifle at well over 3,200 fps — or 2,181 miles per hour — whereas a 9mm bullet might not break 1,200 fps from a typical handgun.

As you can imagine, rifle bullets are designed a little differently to take into account this immense speed and corresponding energy. You still have FMJs for range practice and traditional hollow points, but there are a few more types to learn for rifles:

- » **Open-tip match** (OTM) bullets (shown in Figure 9-8) are essentially FMJs, but each tip has a small opening because of how the jacket is formed around the lead core. This manufacturing process leads to greater consistency between bullets over, say, FMJs, which is why long-distance shooters prefer OTMs. The small openings should not be mistaken for hollow points, though. These rounds perform very much like FMJs, driving into a target — and possibly through it — without expanding.

- » **Soft points** (SPs) have jackets like the previous bullet types, but the inner lead core is left exposed right at the tip, as shown in Figure 9-9. This design allows SPs to expand upon impact like hollow points (though not quite as dramatically) while being a bit more aerodynamic and thus better suited for shooting out to greater distances.

- » **Polymer-tipped** bullets (sorry, no alphabet soup for this one) are also designed for long-range hunting. These bullets have hollow points so that they expand on impact to create large wound channels. But once again, ammo makers cap the hollow points with polymer tips, as shown in Figure 9-10, so that these bullets can travel greater distances. (Leaving the hollow point exposed creates a lot of drag that slows the bullet down as it travels through the air.)

- » **Monolithic or solid** bullets are also specifically crafted for long-range hunting. Here the bullet (as shown in Figure 9-11) is one solid hunk of metal — either copper or a copper alloy — to expand on impact and penetrate deeply into a game animal without fragmenting or losing any weight. Another benefit with these rounds is that there is no lead whatsoever, so you don't have to worry about ingesting a toxic substance.

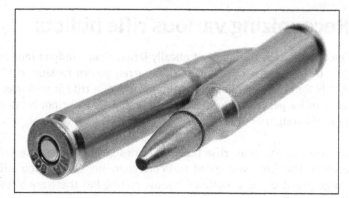

FIGURE 9-8:
Note the small opening at the tip of this .308 Winchester OTM bullet.

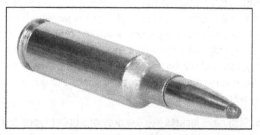

FIGURE 9-9:
Soft points have exposed-lead tips that help drive their expansion.

FIGURE 9-10:
Underneath this bullet's polymer tip is a hollow point.

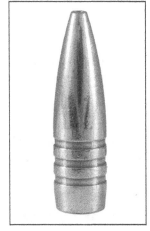

Courtesy of Guy J. Sagi/Shutterstock

To recap, FMJs are good for range practice and training, and OTMs are great for long-distance shooting and competitions. But what about the last three bullet types in the preceding list? Aren't they all designed for long-range hunting?

You have to consider the game you're hunting. For smaller prey like prairie dogs and coyotes — what hunters and Yosemite Sam call "varmints" — that you don't plan on eating, consider a polymer-tipped round that expands rapidly. For larger game like deer, soft points make more sense because they won't damage as much tissue within the animal. Finally, monolithic bullets are powerful enough for the largest, heavy-boned game, but they won't expand properly if they aren't traveling fast enough.

REMEMBER

Hunting ethically means killing the animal as quickly as possible with one shot. That means using the right bullet for the job and shooting from within 200 yards so that the bullet performs as it should, along with a host of other considerations. To learn more, turn to Chapter 15.

Finally, I want to mention the importance of hunting with lead-free, nontoxic ammunition, regardless of your quarry or weapon type. Lead is poisonous to living creatures, including humans and all the other animals that might feast upon the remains of animals you leave in the field after a successful hunt, such as birds and other scavengers. This is why so many states have banned lead ammunition for hunting, and more ordinances are on the way. Do your part to protect the environment; choose unleaded ammunition.

Sorting Out Shotgun Shells

In Chapter 3, I quickly discuss shotgun ammunition to give you a better understanding of how shotguns work. My goal here is to help you see the differences between various shotgun shells.

That's right. Shotguns load and fire *shells* (or simply *shotshells*) — not "cartridges." The name is derived from the outer shell, which was originally made completely of brass and then paper before morphing into plastic in the 1960s to withstand moisture and humidity.

Discerning shell components and naming conventions

The bottom of a shotshell is very similar to a rifle or handgun cartridge. As with cartridges, the brass base is called the head, and you'll find a headstamp that identifies the shell's manufacturer and gauge. A primer is also installed in the center of the base, as you can see in Figure 9-12.

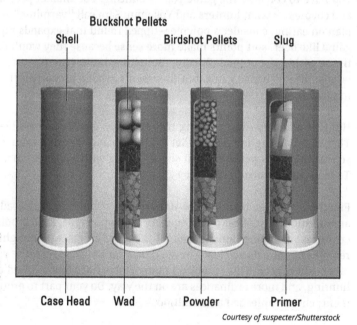

FIGURE 9-12: As this cutaway illustration shows, shotshells are loaded with pellets or slugs.

Courtesy of suspecter/Shutterstock

The primer ignites the gunpowder inside the shell. Ahead of the gunpowder is the *wad*, a disk or cup that seals off the gunpowder from the projectile(s) for increased velocities. Today, the wad is usually made of plastic.

In terms of projectiles, the first option would be several small metal balls known as *pellets* or *shot*. When you fire one of these shotshells, the pellets scatter outward as soon as they exit the muzzle of your shotgun. Several variables — including the size of the pellets and the wad design — determine how far the pellets spread as they travel farther downrange.

The second projectile type is the *slug*, which looks like a giant bullet and performs like one, too.

Shotguns are distinguished by their *gauges*, or bore diameters, which also determine the size of the shot pellets and slugs. The most common shotguns today are 12-, 16-, 20-, and 28-gauge models, and you must use shells that match your shotgun's gauge.

Now, you might be thinking, "Why not use calibers and inches like handguns and rifles?" That would be too easy. Instead, the gun world would rather stick with an antiquated measuring system derived from cannons. *Huzzah!*

TECHNICAL STUFF

Ready for this? If you found a lead ball with the exact diameter of a 12-gauge barrel, that ball would weigh exactly one-twelfth of a pound. To put it another way: 12 lead balls the same diameter as a 12-gauge shotgun bore would weigh one pound. So a smaller 26-gauge barrel could fit 26 smaller lead balls that collectively weighed a pound.

I know. It's truly bizarre. Today, you can use a ruler to measure the inside bore diameter — a 12-gauge shotgun's bore will be approximately 0.725 inches wide, for example — or trust the gauge markings on the outside of the barrel. Just remember that a smaller gauge number means a larger bore diameter, and thus a more powerful gun.

Finally, shotguns can also accept shotshells of various lengths, including 2¾-, 3-, or 3½-inch shells. Figure 9-13 shows some of the shotshell sizes available today. The longer the shell, the more gunpowder and pellets it has, along with recoil. That measurement refers to the length of the shell *after* it has been fired, by the way, but you'll see the number printed on the outside of the shell — and, I hope, on the ammo box — well beforehand.

FIGURE 9-13: Shotshells come in a variety of sizes and colors today.

If your shotgun has a 3-inch chamber, it can safely fire shells up to 3 inches long. A shotgun with a 3½-inch chamber can fire 3½-, 3-, and 2¾-inch shells.

Defining shotshells by use

I know that the previous section is complicated, but this one will make things easier because the projectiles loaded into shotshells can tell you a lot more about the round's intended uses. Specifically:

» **Slugs** are generally reserved for hunting deer and larger game within, say, 75 yards.

» **Buckshot** shells contain the largest pellets made of lead or steel and ranging in diameter from 0.24 to 0.36 inches. The most common buckshot loads contain eight or nine "00"-sized pellets that are 0.33 inches in diameter, and each pellet can leave the muzzle at well over 1,200 fps before eventually losing its effectiveness beyond 50 yards.

These shells are commonly used for home defense and hunting (hence the "buck" part of the name), but only at close range. In fact, some states prohibit buckshot for hunting larger game because hunters might not get close enough for an ethical kill.

>> **Birdshot** shells contain more smaller-diameter pellets for hunting game birds, including pheasants and grouse. Again, because the pellets are smaller, more can be packed into the shell — meaning that you have more lightweight projectiles to knock a fast-flying bird out of the sky.

As with handgun and rifle ammunition, the market is full of different shotshells designed for a range of needs. Consider this chapter a starting point for understanding ammunition. Now it's your turn to do the research and find the right load for your needs. Don't stop at the fine print on the ammo box.

Chapter **10**

Today's Firearm Accessories

Visit any gun shop or sporting goods store and you might notice just how much floor space is dedicated not to firearms, but all the *stuff* that goes with them, like holsters, scopes, lasers, and other gizmos. I know that the array of items might seem overwhelming, but depending on your interests, you're going to need a little more than ammunition and a dependable gun safe.

In this chapter, I detail some of the accessories that gun owners commonly purchase to give you some idea of what you might need — and possibly an idea of what you *don't* need — for activities like hunting, training, and recreational shooting. To hit steel targets hundreds of yards away, you need specialized gear.

The add-ons I describe in the pages ahead will enhance your accuracy at those distances, or help your gun fit you better, or give you more control over it. I also discuss some of today's most common gun modifications, including those you can do at home.

Carrying Your Gun

Holsters and slings are very popular accessories for handguns and long guns, respectively, because they're extremely practical. I know this is the year you finally hit your fitness goals — I can feel it, too! — but you aren't going to be able to hold onto that firearm with your bare hands for hours on end if, say, you're out hunting or practicing your shooting at an outdoor range. You might need to take a break, or bend down to tie your shoes, or make a call, and you can't just drop your gun in the dirt. (Please don't.)

REMEMBER

Along with hunting and recreational shooting, some people carry guns for protection on a regular basis. But there's a lot to consider in that regard, including some important legal aspects. To learn more, turn to Chapter 11.

Choosing handgun holsters

If you've seen too many action movies like me, you've probably lost count of the number of onscreen characters who pick up handguns in the heat of the moment and simply tuck them into their waistbands. That's just a terrible idea all around. A fully loaded handgun can weigh anywhere from 2 to 5 pounds, so you're going to need a bit more than wishful thinking to keep it in place. On top of that, nothing is protecting the trigger, and the gun is pointed directly at some sensitive anatomy. Need I say more?

Instead, invest in a quality *holster* (also known as a *rig*) that can help you carry your handgun and keep it within reach. A good holster will also protect your gun from the elements, but at the very least, it must block off the triggerguard so nothing can touch the firearm's trigger while it's holstered.

Accidents happen when people draw their handguns or reholster them, so you also have to make sure your holster doesn't shift during those maneuvers. It must fit you and your handgun properly, so pay attention to the holster's size, shape, construction, and ergonomics.

Most holsters today are made of leather, nylon, a tough plastic known as Kydex, or some combination of those materials, and formed to fit a specific model of handgun. Here are some of your options:

>> **Belt holsters,** as shown in Figure 10-1, use loops to hold onto to your belt and position your gun outside the waistband (OWB). But you can't use a flimsy old dress belt. As I mention in Chapter 12, you need a sturdy leather or nylon belt built specifically for carrying a handgun.

FIGURE 10-1:
Belt holsters are usually required for pistol training courses at outdoor ranges.

>> **Paddle holsters** are also OWB designs, but instead of attaching directly to your belt, they use a special paddle — clever naming, I know — that slips into your waistband, allowing you to quickly don and doff the holster or reposition it around your waist.

>> **Inside-the-waistband (IWB) holsters** attach to your belt but position the gun inside your pants. These are popular for concealed carry, as I discuss in Chapter 11, but you also have to wear pants that are at least a size larger to accommodate the gun.

>> **Pocket holsters** are designed for carrying the smallest handguns in a dedicated front pocket. (I say "dedicated" because you don't want to carry keys or anything else in the same pocket.) These holsters can prevent your gun from becoming a lint trap and protect its triggerguard.

>> **Ankle holsters** hold a smaller gun against your ankle and under your pants leg. These holsters are a bit old school, however, and drawing your gun from this position requires that you first drop to one knee and lift your pants leg out of the way. Trust me, it's awkward.

>> **Shoulder holsters** feature heavily in old police dramas. Worn under a coat, these holsters use shoulder harnesses to essentially hang the handgun under one of your armpits in a cross-draw position — so the left side of your body if you're right-handed, and vice versa — with the grip pointing forward. Cross-drawing takes some practice, of course.

>> **Specialty holsters** include chest rigs, belly-band holsters, thigh holsters, and yes, even bra holsters — really any option designed for specific outfits and situations. The market is full of unconventional holsters.

UNDERSTANDING HOLSTER RETENTION LEVELS

In the gun world, *retention* is a way of describing how well a holster holds, or retains, a handgun. If there's no retention, the gun slides right out of the holster. Too much retention and the gun is very difficult to draw. Most holsters offer some retention just by being form-fitted to a specific handgun model, and you can usually adjust the retention via a simple screw.

Then there are retention, or security, holsters with mechanisms that lock the firearm within the holster until they are deactivated. These holsters, which offer various levels of retention, were originally developed to prevent criminals from snatching police officers' duty pistols, but they're practical for civilians, too.

- **Level 1 retention holsters** have one security mechanism that has to be disengaged before you can draw the gun, like a strap over the back of the gun's grip that pivots out of the way, or a triggerguard lock that you deactivate by pressing a button.

- **Level 2 retention holsters** use two security mechanisms that must be deactivated beforehand, such as a strap or hood over the back of the gun as well as a triggerguard lock.

- **Level 3 retention holsters**, as you can guess by now, combine three security mechanisms into one rig, providing three layers of safety (at the expense of speed, of course).

- **Level 4 retention holsters** aren't as common because they use four security mechanisms, but they are popular among corrections officers.

WARNING

While the aforementioned holsters are all *on-body* designs, some people prefer *off-body* options like purses and messenger bags with built-in handgun holsters. These are a bit riskier, however, because if you lose your bag or someone steals it, you've also lost your gun. Being a safe gun owner means that you always have control over your weapon.

Selecting a sling for your long gun

If you're planning on hunting with your new rifle or shotgun, or taking a day-long training course, you'll want a *sling* — essentially a strap or harness that allows you to carry the gun on your body when you're not using it. A sling helps to distribute the gun's weight and free up your hands for other tasks.

Slings are a lot simpler than holsters. Most are made from leather or nylon, and they have three basic configurations:

>> **Single-point slings** attach to the gun at one point, usually near the weapon's grip. The other end of the sling is looped over your head and strong-side, or dominant, shoulder.

These slings are primarily used by military and law enforcement personnel because of their retention; they keep the gun close to your body so it's always within reach. They also make it easier to transition from your rifle to a pistol. However, they don't help much when it comes to lightening the load, so to speak, and the front end of the gun isn't secured, so it'll bounce around if you aren't careful when you move.

>> **Two-point slings**, shown in Figure 10-2, are the most traditional of the bunch, and they attach to your rifle or shotgun at two points: the front and the rear. This design provides a lot of stability, allowing you to carry the gun behind your back with the sling over one shoulder or across your chest.

TIP

Two-point slings are also a great way to stabilize your rifle for standing or kneeling shots. The trick is to tighten the sling around your support arm so that it creates tension, and thus a more rigid interface, between you and the rifle.

FIGURE 10-2:
Of the three types, two-point slings are the most common and versatile.

Courtesy of wwing/Getty Images

>> **Three-point slings** are the rarest style, and they're a bit of a misnomer. They attach to your long gun in two places (the front and rear), but an extra loop wraps around your body, providing more retention and stability to hold the long gun in place so you can go completely hands-free. That said, three-point slings are a bit more cumbersome and difficult to use than other slings.

Using Common Shooting Aids

Although I cover the fundamentals of accurate shooting in Chapter 13, quite a few accessories are designed to help you hit targets more often. (Two-point slings are just the beginning!) These add-ons include affordable, low-tech options like iron sights and bipods as well as high-tech gadgets like riflescopes and aiming lasers that will make you cringe when it's time to check out at your local sporting goods store.

I even discuss suppressors, or silencers, in a sidebar later in this section because although they are generally thought of as concealment aids, reducing a firearm's muzzle blast and sound signature can also help your accuracy. You'll be less likely to flinch with a suppressor installed, for example.

Zeroing in with sights and optics

Being accurate with a firearm means lining up your shot so that the projectile goes exactly where you want it to go. Of course, "lining up" requires some unpacking in this context. You have to aim the gun at the precise point you want to hit on the target, hold the gun as steady as possible, and then "break the shot," or pull the trigger.

Quite a few options exist to help you with that first part, aiming, including:

>> **Iron sights** are little aiming appendages on top of a firearm. Modern weapons usually come with adjustable front and rear sights that you have to align with the target, but as always, there are exceptions. Most shotguns only have front sights, for example. Although the sights might be built in, numerous weapons today have notches on top that allow you to add, adjust, or remove sights at will.

REMEMBER

These notch strips are known as *Picatinny rails,* which were originally developed by the U.S. military's Picatinny Arsenal as a means of quickly adding, repositioning, and removing scopes from battle rifles, but you can now find rails on the tops, sides, and bottoms of a number of weapons to host a wide range of accessories, not just aiming devices.

It's common for handguns to feature "white-dot" sights, shown in Figure 10-3, where the front sight has one white dot on its backside, facing the shooter, and the rear sight has two white dots around the sighting notch. These dots are meant to help you align the sights quickly, but the rear dots can also be distracting for some shooters. They're also difficult to use in the dark.

Thus, many shooters upgrade their sights to those that include fiber-optic or tritium inserts, for example, that glow in the dark and are easier to acquire, or pick up, in a hurry.

By the way, although old guns used front and rear sights that were indeed made of iron, most sights today are made from steel or polymer. So you can add "iron sights" to the list of misnomers scattered throughout this book.

FIGURE 10-3:
This close-up shows the white-dot sights on a semi-auto handgun.

Courtesy of Guy Sagi/Adobe Stock

>> **Red-dot, or reflex, sights** (shown in Figure 10-4) are a step up in terms of complexity. Originally designed for aircraft in World War II, a reflex sight will project a small aiming point, or *reticle* — usually a red dot, hence the name — on a clear plastic lens.

Reflex sights, are popular today because, after they're properly dialed in, the shooter simply superimposes the dot on the target and pulls the trigger. You don't have two separate iron sights to align first, for example, saving you time.

Among small arms, these sights were first used on rifles, but as they continue to shrink down, they're becoming more and more common on handguns and even shotguns, too.

FIGURE 10-4:
Reflex sights have become very popular additions on handguns.

Courtesy of Crystal Ricketson/Shutterstock

>> **Telescopic sights**, or simply "scopes," are the most complex of the aiming devices because, just like a telescope you'd use to look at stars or find land if you're lost at sea, they utilize lenses to magnify the image downrange. (This magnification is why scopes are considered *optics,* whereas traditional sights, which offer no magnification, are not optics.)

You might also see scopes referred to as *riflescopes*, like the kind shown in Figure 10-5, which is where these devices got their start in the 1800s, but some models are specifically designed for handguns as well. Shotguns? Not so much.

Fixed-power scopes offer a set amount of magnification, so they'll magnify the image downrange three times (3X), or five times (5X), and so on, but that's it. Then you have variable-power scopes that let you toggle between magnification levels. Rotating a knob or lever on the scope allows you to zoom in from 2X to 5X magnification, for example, or zoom back out. Of course, this feature costs more.

TIP

Why do hunters carry binoculars in addition to the scopes on their rifles? If you search for prey with your riflescope, you'll break the second rule of gun safety and sweep your gun's muzzle over things you don't intend to shoot. Instead, the safest option is to scan large tracts of land with a pair of binoculars and then, after you've spotted your quarry in the distance, transition to your riflescope.

Scope reticles come in a variety of flavors. Sure, there are traditional crosshairs like the kind shown in movies, but long-range shooters prefer reticles that look like Christmas trees with several graduated lines to help you overcome distance and the wind to hit the target. You'll also find knobs on the side and top of the scope to adjust the reticle to compensate for that same distance and wind, too.

TIP

With features like crystal-clear lenses, an illuminated reticle, fine adjustment knobs, nitrogen purging to ensure the scope never fogs up, and a tank-tough outer tube, scopes can get very expensive very quickly. However, you can waste a lot more money buying a few subpar scopes before you finally pony up for a top-notch model. That's why gun aficionados call scope buying a "buy once, cry once" proposition.

Finally, if you're interested in hunting at night, you can spend thousands of dollars on night-vision and thermal imaging scopes that use ambient light and heat signatures, respectively, to illuminate what would normally be difficult to see in the dark.

FIGURE 10-5: This bolt-action rifle is fitted with a variable-power scope and a bipod.

Courtesy of nafterphoto/Shutterstock

Holding steady with monopods, bipods, and more

Your accuracy is directly related to how well you can control your weapon and hold it steady. The more stability you have, the better — as with taking a photo. This is why long-range shooters do as much as they can to remove themselves from the equation. They don't want to miss a shot because of unsteady breathing or the slight vibrations that come with muscle tension.

In fact, long-range shots are best taken from the prone position, lying flat on the ground behind the rifle. What's more stable than the ground below you? (Don't answer that if you live in an area prone to earthquakes.) You'll also see that some of this gear isn't very different from a photographer's.

Here are some devices to increase your shooting stability:

>> **Monopods** are devices either built in or added to the bottom of a rifle's buttstock to steady the rear of the gun so your shoulder doesn't have to do as much work. If you studied Greek or Latin, or have ever visited a podiatrist's office, you know that monopod means "one foot," and that's exactly what you're getting here, though you should be able to adjust the monopod's length and pivot it out of the way when it isn't needed. To keep the gun level, you'll want to pair the monopod with a bipod.

>> **Bipods** are two-legged supports for the front end of your weapon. A good bipod will have a swiveling base and folding, length-adjustable legs. You should be able to lock the base and legs into position as well, making it easier to use the bipod in a few different environments — not just on a benchrest at the range.

REMEMBER

When you attach the bipod to your rifle's forend, you want the legs to fold forward, toward the muzzle. This allows you to put forward pressure on the rifle and "load the bipod" to counter recoil. If the bipod is reversed, the legs might collapse if they can't be locked into position.

>> **Sandbags or shooting bags** can support the front or rear of the rifle in place of a monopod or bipod. So you might see someone use a bipod up front but sandbags at the rear of the rifle, as shown in Figure 10-6, which creates a very stable shooting platform. Of course, sandbags aren't that easy to tote around, and you might need multiple to achieve the desired fit, so they're typically relegated to range duty.

TIP

If the front of your rifle is stabilized by a bipod or sandbags, your support hand no longer needs to hold onto the rifle's forend. In fact, in this situation, it's actually best to use that hand to push the buttstock into your shoulder. So if you're right handed, your right hand will remain on the grip as usual, but your left hand will curl back under the rifle and apply pressure to the bottom front edge of the buttstock. The buttstock might even have a groove or hook there for that purpose.

>> **Tripods** are just like the kind used for cameras. They have three legs, providing the most support for the rifle's front end, though they aren't attached to the rifle like a monopod or bipod. Additionally, because their adjustable legs are much longer than a bipod's, tripods can be used for shooting from sitting, kneeling, and standing positions, so they're commonly used for hunting.

>> **Shooting sticks** can be monopods, bipods, or tripods with adjustable legs, but instead of being attached to the gun, they're carried separately. Then, when a hunter sees their prey, they support their rifle by dropping its forend into the V- or U-shaped yoke on top of the shooting sticks. Grip the sticks with your support hand to keep them in position.

FIGURE 10-6:
For greater stability, this rifle is paired with a bipod and a rear shooting bag.

Courtesy of Guy J. Sagi/Shutterstock

Powering up with lights, lasers, and combination units

I still remember when cops carried flashlights big enough to pull double duty as nightsticks. If you're a fan of the *Terminator* movies, you know that the earliest aiming lasers were as long as the weapons they were mounted to.

Along with contemporary riflescopes, lights and lasers represent the state of the art when it comes to firearm accessories. (Emphasis on accessories. I'm talking about lasers that you install on a gun, *not* laser guns. I'll save that topic for the 14th edition of this book.)

Over time, these gadgets have become significantly smaller and more powerful without wasting a ton of batteries. Most of these types of accessories nowadays are designed to be mounted on a gun's rail and use easy-to-reach activation switches, but some attach to grips, triggerguards, or receivers instead.

Here's a breakdown of these gadgets:

WARNING

>> **Weapon lights** are generally used for military and law enforcement operations as well as for home defense because they can illuminate any dark location, be it a room or hallway or even a forest, giving you more visual information about a situation to process and possibly act upon.

Different colors and modes (like constant-on and strobe) are available, too. But there are a few caveats.

Today's lights are bright enough to blind someone temporarily, which can be a good thing or a bad thing depending on who's on the receiving end. More importantly, however, if you're using a weapon-mounted light to search rooms or something like that, you could potentially sweep your gun's muzzle over an innocent person, violating the second rule of gun safety. That's why a handheld flashlight is a better idea in that situation.

>> **Aiming lasers** can enhance your precision with a firearm, especially if you're in a position that prevents you from using your sights. If the laser has been zeroed properly — or tuned to indicate where a bullet will hit at a given distance — you can use it instead of sights. (With practice, of course.)

Lasers, including those installed ahead of the triggerguard, as shown in Figure 10-7, are mostly helpful in the dark, but I've also tested some that were bright enough to see in broad daylight. Your mileage may vary.

FIGURE 10-7:
Triggerguard-mounted laser sights are available for popular pocket pistols today.

Courtesy of Tom Hirtreiter/Adobe Stock

Red and green are the most common color options. Generally, green lasers are easier to see and pick up, but because of how they're made, they also burn through batteries faster.

>> **Combination units** pair lights and lasers in one small, easily mounted package. These devices usually aren't that much bulkier than traditional weapon lights or lasers, but they cost more, and you have more buttons and adjustment dials to figure out.

And once again, the previous disclaimers apply, so don't use a handgun-mounted light/laser unit to search rooms in your house because your cat decided to knock a vase onto the floor while you were dead asleep.

These accessories require practice and responsibility.

HOW SOUND SUPPRESSORS ACTUALLY WORK

REMEMBER

Gunshots are loud because of the hot gases that escape the barrel behind the bullet. Those gases essentially *pop* or *crack* when they hit the colder, lower-pressure air outside the gun.

Sound suppressors are metal tubes that are attached to or built into barrels and work like car mufflers. They give that gas more room to expand and cool down before hitting open air, thus reducing the sound level or signature.

Note that suppressors are also known as *cans* and *silencers*, but as I discuss in Chapter 18, the latter is a misnomer. Despite Hollywood depictions, no suppressor can completely silence a gunshot. You will still hear a loud *crack*, depending on the caliber, that will damage your hearing unless you protect your ears.

Instead of eliminating sound altogether, sound suppressors greatly reduce the weapon's report and muzzle flash — the bright light produced by a gunshot — making it very difficult to figure out where the shot came from. This is why military snipers typically use sound suppressors.

These benefits also make suppressors great accuracy aids. Because they reduce noise and eliminate flash, you're less likely to flinch when you break the shot.

(continued)

(continued)

There are three main types of suppressors:

- **Traditional suppressors** use several *baffles,* or expansion chambers, wrapped in metal tubes. Remove a conventional suppressor's outer tube and you'll find a series of baffles in what's commonly called a *stack.*

- **Monocore suppressors** are modern designs in which one solid unit holds all the expansion chambers (see the following figure). These suppressors are easier than traditional suppressors to take apart and clean, and they're easier to manufacture with CNC machines or even 3D printers.

Courtesy of Guy Sagi/Adobe Stock

Suppressor components are typically made of steel, aluminum, titanium, or an alloy like Inconel. Some models are caliber specific, whereas others work with several calibers, as long as none are larger than the suppressor's highest caliber rating.

- **Integral suppressors** combine barrels with sound-dampening expansion chambers. From the outside, you might see one long barrel, but internally, baffles are positioned in front of where the barrel technically ends.

No matter the style, every sound suppressor is federally regulated by the National Firearms Act of 1934, meaning they can be difficult to obtain. To learn more about their ownership requirements and other federal regulations, turn back to Chapter 2.

Customizing Your Gun

The next time you're waiting at a stop light, look at the vehicles around you and keep a tally of all the customizations you see: aftermarket wheels and paint jobs, bumper stickers and "mufflers" that only make cars louder. People like making things their own, even when it comes to firearms.

Hundreds of companies produce parts to help you or a qualified gunsmith customize your weapon to fit your needs. That could mean altering the gun's ergonomics, upgrading its performance, or changing how it looks.

Upgrades you can do at home

Obviously, you know yourself better than I do. (We're still getting to know each other!) But even if you're "all thumbs" when it comes to repair jobs and handi-work, there are some gun modifications you can perform at home before you need to schedule an appointment with a gunsmith. To help, I've listed some common adjustments people make to their guns.

REMEMBER

That said, even though everything I list here is legal on the federal level, you are responsible for understanding what is and isn't allowed according to your local and state laws. For example, Californians should not change out the grips or stocks on their rifles for those that might be prohibited. And as I caution in Chapter 7, if your gun has a warranty, consult the fine print before you go through with any of these alterations. I don't want you to void it.

The good news is that all of these do-it-yourself modifications are completely reversible. So what can you do?

>> **Replace the iron sights.** As I mention earlier in this chapter, some guns come with rudimentary sights that aren't conducive to aiming quickly or in low light. So you can always replace your handgun's white-dot sights for those with fiber-optic inserts, for example.

To start, check with your gun's original manufacturer and see if they offer upgraded sights for your model. That way, you know you're getting a compati-ble set. Aftermarket makers are your next stop.

Your gun's manual might also tell you how to replace the sights. Just know that it could take several fine adjustments and trips to the range to get the new sights lined up properly so that your *point of aim* (POA) matches the *point of impact* (POI) with a given ammunition type. A gunsmith can help if needed.

>> **Adjust the grip.** Your gun's grip should fit your hand properly and provide the right level of traction. Otherwise, you're not going to be as accurate or in control of the gun as you could be.

Of course, altering the grip is different for every gun. For shotguns and rifles, you might be able to replace the grip entirely, or if it's an integral part of the stock, you can add grip tape to increase the traction.

For older handguns, including 1911s and revolvers, you can replace the grip panels to attain the desired fit and feel for your hands. In contrast, most modern polymer-framed pistols come with interchangeable *backstraps* so that you can customize the back of the grip to fit small, medium, or large hands. If that's not enough, you might be able to add a rubber grip sleeve or grip tape, or replace the entire frame.

WARNING

With that latter option, a new frame means a new serial number, so the sale will have to go through a licensed gun dealer and will be subject to a background check. To learn more about that process, turn back to Chapter 4.

>> **Alter or replace the furniture.** No, I don't mean couches and ottomans. In the gun world, *furniture* means a weapon's grip, stock, or forend — parts that interface with the shooter. I've already discussed the grip modifications available to you, but the stock and forend deserve some attention, too.

With rifles and shotguns, you might only need a screwdriver to replace the handguard for one that accepts more accessories; add shims to the stock to adjust the *length of pull,* which is the distance from the trigger to the rear of the stock; or swap a fixed stock with a collapsible version to fit your frame more comfortably. You just have to make sure that the change doesn't interfere with the gun's operation or run afoul of the law.

If you have any questions about a replacement part's compatibility, check with the manufacturer — original or aftermarket — before you purchase it.

>> **Replace the controls.** If the magazine release is a bit too small for your hands, look for an replacement. The same goes for charging handles, slide releases — any of the gun's smaller controls. I'd once again start by checking with the original manufacturer and then try reputable aftermarket part makers with good reviews.

WARNING

You can also find drop-in replacement triggers for a number of semi-auto handguns and rifles these days, but I must caution you against choosing a trigger with a pull weight that is too light, or below 5 pounds. No accuracy gains are worth the increased risk of accidental discharges. Instead, consider a trigger that feels smoother in operation, has a crisp break, or has a shorter reset. These qualities will feel like a big improvement without needlessly making your gun more dangerous.

>> **Replace the barrel.** For this book's purposes, this upgrade only really applies to modern semi-auto pistols, for which you can order a compatible replacement barrel from the factory, and 99.9 percent of the time, it'll slide right into the old barrel's position without causing any issues. So if you want the same barrel but with muzzle threading for a sound suppressor, or a gold version because you're fancy, this is an option for you.

(By the way, if you order a gold barrel that hasn't been titanium nitrided, don't expect it to stay gold beyond your first range outing.)

Upgrades that require gunsmithing

Certain firearm modifications require a gunsmith. There's no way around it. You don't want to wing it on something that could potentially injure or kill yourself or others. (These upgrades will also void your gun's warranty.)

The goal is finding a certified professional who has been altering and customizing guns for years and will guarantee their work. The best gunsmiths will try to get a better understanding of what you want changed and why, and they'll offer you several options to achieve that dream. Some common gunsmithing tasks include:

>> **Action tuning:** This is kind of a catchall term for smoothing out the firearm's internal parts so that they work together better for optimum accuracy and reliability. This tuning includes getting the grittiness out of a trigger's movement.

Mass-produced firearms have come a long way in terms of quality, but sprawling assembly lines and computer-controlled machinery can only go so far. A skilled gunsmith knows exactly which components need to be fitted by hand (lapped, filed, and so on) to make a gun run like a top with specific ammunition types.

>> **Barrel modifications.** A gunsmith should be able to replace the barrel on any gun, including semi-auto pistols, but a skilled one can also take the original barrel and add threading for various muzzle devices, small ports to reduce muzzle rise, or fluting to reduce weight. They can resize the barrel or even rechamber it for a different caliber.

Obviously, the laws of physics still apply, but the gunsmith should be able to tell you what is and isn't possible with your specific weapon.

>> **Grip and slide modifications.** With handguns, gunsmiths might be able to add texturing to the grip — *checkering* for metal frames; *stippling* for polymer frames — for enhanced traction. With the slide, they can adjust or replace the front and rear sights, add cocking serrations, relieve metal to reduce weight, or cut the slide to accept a miniature reflex sight.

>> **Furniture adjustments and replacements.** Gunsmiths offer a lot of services in this regard. For example, not only can they customize or replace the stock on your favorite bolt-action rifle, but they can also *pillar bed* the action so that it's mounted rigidly within the stock for enhanced accuracy downrange.

>> **Custom finishes.** For better or worse, any number of gunsmiths can add a camouflage pattern, tiger stripes, or some version of the American flag to your gun. (Hey, I won't judge you . . . too much.) But instead of using paint that could easily rub off, they'll use a ceramic-based finish like Cerakote that will survive rough handling. So I hope you love tigers!

If your tastes are a bit more reserved, gunsmiths can also restore wood and metal components to their former glory.

REMEMBER

THINGS YOU CAN'T LEGALLY DO TO A GUN

Before you head to the garage to grab a hacksaw, I must warn you about some of the gun modifications restricted by federal regulations. For example, because of the National Firearms Act (NFA), which regulates easily concealable weapons, you can't cut a rifle or shotgun barrel down below 16 or 18 inches, respectively, without receiving prior approval from the ATF. If you skip the NFA registration process and create a short-barreled rifle or shotgun anyway, you face 10 years in prison, a $10,000 fine, or both.

The NFA even defines rifles and shotguns as two-handed, shoulder-fired weapons, whereas handguns are defined as weapons that can be fired with just one hand. So if you add a shoulder stock to a handgun, for example, you've just created a short-barreled rifle.

The NFA also restricts fully automatic weapons, so if you tinker with your firearm's internal components and enable it to fire more than one shot per trigger pull, you're facing 10 years in prison, a $250,000 fine, or both.

Finally, because of the Gun Control Act (GCA) of 1968, if you attempt to alter or remove your firearm's serial number, you're risking five years in prison.

These are just a few examples on the federal level. The penalties will compound if you've broken state or local laws as well. But as you can see, altering a firearm can be a risky endeavor. To stay on the straight and narrow, make sure you read Chapter 2, and consider talking to a gunsmith or lawyer before you make any major changes to your firearms. Better safe than sorry, right?

Looking at Other Helpful Accessories

Although I've dedicated a good portion of this chapter to on-gun accessories like scopes and sound suppressors, I want to recommend a few off-gun items that will save you some trouble the next time you hit the range:

>> **A range bag** helps you keep all your shooting accessories in one easy-to-transport place.

>> **Electronic hearing protection** includes earmuffs and earplugs that cancel out the sound of gunfire while amplifying ambient sounds, including conversations. To learn more about these miraculous devices, check out Chapter 12.

>> **Magazine loaders** save you a lot of time and effort when it comes refilling detachable pistol and rifle magazines with fresh ammo. I cover these lifesavers in Chapter 12.

>> **Recoil shields** are shoulder pads that incorporate rubber to take some of the sting out of a long gun's recoil, much like the grip sleeves and recoil pads installed on guns. I recommend recoil shields for those who might be sensitive to recoil or plan on shooting shotguns or high-caliber rifles for extended periods of time.

>> **An armorer's kit** provides several tools to help you take down, modify, or reassemble a firearm, including punches, a torque wrench, and screwdrivers. Additionally, the best kits include cleaning tools like bore brushes in case your gun starts jamming from fouling.

>> **A sight adjustment tool** is a great idea if you've replaced your iron sights and need to fine-tune the new ones for your particular ammunition. If your rounds are hitting left or right or where you're aiming, you might need to adjust the sights left or right, for example.

>> **A quality safe** to lock up your gun. I know I said these were all range accessories, but as I mention several times in Chapter 6, it is absolutely critical that you secure your firearm when you aren't using it. A little reinforcement never hurts, right?

Chapter **11**

Leaving Home with Your Firearm

There are plenty of legitimate reasons for leaving your home with a gun. Maybe you want to practice your marksmanship at the range or compete in a shooting match, or go hunting, or take your firearm in for repairs.

Some people also choose to keep guns in their vehicles, or carry them on their person, for protection. But doing so is risky, even if you have the best intentions. Your gun could be stolen and used to commit a crime, or you might tempted to grab your gun when it isn't warranted. In 2021 alone, there were an estimated 728 road-rage incidents involving a gun, and 68 percent of those cases led to an injury or death. Of that number, 131 people were killed.

Traveling farther? The Transportation Security Administration (TSA) discovered 5,972 firearms in carry-on luggage at airport security checkpoints across the U.S. in 2021, and 86 percent of those guns were loaded at the time.

Those are startling numbers.

I don't want you to add to the problem or become another statistic. So this chapter is all about teaching you how to leave your home with a gun *the right way*. I cover everything from driving and flying with a gun to concealed carry and all the legal aspects in between.

WARNING

If you're ever in doubt about how to get a firearm from Point A to Point B and back again in a safe, responsible way, leave the gun locked up at home until you can do your research, learn the applicable laws, and invest in a car safe, for example. When in doubt, do without.

Transporting a Gun in a Vehicle

Your home is your castle — at least metaphorically, until you find the mansion of your medieval dreams with turrets, stone walls, and a drawbridge on your favorite real estate website.

(No, a gun doesn't necessarily make your home safer, but you can mitigate some of that risk by teaching the safety rules to your family and investing in a sturdy safe. For more on those topics, read Chapters 5 and 6.)

WARNING

Everything changes when you try to step off of your property with a firearm, however. All of a sudden, you're out in public, and you need to know the rules of the road — literally and figuratively.

Understanding relevant laws

Every state has its own laws regarding how and when you can transport a firearm in a vehicle. In most states, the gun must remain unloaded and some distance away from you while you're driving (unless you have a concealed-carry permit, which I discuss later in this chapter).

For example, in Florida, the firearm can't be "readily accessible" to you, so you might be able to keep it in a gun case on the back seat, but not the passenger seat next to you. In Minnesota, you have to keep the weapon in the trunk of your car or completely enclosed inside a gun case. Other states require that the gun be locked inside a container.

People cut each other off in traffic all the time. They bend fenders. They get angry. The idea behind these laws is to prevent someone from brandishing their gun to threaten someone else, or retaliate, in these heated moments.

REMEMBER

To learn your state's laws when it comes to transporting a firearm in a vehicle, check the websites of local and state law enforcement agencies, including state patrols or departments of public safety.

Examining vehicle storage options — and their risks

Think of your state's laws as the bare minimum. When it comes to safety and security, you can do a lot better than simply keeping the gun in a case on your car's back seat or in the trunk. Not to date myself, but I grew up in a time when people — thieves and those unlucky souls who accidentally locked their keys inside their cars — could break into vehicles with coat hangers or even bits of string. (Okay, I'm old.)

Yes, today's vehicles are much more secure than ever before, but that doesn't mean that someone can't smash a window or pry open the trunk and escape with your firearm before police arrive. So what should you do? Before I get to that, let me tell you what *not* to do and why.

WARNING

>> Avoid any decals or bumper stickers that might tell a thief that you have a gun in your car. (Say goodbye to that Gadsden flag.) You want your vehicle to blend in with everyone else's. Make it less of a target.

>> Please don't leave your gun out in the open on a seat (as shown in Figure 11-1) or the dashboard, or inside the trunk. This is extremely dangerous and irresponsible. Not only is this illegal in most states, but anyone could steal your gun in a handful of seconds if the opportunity presents itself. And this might seem obvious, but you really don't want your gun to fly around if you have to slam on the brakes.

>> Even if you store your gun inside a case, don't then leave the case out in the open. Gun cases are extremely easy to recognize. If a thief does mistake your handgun case for something else, it'll only be for another expensive purchase, like a camera, and be stolen. Rifle and shotgun cases are even harder to confuse for other items.

   As a responsible gun owner, you must do everything you can to prevent someone from stealing your gun. When in doubt, leave the gun at home.

>> Don't try to slide that case under a seat, or tuck your handgun inside your vehicle's center console or glove box. These locations are still "readily available" to you *and others*. How often do you ride with passengers? Do they ever look in your console or glove box?

   Now think about thieves. These are the first places they'll check if they gain access to your vehicle.

   As I discuss in Chapter 6 in relation to secure gun storage at home, concealment alone isn't enough of a safeguard for your weapons.

>> I've seen ads for companies selling magnets that allow you to stick a handgun under your dashboard so that it's within easy reach. That's part of the danger, though. The gun is *too* easy for you to reach in an altercation, and for others to reach if they gain access to your car.

Again, this position is also illegal in many states, so avoid it.

>> If you live in a rural area, you might see trucks with rifle racks in their back windows. I know I won't win any fans in Texas for writing this, but you really shouldn't display a "truck gun," or any firearm, in such a way. It's irresponsible and just invites trouble.

FIGURE 11-1:
Never leave your gun out in the open on a car seat.

To reduce the risk of theft or some other mishap, invest in a dedicated gun safe for your vehicle, even if you have a concealed-carry permit and can legally carry a loaded weapon on your body as you drive. (Which can be pretty uncomfortable, by the way.)

For handguns, it's easy to find a small lockbox or vault that can be installed under a passenger seat or in the trunk. The safe doesn't necessarily need to be made for a car or truck, but it does need to be hidden and mounted to the vehicle's structure, like the floor or frame. Otherwise, a thief can simply steal the entire safe.

WARNING

Some companies make handgun safes that can be installed under your vehicle's dashboard, alongside the console, or inside the center storage compartment, but I must warn you against them. They're too "readily accessible" to be legal in some states, and more importantly, they make it too easy for you to draw your gun and escalate a situation into something far more dangerous. I know you're always on your best behavior, but remove the temptation.

If you have to transport a rifle or shotgun, look for a dedicated long-gun safe that can be installed in the trunk of your vehicle, or if you have a truck, under the rear bench seat.

WHAT TO DO IF YOU'RE STOPPED BY THE POLICE

Say that a police officer pulls you over while you have a gun in your vehicle. What do you do?

- Start by taking a few deep breaths. I know these situations can be tense, and you never know what mood the officer will be in. Breathe.

- Turn off any music you're listening to, roll down your windows, and keep your hands in sight. I recommend placing them at the top of the steering wheel.

- When the officer steps up to your window, try your best to be courteous. (Ugh! I know. Just remember that traffic stops are the most dangerous things cops do on a day-to-day basis.)

- Now here's the important part: Tell the officer that you have a gun in the car and where it's located. Say, "Officer, I would like to inform you that I have a firearm in my vehicle. It's in a safe in my trunk." Avoid "I've got a gun!"

  Again, I know this is stressful. I've met a ton of cops who fear these situations, too, but they would rather know up front instead of being surprised later.

  In addition, many states have "duty to inform" laws requiring that you disclose the presence of a gun to law enforcement if you're stopped. Some of those states stipulate that you have to tell an officer immediately; others require only that you tell the officer if they ask if you have a gun in your possession.

- After you notify the officer about the firearm, answer their questions and listen to their commands. They might tell you to leave the gun in place — this is another benefit of storing the gun in a safe under a passenger seat — or attempt to take the gun from you temporarily. Go with the flow. They might also ask you to retrieve the pistol, but this is the most precarious option for everyone involved. In that position, be slower than slow.

WARNING

No matter what safe you purchase, understand that it is a *temporary* solution. No security device is 100-percent tamper-proof forever, especially if someone steals your car and has hours, if not days, to break into your gun safe. So if you plan to park and leave your car unattended for more than an hour or so, keep your gun locked up at home.

Crossing State Lines with a Firearm

REMEMBER

If you're thinking about traveling to another state to, say, hunt or attend a firearms training course, the first thing you must do is research and follow the laws pertaining to the transportation of firearms and ammunition wherever you're traveling to.

As I discuss in the pages ahead, there are federal regulations concerning driving and flying with a gun. With the latter, you also need to know the airline's rules and your destination's — unless you want to be detained the moment you step off the plane.

If you're driving, you also need to know the gun laws for every state you intend to pass through and stop in — and even those of neighboring states in case you have to take a detour. State laws vary considerably, and I want you to stay on the right side of the law the entire route.

Traveling by road

If you've ever taken a civics class, you know that the U.S. federal government is involved anytime the word "interstate" pops up. When it comes to driving, you're looking at Title 18, United States Code 926A, which covers the "interstate transportation of firearms."

Where are my 926A fans? Anyone?

Basically, the law states:

>> You can transport a firearm or ammunition into another state only if you can legally possess those items in that other state.

>> The firearm must be unloaded while it's in transit.

>> Your gun and ammunition must not be "readily accessible" or "directly accessible from the passenger compartment" of your vehicle.

>> However, if the driver and passenger compartments are not separated (which covers most vehicles today), the firearm and ammunition can instead be kept in a locked container that does not include the glove box or console.

In other words, if you follow my advice in the previous section on vehicle storage and use a gun safe mounted under a passenger seat or in your vehicle's trunk, you should be fine. (Look at that. It's like I'm clairvoyant.)

Just make sure to follow any additional state laws wherever you're driving.

Traveling by air

I'm not going to break any new ground or win a Pulitzer (sorry, Mom) writing about the stress of flying today, so I'll just throw out some words to set the mood: Busy airports! Security lines! The awful boarding process!

TIP

How do guns fit into this scenery? The TSA is in charge of protecting American flyers and keeping airports as safe as they can be, so the agency's website (www.tsa.gov) should be your first stop in learning the federal guidelines regarding air travel with firearms and ammunition.

There are several rules to follow here:

REMEMBER

>> You can only fly with an unloaded firearm locked in a hard-sided container that is checked with the airline, not in a carry-on bag.

When I say unloaded, I mean it. No ammunition should be in the gun's chamber or magazine.

>> The container must be TSA approved, which means that it's durable and lockable in a few different places.

The hard case that came with your gun may work, but you might also want to invest in a sturdier, TSA-approved case that will accept anywhere from two to four locks that fit snugly into place.

There are no specific requirements about the locks themselves — only that the case is secure.

>> You must declare the firearm when you check in for your flight at the airline's ticket counter. Be prepared for the agent to open the case to inspect its contents, so keep those keys handy.

TIP

Try to be polite. I know you're an angel in every other situation, but really turn on the charm here, okay? You might be dealing with a new employee who hasn't learned the process of checking a firearm yet. And I recommend saying, "I'd like to declare a firearm," instead of "I've got a gun!"

>> You'll then sign a declaration card saying that your firearm is unloaded before it's placed in the case.

>> If you're also bringing along ammunition, it'll also need to be checked. You can keep it in its original box if it's durable enough (not one of those paper boxes that falls apart as soon as you pick it up) or resort to a plastic ammo box.

Airlines might also have a weight limit for ammunition — 11 pounds is the current standard for American Airlines, Delta, and United — or require that you separate the ammo from your gun, so be prepared to put it in a checked bag or suitcase.

TIP

To make your life easier, give yourself plenty of time to check in your firearm and luggage at the ticket counter, make your way through security, find your gate, and so on. If you're short on time, you're more likely to be short on patience.

My favorite airport is Missoula, Montana's because it has one terminal with six gates. That's it. At its busiest, it has a few dozen people inside. You can check in and glide through security in moments. But I know this example is the exception. Prepare accordingly.

THE RIGHT WAY TO SHIP A FIREARM

In the course of owning a gun, you might need to mail it to a manufacturer or gunsmith for repairs, or send it to an out-of-state training academy or hunting destination ahead of time so that you don't have to worry about the hassle of checking a firearm in at an airport ticket counter.

If you're sending a gun back to a manufacturer, contact the company and have them provide you with a packing slip. Then take the gun to FedEx or a UPS Customer Center (the counter of a larger UPS shipping facility, *not* your local UPS Store). Each company has different rules, but in general, you'll want to ship the gun unloaded, without any ammunition, and in a box that doesn't indicate that a gun is inside. You must also notify the carrier that you are shipping a firearm.

You can only use the U.S. Postal Service to mail long guns to others within your state or to yourself (in care of someone else) out of state if it's for hunting or "other lawful activity." Once again, the gun must be declared, unloaded, and packed discreetly, and for out-of-state shipments, you are the only one who can open the package and take possession of the long gun. With few exceptions, handguns are verboten.

If you're mailing a firearm out of state to another individual, you can only send the gun using FedEx or UPS — again following their rules — to an entity like a gun shop with a Federal Firearms License (FFL). The intended recipient will then fill out ATF Form 4473 and undergo a background check before taking possession of the firearm. To learn more about that process, turn back to Chapter 4.

For those FedEx and UPS shipments, ask the gun shop ahead of time for a copy of its FFL paperwork, which you'll print out and include in the package (after you let the shipping company see it) along with a photocopy of your ID. Also include a packing slip with your contact information as well as the intended recipient's. That way, the FFL can contact you if they have any questions and notify the recipient when the firearm arrives.

That covers the federal regulations. Your state might have its own laws regarding how firearms may be shipped and transferred, so do your research before you whip out the bubble wrap.

Carrying a Firearm on Your Person

If you bought a gun to defend yourself, you might be tempted to carry it with you as you step out into the world, either displayed openly or hidden on your person. Every state has various laws concerning open carry and concealed carry, as they're known, but I have to start with the risks.

WARNING

You might *feel* like you need the protection a gun provides, and I understand that. But you must look carefully at your circumstances and ask yourself whether you really need that gun. I mean it. Will introducing a deadly weapon — one that doesn't offer second chances — into a situation make it any safer?

Try playing it out. Say you're getting into your car after buying groceries when a man steps up to your door and tries to wrestle you out of the car so that he can steal it. If you have a gun, your first instinct might be to grab it and scare away the carjacker. But unless your life is threatened, grabbing a gun during an attempted robbery is a dramatic escalation.

Now think about it from the carjacker's point of view. When he sees the gun, he's going to want to defend *himself*, and all of a sudden there's a fight for control of the weapon. Or he could have his own gun. What will happen?

REMEMBER

The statistics aren't in your favor. A study published in the *American Journal of Public Health* in 2009 shows that having a gun in a confrontation more than quadruples your chances of being shot.

I don't like those odds. You shouldn't like those odds.

However, if you've assessed your situation and still think that carrying a gun is the right choice for you, you must understand that guns should only ever be considered *a last resort* when it comes to protection. Your next step is then learning more about the carry laws where you live.

Getting to know your state's carry laws and off-limit locations

Every state and county has different gun laws, especially when it comes to open carry (which I and other experts strongly warn against, as I discuss in the pages ahead) and concealed carry. Some states prohibit open carry altogether, or require that you first obtain a permit to do so. Concealed carry is allowed in all 50 states, but the requirements differ. Many stipulate that you obtain a permit first, which might entail a background check as well as firearms training. Every state's different, and these laws change frequently.

You might live in a "may issue" state, which means the state *may issue* you a "Concealed Carry Weapon" (CCW) permit or "Concealed Handgun License" (CHL) if you meet all the state's requirements, pass a background check, and have a legitimate reason for carrying a weapon on your person, like if you're a security guard or transport diamonds for a living. The implication here is that the state may *not* give you a carry permit. Don't take it personally.

That said, just before this book was published, the U.S. Supreme Court ruled that New York could no longer require residents to demonstrate "proper cause" to obtain a carry permit, and the decision may affect other "may issue" states.

In a "shall issue" state, the state *shall issue* you a concealed-carry permit if you meet the state's requirements and pass a background check. In other words, these states aren't as strict when it comes to processing carry permits.

Finally, as of this writing, 25 states allow their residents to carry concealed weapons without a permit or background check. This is known as "permitless carry." Yes, you have to undergo a background check when you buy a gun from a licensed dealer, but a number of states also allow for private sales between *unlicensed* individuals without any background checks. So, there aren't any safeguards in place to stop someone who legally may not own a gun from buying one from a neighbor, for example, and carrying it around in public. Kinda scary, eh?

TIP

To learn more about the concealed-carry laws where you live, check the websites of your local and state law enforcement agencies, as they're usually the ones in charge of processing carry permits. Look for that .gov at the end of the website's URL, and pay attention to the "last updated" dates. If you're still in doubt, talk to a lawyer in your area.

These websites should also be able to tell you where you *can't* carry a gun even if you have a valid permit. On the federal level, you can't bring a gun into courthouses or other federal property, airports, prisons, visitors centers at national parks, military bases, and post offices, to name a few examples. The Gun-Free School Zones Act (GFSZA) of 1990 also prohibits guns on school grounds across the country.

Depending on the city or state, you also can't bring a gun into a state courthouse, a religious center, a bar, and other sensitive places. Private establishments, including bars, restaurants, and shopping malls, can also choose to prohibit guns.

TIP

Find out what "gun-free zones" exist wherever you live, follow the law, and pay attention to "no gun" signs near the front doors of buildings. Don't even think about bringing a gun into one of these locations. And if you're ever in doubt, do without. Leave the gun locked up at home or, at the very least, secured out of plain view in your vehicle.

THE DANGERS OF OPEN CARRY

The gun world is full of disagreements on things like the "best" caliber and the "right" way to accessorize a firearm. But most of the firearms experts I've had the pleasure of meeting and working with agree that open carry, which means you carry a gun out in the open so that everyone can see it, is downright dangerous — if it's even legal in your state in the first place. Here's why open carry is dangerous:

- First off, wearing a handgun on your hip, or a rifle slung over your shoulder, paints a target on your back. I know that some open carriers think they are deterring possible attacks, but criminals might see your gun and single you out as their first victim.

  In other words, you're giving up the element of surprise *and* your ability to walk away and not be involved.

- An attacker might even attempt to disarm you, which happens to police officers quite frequently. According to the FBI, of the 503 cops who were killed in the line of duty between 2011 and 2020, 51 (or 10.1 percent) were first disarmed of their weapons, and 16 (3.2 percent) were killed with their own weapons. This is why officers increasingly wear security holsters and receive special training to prevent people from snatching their sidearms.

- If something happens, responding police officers might not be able to distinguish you from the bad guy. This is a dangerous position to find yourself in.

(continued)

(continued)

- Studies have shown that carrying a gun can make someone more aggressive, and thus more likely to escalate situations. This is known as the "weapons effect."

- You could also intimidate others who aren't used to firearms or, frankly, don't want to see them while they're shopping for groceries. They have that right.

  In the end, you never know how others will react to the sight of your gun, and scaring people with a firearm is extremely irresponsible. So think twice before you decide to carry one in public.

Recognizing common carry positions

In Chapter 10, I offer a quick overview of some of today's most popular *holsters*, or *rigs*, crafted from leather, nylon, plastic (often called Kydex), or some combination of these materials, and formed to fit a specific make and model of handgun.

For concealed carry, your holster must protect your gun from the elements (including your own sweat), keep it secure, and prevent anything from entering the triggerguard, thus helping you avoid an accidental discharge. It'll also help if the holster breaks up the gun's outline under clothing.

Although I won't recommend any specific holster or carry position, it might be helpful to know about some of the *on-body* options out there:

>> **Inside-the-waistband (IWB) carry** lets you keep a gun holstered on the inside of your waistband and is probably the most popular choice. IWB holsters usually clip onto a belt, so along with having to wear pants that are at least one size larger than you normally would to accommodate the gun, you'll also need a stiff leather or nylon belt designed for carrying a handgun as well as a loose shirt, sweater, or other "cover garment."

   Although many IWB holsters, including "belly bands," position the gun around your hips or in the "small of the back," some allow for "appendix carry," which positions the gun toward the front of your waistband. This position has some drawbacks, though.

   First, you can't have a tummy. So if you're like me and still working on your New Year's resolution from 2015, appendix carry is already off the table. Second, the gun will point at some sensitive anatomy — not only *those* parts, if you catch my drift, but also your femoral arteries.

>> **Outside-the-waistband (OWB) carry**, as you can guess, means that you secure your holstered gun on the outside of your waistband. OWB holsters typically use belt or paddle attachments. But this carry position isn't great for concealed carry unless you wear a longer jacket or coat.

"Concealed" is the operating word here; you don't want to expose your gun every time you reach up, bend over, or kneel down to tie your shoes.

>> **Pocket carry** is another common choice, but it really only works if you find a small enough gun or have giant pockets. (JNCO fans, rejoice!) A front or cargo pocket would be ideal here — not a back pocket, because sitting on a gun can be painful. You also need a pocket holster that breaks up the shape of the gun in your pocket, prevents lint from accumulating inside the gun, and protects the triggerguard.

   To prevent any interference with your gun, don't stash anything else in that pocket, like your keys, phone, or wallet.

>> **Ankle carry** means that you hide a handgun under your pants leg, in a holster strapped to the ankle opposite your strong hand. So if you're right handed, the holster will be on your left leg. The gun has to be pretty small, however, so adherents to this carry position usually stick with snub-nose revolvers.

   You'll need wide-legged pants for ankle carry, too, which is why this method is popular for those wearing dress suits.

>> **Shoulder carry** is another method that requires a cover garment — in this case, a roomy coat or jacket to hide a shoulder holster that suspends your gun under one armpit, against your torso, and spare magazines under your other armpit. You have to be careful that the gun isn't exposed if your jacket flaps open, however.

If you decide to carry a gun — after honestly assessing your situation, examining your state's laws, taking a training course, obtaining a permit — you'll probably have to experiment with a few of these carry positions to find the one that works best for you. This is why gun owners tend to amass holsters over the years.

REMEMBER

No matter the position, your gun must stay hidden and secure. After you've settled on an outfit, confirm that your gun doesn't peek out from your clothes when you move around or bend over. Then check to make sure that the shape of the gun isn't visible through whatever cover garment you've chosen. If your gun "prints," as it's known, try a looser fit.

Most important is keeping your firearm locked in place. You don't want your gun to become visible or, worse yet, spill out of your clothes and fall onto the ground when you hustle across the street, for example. If that happens, your embarrassment will be the least of your worries.

To prevent those mishaps, use a holster that securely attaches to you — whether it's your belt, the interior of your pocket, or your ankle — and is built for your exact gun model. Also consider a holster with an extra layer of retention, like a strap or release button, as I mention in Chapter 10.

And don't get too set in your ways. After you've gone through all the hassle of finding the right clothing and carry position, the weather will change and you'll have to start back at square one. People will notice if you stick with a parka in 80-degree heat.

WARNING

Finally, although some people carry their handguns *off-body* in purses, backpacks, messenger bags, or super-stylish fanny packs, I must warn you against this route. I would hate for you to drop the bag and damage the gun, or have it spill out onto the sidewalk. More important, however, if you lose the purse or bag, or someone cuts the strap and steals it, you've also lost your gun. Safe, responsible gun owners always maintain control over their weapons — and avoid unnecessary risks.

Avoiding injury while unholstering

Drawing a handgun from a holster might seem like a simple proposition. You just grasp the grip of the gun and pull it straight out, right?

Not quite. Westerns make it look deceptively easy.

In reality, unholstering a gun is dangerous. You have to pay very careful attention to several things simultaneously, including your strong-hand grip and trigger finger, where the gun's muzzle is pointing as you lift it out of the holster, and the location of your nondominant hand. It's hard enough learning to draw a gun from an OWB holster on your hip before you throw in a cover garment.

WARNING

Because of the muzzle and trigger discipline required, only a certified firearms instructor can teach you how to draw a handgun from a holster in a safe, controlled environment, and if you're focused on concealed carry, look for "CCW" or "CPL" training courses in your area to learn the extra steps that are required. I only offer a few pointers here.

In other words, you need to be on the firing line at your local shooting range, using a completely empty gun, and under the watchful eye of an experienced instructor to practice drawing and reholstering a handgun. Don't just read a book — even a masterpiece like this one — or watch a YouTube video and think you've got it.

Drawing from an open holster

Every instructor has a different procedure, but they'll show you how to draw a gun in a handful of steps. Some of the following actions take place simultaneously:

>> The basic drawing process, or *drawstroke,* from an OWB belt holster begins with placing your nondominant hand on your chest like you're saying the Pledge of Allegiance.

>> You then grasp the grip of your handgun with your strong hand, placing your index finger along the outside of the holster.

>> Draw the gun straight up out of the holster. As it comes up, let your index finger drop onto the handgun's frame, just above the triggerguard.

>> As you lift the gun, begin rotating it so that the barrel points downrange, toward your target.

>> When the gun is near the center of your chest and pointing downrange, add your nondominant hand to the grip.

>> Drive the gun forward and align your sights. Only when you're on target and ready to fire will your index finger make contact with the trigger.

REMEMBER

The process is deceptively simple, and it changes based on where your gun and holster are positioned. A trainer can help you iron out the kinks.

Now, you might be wondering why your nondominant, or support, hand stays on your chest for most of the drawstroke. Put simply, this ensures that it doesn't cross in front of your gun's muzzle at any point in the drawstroke. In the past, cops and gun owners have been documented shooting their own hands because, in a deadly encounter, humans become threat focused and lose some of their fine motor skills. So, keep those digits!

Another helpful bit of advice: Slow is smooth, and smooth is fast.

This saying, often attributed to the U.S. Navy SEALs, applies to any maneuver that requires skill, whether it's drawing a gun or fly fishing. Practice the motions slowly until they're smooth — and safe — and then you can speed up. Conversely, if the motions aren't smooth, slow down.

Drawing from concealment

What if you need to draw your gun from concealment? Again, a good trainer will walk you through the details based on the carry position, but in general, your support hand will be in charge of dealing with the cover garment. Keep these techniques in mind:

>> If you're using an IWB holster, your support hand will grab your shirt or sweater and pull it up, out of the way (as shown in Figure 11-2), as you grip your firearm with your strong hand.

>> If you're using an ankle holster, step forward with your nondominant leg (the one with the holster on it) and either bend over to reach the holster or

drop down into a kneeling position. Then pull up on your pants leg with your support hand and draw your firearm with your strong hand.

>> If you're using an IWB, OWB, or shoulder holster with a jacket or coat, you'll sweep the jacket flap on your strong side away from the gun and holster with your strong hand like an Old West gunslinger before you grasp the firearm.

>> If you're using a pocket holster, you'll draw the gun as you normally would with your strong hand. Hopefully the holster will stay in place. If not, resist the urge to hold it in your pocket with your support hand. Again, you don't want to sweep your hand with the muzzle of your gun.

TIP

If the holster comes out of your pocket with the gun, it's time to get a new holster — one with a stickier outer material so that it'll stay in position.

FIGURE 11-2:
This shooter draws from an IWB rig after lifting his shirt with his support hand.

Courtesy of Ambrosia Studios/Shutterstock

Reholstering your gun safely

Please be extra careful when you reholster your firearm. When you're first learning to return your gun to its holster, pay attention and watch what you're doing. Look at the gun as you guide it back down into position, and please keep your fingers away from the trigger!

WARNING

In fact, keep *everything* away from the triggerguard. I've heard of incidents in which gun owners have shot themselves because little jacket toggles or zippers caught on their guns' triggers while they were reholstering. Yikes!

So hold your cover garment up and out of the way as you reholster your gun, and watch what you're doing. Professional shooters can stay focused on targets downrange while they reholster their guns because they've practiced thousands of times. And they aren't wearing bulky clothing.

You'll get there eventually. Start slowly.

3

Discovering How to Use Your Firearm

Locate a reputable firearms training course near you and pack the best gear for classes.

Build your shooting and gun-handling skills while staying focused on safety.

Find out how to reload and troubleshoot common pistol malfunctions.

Chapter **12**

Basic Training

Think of this book as a good starting point when it comes to understanding guns. Reading every single page — and I hope you will! — should give you a solid foundation of knowledge *to build upon.* A book can go only so far, though. You need hands-on experience, one-on-one instruction adapted to your particular learning style, and lots of practice to build muscle memory with firearms. That's why it's time to invest in formal training.

No, not *that* formal. Please don't show up to the firing range dressed like James Bond. Instead, I'm talking about attending an official training course at a dedicated shooting facility or academy and taught by a certified instructor — someone who puts safety first and has years of experience in both firearms and teaching. Not that friend or neighbor who's obsessed with action movies and regularly posts pictures of their growing arsenal on Instagram. We deserve better.

That said, I know it can be a little intimidating to step into a gun shop for the first time, let alone sign up for a "Firearms 101" class, but with a little forethought, you can take the anxiety out of the equation. This chapter helps you pick the right training course so that you can learn lifesaving skills.

WARNING

You might be tempted to forego live, in-person training and instead head to YouTube to watch countless videos of gun "experts" sharing their favorite tips and tricks — while also advertising various products. But it can be difficult to discern hobbyists from certified professionals, and even if you do luck out and find a real expert (without quotation marks), they might skip important topics or assume that their viewers are already well versed in firearms. So, at the risk of sounding like an old grump, be wary of learning from YouTube.

Understanding Why You Need to Attend a Training Course

Think back to driver's ed for a moment. You might have already learned the basics of driving from your parents or friends before you took the class, but did they explain all the road signs and traffic laws out there? What about defensive driving techniques? Did they help you practice parallel parking in a safe, dent-free environment? If so, what's your insurance premium?

It's undeniable that driver's ed courses — required in a majority of states — have made our roads safer. But according to a 2015 survey published in *Injury Prevention*, only 61 percent of U.S. gun owners, or roughly three in five, have received some type of formal firearms training. That number is a bit low for comfort, and I think we can do better for ourselves, our family members, and our communities.

Like driver's ed courses, a few states require that their residents take training courses just to purchase or possess a firearm, as shown in Table 12-1 below.

TABLE 12-1   **States with Firearms Training Requirements**

State	Training Needed For
California	Purchasing any firearm
Connecticut	Purchasing any firearm
District of Columbia	Owning any firearm
Hawaii	Purchasing a handgun
Maryland	Purchasing a handgun
Massachusetts	Owning any firearm
Rhode Island	Purchasing any firearm
Washington	Purchasing a semi-auto rifle

In addition, many states and Washington, D.C., require some form of firearms training to obtain a concealed-carry permit. To learn more about that aspect of gun ownership, head to Chapter 16.

State gun laws change all the time, so it's important to check with your local and state officials, including state police and county websites, regarding licensing requirements. If you have questions, consult a lawyer in your area. Currently, there are no federal regulations that require firearms training.

But even if you live in a state that doesn't require training, it's still a good idea to enroll in a course. Otherwise, you'll miss out on tons of critical information. A great entry-level training course will:

>> Reinforce the four rules of gun safety (see Chapter 1) and show you how they work in the real world, with additional lessons on child safety and proper storage

>> Teach you to safely handle firearms and ammunition and identify basic firearm components

>> Explain federal laws as well as your state's laws regarding self-defense, deadly force, permitting requirements, and more

>> Provide techniques to help you avoid conflicts and de-escalate potentially violent situations

>> Demonstrate the fundamentals of marksmanship and overcoming recoil

>> Provide one-on-one support to help you hit targets on the range, and just as importantly, help you understand why you *aren't* hitting targets

>> Coach you to reload and clear malfunctions in a safe, controlled environment

>> Show you several drills to help you safely practice everything you've learned on and off the range

>> Help you gain confidence with firearms, especially your own

As you can see, training courses can be revolutionary for new shooters. But what about seasoned veterans and old pros? Even if you grew up around guns, or have been hunting, or hit the shooting range regularly, it never hurts to take a refresher course or add to your toolbox, so to speak.

When it comes to your marksmanship and gun-handling skills, are there areas that need improvement? Have you picked up any bad habits? Would you be able to spot them if you did? A good instructor can improve your accuracy, for example, or teach you new shooting drills so you can make the most of your range time in the future.

In other words, it's never too late to take a training course.

Knowing What to Expect from a Training Course

The idea of attending a training course may be overwhelming. You think it's a good idea because you want to be a responsible gun owner, but how do you know which course to register for, and how can you assess a course or trainer's quality? Take a deep breath and keep reading. I answer these questions and others in the following sections.

Breaking down the types of courses

I've attended different training courses over the years, from basic range safety and firearm orientation sessions that lasted a few hours to weeklong classes combining several interrelated topics. Each style has its benefits, drawbacks, and requirements, so it's important to break them down a bit further.

First, here's an overview of some entry-level options, which I've ranked in terms of difficulty and commitment:

>> **"Basic Gun Safety" or "Home Firearm Safety" seminars** are the most rudimentary of training courses. In fact, you might see them called "orientations." Here you'll learn the four rules of gun safety, firearm parts, and how to unload and take care of weapons. But notice that I wrote "seminar" above. These courses, which can last up to four hours, tend to take place in classrooms and don't include live fire on a range.

>> **"Basic Rifle" or "Rifle 101" courses** are designed for those new to firearms and don't necessarily want to own a handgun. This course will build on the information of the previous seminar style but should include some range time.

TIP

If you're intimidated by weapons, I highly recommend a Basic Rifle course because rifles are much easier to handle and shoot than handguns.

>> **"Basic Pistol" or "Pistol 101" courses** are a great starting point for most people. They begin in the classroom like the basic seminars above but include range time so you can build muscle memory with your pistol or a rental. I recommend attending a class like this in your area that lasts at least eight hours, or one day. As the name implies, the focus is on handguns, but many of the same lessons apply to rifles and shotguns.

>> **"Concealed Carry Weapon" (CCW) or "Concealed Handgun License" (CHL) courses** are very similar to the Basic Pistol courses above, but they're more common in states that require formal training to obtain a concealed-carry

permit. The names change based on what each state calls its permit or license, but these courses focus on handguns and usually last one to two days.

You'll also find intermediate and advanced versions of the aforementioned classes that generally last longer — anywhere from two to five days — as well as those dedicated to rifles, shotguns, and hunting, to name just a few options. Instructors and academies typically provide detailed course descriptions on their websites so you can see whether a shotgun course is dedicated to skeet shooting or home defense, for example.

Considering three major factors: cost, time, and format

So how do you choose between all the various options? Looking at a few different factors can help you narrow down which training course is best for your situation and needs.

» **Cost:** Welcome to life, where money is always a consideration. Training courses that last one to two days can cost anywhere from $150 to $500, and I've seen weeklong courses approach $2,000. This might seem expensive, but at the risk of sounding like an insurance salesman, what would you pay for peace of mind? Quality training provides you with lifesaving information that you can pass along to your family members. I can't stress that point enough. You should also come out of the class with drills to practice on your own time to develop and maintain your skills.

» **Time:** We all know the saying about time being money. In this situation, you need to ask yourself how much time you're willing to devote to your firearms education. Obviously, the more the better. But at the very least, I recommend attending an eight-hour course, which also happens to be the bare minimum for a few states that require training. Any shorter and you're risking valuable range time. If eight hours seems like too much — if you don't want to give up a Saturday for training — you might not be ready to own a firearm.

» **Format:** Every training course starts in a classroom-style setting where the instructor(s) provides lessons on a range of topics. The "classroom" itself might be indoors or outdoors; it might be attached to a shooting range or in a separate location.

REMEMBER

You should receive a packet or handbook that explains and reinforces all the topics that are discussed. Feel free to ask questions and take notes because there could be an exam at the end of the class.

Unless you're taking a basic safety or orientation course, your instructor(s) will then take you to the range to practice the concepts you discussed in the classroom. Ideally, you want to attend a course with a lead instructor and assistants who can work with a few students at a time and ensure that everyone is following the safety rules.

The instructors will decide how the classroom and range time are divided. If you're taking a two-day Basic Pistol course, for example, you might spend the first day in the classroom and the second on the range, or the first half of each day in the classroom and the second half on the range. Either way, you should look for a good mix of classroom instruction and range time. If you do one without the other, you're sacrificing valuable knowledge or experience.

TIP

Some trainers and academies now offer the classroom portions of their courses online. Although this is a convenient option, I don't recommend it for someone who is easily distracted or unaccustomed to e-learning. (Be honest with yourself!) It also might be harder to interact with the instructor or fellow students as well. However, no matter what you decide, the range portion will still be held — you guessed it — at a range.

Understanding common course requirements

Ever have nightmares about missing a test in high school, or not turning in your homework on time? I'm truly sorry if all this classroom talk brings back bad memories. But I know one thing for certain: Whether it's for A.P. Bio or Basic Pistol, you never want to be that student who shows up unprepared. Not only could you slow the class down in some way, but your instructor might make an example of you. *Yikes.*

Thankfully, it's pretty easy to avoid this scenario. After you've enrolled in a training course online or over the phone, simply check the trainer's or academy's website beforehand to see what is required to attend. Obviously, every class is different, but I can offer a few pointers.

For the basic safety and orientation courses that only take place in a classroom-style setting, you just need to bring your ID, a good attitude, and comfortable clothes. You will be sitting for several hours at a time. Consider bringing along your favorite pen or pencil and possibly lunch.

For beginner's courses that split time between the classroom and range, you'll most likely be asked to bring the following:

>> **A firearm:** Some ranges will allow you to rent one for the course, though. If you bring your own, make sure it's clean and well lubricated beforehand to avoid jams and malfunctions during the class. (See Chapter 8 for information on cleaning and maintaining your gun.)

>> **Ammunition:** The course website should tell you how many rounds to bring along and whether any special types are required, such as frangible rounds for close-quarters training. If you don't see this information on the course website, call to confirm the details. For handgun courses, you will most likely use FMJs. But no matter what, make sure that your ammunition works in your particular gun. Now is not the time to test a new load in your weapon. Again, you're trying to avoid jams and other malfunctions.

>> **Comfortable shoes and clothes:** Wear clothes that you won't mind getting a little dirty. I say this because the combustion of firing a weapon creates gunpowder residue and soot that might ruin a white shirt, for example. I discuss dressing appropriately in greater detail later in this chapter.

>> **Eye and ear protection:** I cover this topic later in the chapter.

For more advanced handgun courses, including those dedicated to concealed carry, you will probably need those previous items as well as these:

>> **A holster** if you will be learning how to draw your pistol. If it's a concealed-carry course, the instructor might want you to bring a holster designed specifically for that purpose. Otherwise, you will most likely have to bring a belt holster with an open top and no retention devices, meaning no levers or buttons that must first be deactivated for the gun to be drawn. Although retention holsters are highly recommended in every other setting, their security devices are not conducive to training.

>> **A gun belt,** which should be sturdy and purpose-built for carrying firearms, ammunition, and other gear — not the dinky dress belt you throw on with khakis. Several companies offer leather and nylon gun belts that provide plenty of support while still being flexible. Just make sure that the belt fits properly before you step onto the range.

>> **Spare magazines** so you can practice reloading. I recommend having at least three spare magazines for any training course.

>> **Magazine carriers** so you can keep spare magazines within easy reach on your gun belt.

>> **A magazine loader** to help you replenish all those spare magazines between drills, when you're off the firing line. For longer courses, you'll fire hundreds of rounds that need to be pushed down into magazines while fighting spring tension. (Your thumbs can thank me later.)

>> **A small cleaning kit,** because even if you've done everything right — paid your taxes, held doors for strangers, tipped every waiter at least 20 percent, and so on — your gun still might jam and need a thorough cleaning.

>> **Kneepads,** because if the course covers positional shooting, you'll have to kneel, presumably on a hard surface like concrete or gravel, over and over again. So save those knees and thumbs!

Again, these are common, handgun-specific requirements. For rifle and shotgun courses, for example, you'll need a sling instead of a holster. So make sure that you understand the course requirements well in advance.

These are also *my* recommendations from *my* experience. You know yourself and can decide whether you need to, say, pack a back brace because you'll be on your feet for hours on end. You should push yourself, not hurt yourself.

Whatever course you decide on, the most important requirement is going with an open mind. Ask any instructor, and they'll tell you that the best students are actually those with the *least* firearms experience because they aren't saddled with pre-conceptions. In other words, if your dad taught you one way to grip a handgun, don't let that get in the way of learning a new — and possibly better — method.

Evaluating course options

It's very likely that the instructors and academies in your area offer similar courses. So how do you decide between a Basic Pistol class at Facility A and another at Facility B? The last thing I want is for you to sign up for a course, pay the tuition, and simply "hope for the best," only to be disappointed.

The best decisions are informed decisions, so consider the following steps:

1. **Start by reading the course description on the trainer or academy's website.**

   Is the class too expensive or time consuming? Can you make it fit into your busy schedule? Does the format seem reasonable? If the description doesn't mention live fire on the range, for example, you might want to pass on it. Again, it's important to understand your needs.

2. **Compare the course description to the list I provided earlier in this chapter of what a "great entry-level course" should offer.**

   Will the course review the four safety rules and your state's gun laws? What about conflict resolution and safe storage?

If these topics aren't specifically mentioned on the course website, feel free to call the instructor or academy — I know, what an outdated idea! — to obtain more information. I say this because trainers aren't exactly known for keeping cutting-edge websites. If the course still doesn't appear to cover some of those topics, however, consider avoiding it.

3. **Ask about the class size.**

   Just like with any other school, you want a smaller class or a low student-teacher ratio, generally no more than five students per trainer. Too many students and you might not get enough one-on-one time with an instructor or, worse yet, they might have a hard time ensuring that everyone is handling their weapons safely.

4. **Read Google and Yelp reviews to see what past students have said about the instructor, the facility, or the course itself.**

   Obviously, you're looking for highly rated trainers and academies with at least four stars. If someone gave an instructor only two stars, for example, try to find out why. I'm sure you'll see some red flags.

   WARNING

   Be wary of the testimonials trainers and shooting facilities post on their not-so-cutting-edge websites and social media pages. They might publish only positive reviews and ignore or delete negative ones.

5. **Learn more about the facility.**

   If the course is being held at a local gun shop with an attached range, go visit and see what it's like. Is it a busy location? Is it relatively clean? Those are good signs. Is it empty, dirty, poorly lit? Obviously, those are bad signs.

   Air quality is another important consideration. Newer indoor shooting ranges will advertise that they have advanced air filtration systems to get rid of the toxic substances produced by firing guns, including poisonous lead. So if you can't find any information about the range's air quality, don't sign up for a class there — unless you want to wear a gas mask.

   Outdoor ranges don't have this problem, and they're better suited for training that involves positional shooting, movement, and drawing from a holster, for example. On the flip side, outdoor ranges are, well, outdoors, so you'll be exposed to the elements. (I talk a bit more about dressing for the weather later in this chapter.)

   Outdoor ranges also aren't known for their amenities. Don't expect spotless, climate-controlled bathrooms with marble countertops. Case in point: Several years ago, I attended a training course with "Beware of Rattlesnakes" signs decorating the outhouse walls. Talk about pressure!

   Thus, the facility has a big effect on the course's content and quality.

6. **Get to know the instructor.**

First and foremost, they must be certified by a national training organization or state authority, and they must be open about their professional experience. Good trainers publish their credentials, including their certifications, on their websites. They also explain their previous positions in, say, the military or law enforcement as well as the classes they've taught over the years.

In other words, you shouldn't have to dig through their LinkedIn profiles to find out what they've accomplished.

It's also absolutely critical that instructors exhibit safe gun handling at all times. I cannot stress this enough. If, during your research, you see a YouTube video of the instructor pointing a gun at students — even if it's unloaded — during a demonstration, avoid that trainer at all costs.

Instead, a good instructor *safely* demonstrates everything they teach. They can't just tell you how to handle and shoot a gun accurately; they have to show you.

On paper, these are some of the most basic requirements of a firearms instructor, but reviews and testimonials from past students should give you a better idea of the trainer's style and demeanor, making it easier to pick one over another. It's hard to ignore dozens of glowing reviews.

FIVE MORE INSTRUCTOR RED FLAGS

The gun world is rife with disagreements and contentious subjects. Experts argue over different calibers or the right way to hold a flashlight and a handgun at the same time. But there's no debate over what makes a bad instructor because bad instructors are objectively dangerous. Not only can they waste your time and money, but they can also teach you unsafe techniques and even get someone killed.

So how do you spot a bad trainer? Look for these red flags:

- **The instructor doesn't mention an emergency medical plan.** At the very beginning of a course, the trainer should let everyone know what to do if someone gets hurt. At a minimum, every student should know where the first-aid kit is and who is in charge of dialing 911 in an emergency.

- **The instructor doesn't take firearms seriously.** Sorry to be a buzzkill, but as I've mentioned elsewhere, guns are inherently dangerous and demand respect. Instructors must set an example and show their students that they take such responsibility seriously. So, to me, red flags include jokes about guns, sloppy gun handling, and even "Welcome to the Gun Show" tank tops.

- **The instructor has a "shoot first" philosophy.** This means that guns are their first resort in an altercation. But as a safe, responsible gun owner, you shouldn't *want* to use your gun for self-defense; it is your last resort in this regard. So if the instructor doesn't teach you how to de-escalate confrontations or avoid them altogether, it's time to find a new trainer.

- **The instructor doesn't use an inert training gun.** Remember what I said about safe demonstrations earlier? One surefire way to display techniques without having a real gun in the mix is to use an inert training gun. These non-functioning "guns" are made of bright red or blue plastic so that they're easy to identify and won't be confused for the real thing. On top of that, they're super cheap.

- **The instructor acts like a drill sergeant.** If you want to be yelled at, enlist in the Marines or join a "boot camp" fitness class. That supercharged teaching style doesn't make much sense among civilian firearm students, however. Call me a "softie," but I think you'll respond better to a courteous and professional instructor who listens and believes in constructive criticism, not forced marches.

- **The instructor doesn't prioritize your education.** Most trainers love teaching others, sharing their knowledge. But some effectively turn their training classes into sales presentations, recommending specific products — their preferred guns, ammunition, and accessories — or organizations as unofficial recruiters. In turn, they may receive discounts and other financial incentives. But remember, you're paying for training, not an eight-hour commercial.

Finding a Training Course Near You

The previous section establishes what makes a good training course and discusses common requirements. In this section, I offer tips for finding a class near you. Just bear in mind that "near you" might still entail driving a few hours, especially if you live in a big city and want to train at an outdoor range.

So where do you start? Instead of picking the first option you stumble on, I recommend building a list and then using the criteria discussed earlier in the chapter to find the best choice from all of the available options.

Here are some ideas to begin your list:

>> Ask gun-owning friends and families members if they have any recommendations for training courses. You might luck out. However, if they can't offer any help and you do end up finding a great course, make sure you circle back and recommend it to *them*.

>> Although big box stores won't be as helpful in this regard, smaller gun shops usually offer training courses. But even if they don't, the staff will be happy to recommend nearby trainers and academies. Obviously, this is a great starting point if you purchased your firearm at a local gun shop. So if this is an option for you, add it to the list.

>> Tap into the power of your favorite search engine, like Google, Yahoo!, or Bing. (I'm not here to judge.) But before I win the award for laziest author, here are some search tips:

- Searching for "firearm training near me" will provide results, but try including the name of the course, like "Basic Pistol" or "CCW," to get specific. If you aren't seeing as many results with "near me" or your zip code in the search bar, zoom out and add your state (for example, "Basic Pistol training Georgia").

- If you Google "firearm academies," the search engine will let you filter results by rating and operating hours.

- Search for local gun shops to then find training courses, as I mentioned at the top of this list.

- Finally, Yelp is another resource that can help you build a list quickly. Simply type **firearm training** into the search bar and include your city or zip code to see the highest-rated trainers and academies in your area.

WARNING

Some third-party websites promise to help you find training courses — while also phishing for your email address or personal information for marketing purposes. Instead, try going directly to the trainer or academy's website.

After you've compiled a list of options, go through and remove those classes that don't fit your cost, time, or format constraints. Then, with the remaining classes, read reviews and learn more about the instructors and facilities, as I mention earlier. You get the idea. Obviously, you don't have to follow this exact order to narrow down your options. Just remember that these courses fill up quickly, so as soon as you find the one that feels right, sign up.

TIP

If you're looking to spread your wings and travel for training, read Chapter 11 for advice on traveling with a firearm.

Range Safety Fundamentals

Whether you're heading to the range for training or just some fun recreational shooting, it's important to understand the facility's safety rules. Depending on the location, these rules might be listed on the range's website or even printed on big signs displayed around the facility, kind of like those posted at public swimming pools.

Raise your hand if you read all of the pool safety rules before diving in. Anyone? Anyone who isn't a lawyer?

With shooting ranges, you must understand and follow the rules. If not, the life-guards here — range officers, or ROs — will ask you to leave. Every range has its own rules, however, so the following section focuses on the most common examples you might come across.

Explaining common range rules

Most range rules build off of the four rules of gun safety that I refer to repeatedly in this book, but there are a few adaptations and several additions:

REMEMBER

>> **Always treat firearms like they are loaded.** However, ranges also stipulate that the gun must be fully *unloaded,* with the action open and the magazine removed, if it's not on the firing line.

The firing line is where you step up and fire your gun. At an outdoor range, it may be a literal line on the ground or a row of benches to sit and shoot from. You will only ever cross the firing line to, say, set up a new target *after* a range officer calls the range "cold" and gives you permission to move forward.

At indoor ranges, the firing line is essentially a countertop divided into several lanes, and you never cross it. Instead, you retract or extend your paper target using a system not all that different from a clothesline.

>> **Always keep the muzzle pointed downrange.** See the difference here? Although the second rule of gun safety is "Never let the muzzle cover anything you aren't willing to destroy," range officers have to account for several people operating firearms in a small area. The easiest way to keep everyone safe is to make sure that everyone points their guns downrange, toward the targets, and no one should ever cross in front of your muzzle.

>> **Always keep your finger off your firearm's trigger** and outside the triggerguard until you're ready to shoot.

>> **Be aware of your target and what's behind it.** Most ranges also add that you should not shoot at other people's targets.

>> **Always listen to range officers.** They are there to help you and ensure that everyone is following the safety rules, which is why they reserve the right to inspect your gun and ammunition. If something goes wrong — say, your gun has a malfunction — notify them and let them deal with it.

In that same vein, if a range officer says that the range is "hot," that means people can fire their weapons at will.

If the range goes "cold," or the range officer yells "Cease fire!" everyone must stop firing and step away from their weapons. How can you hear these commands over the sound of gunfire? I get to that in a minute.

>> **Report any unsafe activity or conditions to a range officer.** They may catch the problem before you; they may not. Err on the side of caution.

>> **Do not draw your gun from a holster** unless you have been given express permission to do so. This is another way to limit movement and ensure that guns are only ever pointed downrange.

>> **Never try to catch a falling handgun.** This might seem counterintuitive, but if your gun slips out of your hand, *let it go*. Most modern firearms won't discharge if they are dropped. But if you fumble with the gun while it's falling, there's a chance you could accidentally pull the trigger.

>> **Do not use ammunition prohibited by the range.** This one varies by range, but most ban tracer rounds, for example, which can start a fire, or steel-core ammunition that can penetrate the range's back wall.

>> **Do not bring food or drinks onto the range.** No, you don't want to ingest those toxic substances I mentioned earlier, like gunpowder residue and lead. And wash your hands as soon as you're off the range!

>> **Do not even think about touching alcohol or drugs before hitting the range.** You should only ever handle firearms if you are completely sober. So save that beer for *after* the range.

Dressing appropriately

A few pages ago, I mentioned that if you're heading to the range, you should only wear clothes that you won't mind getting a little dirty. This is because guns emit burnt particulates and soot when they're fired, so I don't recommend wearing a pristine white shirt, for example.

If you use a semi-auto firearm, you also have to watch out for the spent casings that fly out of the gun after it's fired. Again, you're creating a tiny explosion within the weapon, so these casings will be piping hot the second they eject from the action — so hot that they will burn you if they touch your skin. Sadly, the dividers between shooting lanes create the perfect surfaces for casings to bounce right back at you.

In other words, you'll save yourself a lot of pain if you avoid open-toed shoes as well as sleeveless or low-cut shirts.

TECHNICAL STUFF

If you're a leftie like me, hot casings are harder to avoid. Although gun manufacturers have begun to introduce more models with ambidextrous controls in recent years, most semi-auto rifles and shotguns are still designed for right-handed shooters, meaning that they eject spent casings from the right side — and into your face or down your shirt if you aren't careful.

Protecting your eyesight

I've seen far too many shooters break the safety rules, either by inadvertently pointing their guns at others or putting their fingers on the trigger before they're ready to fire. It's terrifying behavior. But I've also lost count of all the shooters I've seen not wearing eye protection, especially hunters.

Thankfully, shooting ranges explicitly require eye protection. How else are you going to keep spent casings, gunpowder residue, and other particulates out of your eyes?

Now, if you've been blessed with four eyes like me, you can simply wear your regular, everyday glasses to the range. They should provide adequate protection from the hazards I keep mentioning. If you're outdoors, sunglasses are a viable option as well.

If you're of the 20/20 persuasion, you can rent plastic safety glasses from the range staff. They won't win you any style points, but they work.

Finally, you can also bring your own safety glasses. If you're considering this route, I recommend purchasing those specifically designed for shooting that meet (or surpass) ANSI Z87.1 standards, which means that the lenses have passed high-impact and industrial safety testing requirements. No, these glasses are *not* bulletproof, but they will help keep debris and other environmental hazards out of your eyes. You can find pairs for less than $30.

Protecting your hearing

According to the Centers for Disease Control and Prevention, any noise over 70 decibels can damage your hearing if it lasts for a prolonged period of time. Normal conversation comes in at around 60 decibels. But a quick, loud noise over 120 decibels can immediately damage your hearing and cause serious pain.

Gunshots start at 140 decibels and can reach well into the 160-decibel range depending on the caliber, your distance from the gun, and other factors. At this level, exposure to a single blast without any protection could lead to tinnitus and permanent hearing loss. So you can see why it's important to wear some form of hearing protection around guns, and why shooting ranges — both indoor and outdoor — require it.

Consider earplugs the bare minimum for your ears. You'll still hear the gunshot, but it won't be as loud or as painful as it would be to the naked ear.

Earmuffs that completely cover your ears are a big step up from earplugs in terms of protection. Most ranges have very basic earmuffs (also known as "passive earmuffs") available for rent, and you should consider wearing earplugs underneath these earmuffs for added insulation.

TIP

How do sound suppressors, or silencers, play into this equation? Are they as quiet as they're depicted in movies? To learn more, turn back to Chapter 10 and see the sidebar "How sound suppressors actually work."

But if you want the most *bang* for your buck (or should I say *least?*), invest in electronic shooting earmuffs. Honestly, I own seven different pairs now, and they are still the best firearm accessories I've ever purchased or been gifted. They not only cancel out the sound of gunfire, effectively muting it, but also amplify other ambient sounds below a certain threshold.

In other words, with electronic shooting earmuffs, you can hear conversations around you, including range commands, but not gunfire. Amazing, right? These earmuffs are especially invaluable for those who might otherwise be intimidated by firearms, because they take some of the bark out of shooting a gun, so to speak. On top of that, these earmuffs are pretty affordable — typically less than $60 — and even if the batteries die, they still protect your ears.

TECHNICAL STUFF

When you shop around for electronic shooting earmuffs, look for highly rated models that use easy-to-find AAA batteries and aren't too bulky. You also want a "noise reduction rating" (NRR) of at least 22 decibels and an "attack time," or how quickly the earmuffs register a loud noise and cancel it out, of 150 milliseconds (0.15 seconds) or faster. Finally, electronic ear*plugs* that work the same way are available, but they cost a lot more.

Preparing for All Types of Weather

With outdoor shooting ranges, you are at the mercy of Mother Nature. There might be a roof over the firing line, but you shouldn't expect walls, insulation, ceiling fans, air conditioning, or any of the other basic amenities we've come to rely upon. And before you ask, no, you can't just stay under the roof — if there is one. You will have to step out from under it to replace your target, for example, or grab something from your car. So, if it's a blistering hot day, expect to sweat. If it's pouring rain, expect to get wet.

In addition, most firearms trainers and academies have policies stating that their outdoor courses will go on "rain or shine" because of how difficult it is to reschedule them. Believe me, I've trained in every condition, from hot summer days to windy, bone-chilling nights.

To make your life easier, the upcoming list suggests some items to bring that can help you deal with inclement weather. The first step is to check the weather forecast several times beforehand in case it changes, and understand that despite the best advances in technology, the forecast might be completely wrong.

As mentioned earlier, you should wear comfortable clothes and shoes that you won't mind getting dirty and that prevent spent casings from burning your skin. Regardless of the weather, I also recommend packing water, snacks, a hat, and lip balm. Seriously. You don't want painful, cracked lips.

For hot, sunny days, you should bring:

>> Sunglasses

>> Sunscreen

>> A small towel to dry your hands

>> An extra shirt in case you sweat through the first one

For cold or wet conditions, consider:

>> Thermal undergarments

>> Waterproof outer garments

>> Hand warmers

>> Waterproof shoes

>> Gloves

I know this list seems a bit obvious, but there are some caveats that come with using firearms. For instance, I personally don't like to wear gloves while shooting because it's harder for me to feel the trigger with my trigger finger. That's why I keep hand warmers in my coat pockets for when I'm not shooting. But if you need them, I suggest thin gloves that fit tightly. You don't want bulky gloves that interfere with your trigger control. If you want to be really hip, you can wear fingerless gloves or simply cut off the tip of the glove's index finger. Just don't do it while you're wearing the gloves!

You want waterproof outer garments in case it starts raining or snowing. But is it warm enough for a lighter jacket, or do you need a thicker coat? Whatever you decide, you generally don't want to wear a heavy winter coat like a parka that might hinder your movement. More importantly, if your training involves drawing a handgun from a holster, your coat shouldn't interfere with those motions. It should be relatively short and tight-fitting.

I learned this lesson the hard way when it snowed during my first training course. My coat was too long and too heavy. Before any drill requiring that I draw and fire my gun, I had to unzip the coat and get it out of the way by tucking the loose front ends behind my holster on my left side and my spare magazines on my right. In other words, I looked like a cowboy about to lose the shootout in a terrible Western — every single drill. So learn from my pain: Make sure that your coat won't interfere with your gun belt or holster.

Likewise, you should avoid coats with zippers or toggles where your handgun passes during the drawstroke. Trust me, you don't want a zipper getting caught in the triggerguard of your pistol as you're reholstering it.

Finally, it's worth noting that freezing conditions can impact your firearm's performance. If condensation builds up inside the gun, the internal mechanisms can freeze and cease operating. Similarly, lubricants lose their viscosity in subzero temperatures and can "gum up" the action. To avoid these situations, make sure to wipe off any excess condensation and keep the gun oil to a minimum. Or use an oil made for subzero conditions.

Continuing Your Education

At the end of a training course, take a moment to appreciate all that you've learned along the way. Remember where you started in terms of skill?

You should walk away from the course with a packet of all the material you covered that you can hold onto, like an old textbook, a certificate proving that you passed, and drills that you can safely practice on your own, either at home or on the range, to work on your skills and techniques. In this way, the best instructors ensure that you grow as a shooter even after the class ends.

Revisiting what you learned and practicing on your own is the first part of continuing your firearms education. If you only take one class and never hit the range again, however, your gun-handling skills will eventually diminish over time. As any instructor will tell you, these skills are perishable and need to be refreshed on a regular basis.

The second component is signing up for another class. If you liked your instructor and want to take another course with them, ask what they'd recommend for your next steps. If you liked the academy or facility, they might have created a curriculum or course lineup for you to follow.

Otherwise, if they don't recommend any particular path to take next, ask yourself the following questions:

>> Do you want to take another handgun course, perhaps the intermediate-level "201" edition? After all, you now have the prerequisite of having passed the beginner's course.

>> Do you want to branch out and take another entry-level class in a different category, like a hunter education course or Basic Shotgun?

>> Do you want to try out a new trainer or academy? You might be tempted to stick with what you know, but it never hurts to round out your education with classes taught by different instructors. In this way, you can learn various techniques to accomplish the same task, and then pick whatever works best for you.

For example, the instructors of the first course I attended preached the gospel of the Weaver shooting stance, and I didn't learn about the isosceles stance until I went to a different academy. If I had stuck with those first trainers, I wouldn't have learned of the style I prefer today.

Take your time and think about the next course whenever you're ready. In the meantime, hit the shooting range every so often to retain what you've learned.

At the end of the day, the only wrong decision here is to not continue training in some way. Never stop learning.

IN THIS CHAPTER

» **Increasing your accuracy at the range**

» **Working with shooting stances, grips, and more**

» **Aiming like a professional**

» **Practicing safely on the range**

Chapter **13**

On the Mark

N o, you might not ever be a sharpshooter or crack shot like Annie Oakley, who could shoot dimes out of the air and split playing cards along their edges. But you can become a skilled shooter by learning all the right mechanics and practicing them regularly.

In fact, learning to shoot a gun accurately isn't all that different from learning any other sports technique, like throwing a football or serving a tennis ball. So in this chapter, I put on my coaching hat (go team!) to help you hit the *bullseye*, or center, of every target. I show you all the basics — the best grips and stances, how to align your sights properly, what it means to truly control your trigger as you break the shot, and more.

TIP

To get the most out of this chapter, read it slowly (trying to follow along with some of the instructions might make you feel as though you're playing a game of Twister) and practice without having a gun present. Then, when you hit the range, start with an unloaded weapon to make sure you have everything down pat. Safety first and always!

WARNING

Remember: Nothing in this book (or whatever you find on YouTube) should be considered a substitute for in-person firearms training on a shooting range. Although I share as much as I can here, a good trainer can give you invaluable feedback and one-on-one instruction as well as more advanced tips that I simply don't have room for in this chapter.

Learning the Basics of Accurate Shooting

Being accurate on the range means that your shots hit exactly where you want them to hit. You aim for a point on a target and then hold the gun as still as you can while you squeeze the trigger. Yes, that's a wild oversimplification, as you'll soon find out, but you have to start somewhere!

REMEMBER

I discuss various firearm components in the pages ahead, like slides, grips, and stocks, so if you need a refresher on what those terms mean and how to locate them, turn back to Chapter 3.

WARNING

The four safety rules always apply, so even while you're learning the basics at the range with an unloaded firearm, keep the gun pointed downrange and your fingers outside the triggerguard. Until you're ready to shoot, your index finger should be resting along the side of the frame or receiver, well above the trigger, as shown in Figure 13-1.

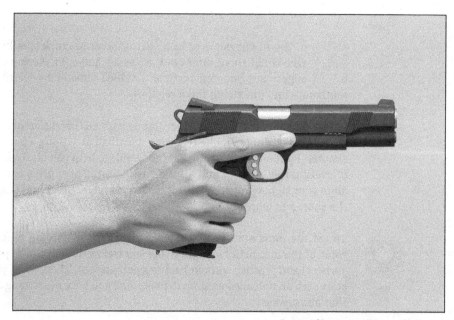

FIGURE 13-1:
Place your trigger finger alongside your gun's frame or receiver until you're ready to fire.

Courtesy of Rattanapon Ninlapoom/Shutterstock

Establishing a firm grip on a handgun

Think back to high school physics for a brief moment. Remember Newton's third law of motion? For every action, there is an equal and opposite reaction.

Firing a bullet — launching a projectile forward — causes the gun to recoil backward. If you could run this experiment in a vacuum, with no human interaction, it would be entirely linear. The bullet would go forward, and the gun would travel backward.

Of course, you aren't firing a gun in a vacuum. You aren't in outer space. You're stuck on *terra firma* like the rest of us, so you have to hold onto the gun. And your grip on the gun is what causes it to tilt upward as it recoils. This movement is called *muzzle rise*. The bullet goes forward; the gun kicks backward *and* upward.

The correct two-handed grip will help you overcome that recoil and muzzle rise:

>> Start by gripping the gun with your dominant, or strong, hand. Regardless of the gun type — handgun, rifle, or shotgun — your hand will naturally fall onto the grip so that the gun lines up with your wrist.

Think of it like throwing a punch or pointing at something. Your hand, wrist, and forearm should create a straight line.

When you wrap the four fingers of your strong hand around the grip, your proximal knuckles (the next joints up from the palm) should be pointing forward, toward your target, and there should be no space between your fingers and the gun's grip.

You also want your strong hand to be as high up on the grip as possible to limit the gun's muzzle rise as it recoils. However, if you're using a semi-auto pistol, you have to make sure that the web of your hand isn't so high that it'll be cut by the slide as it reciprocates backward. Trust me, you don't want to join the "slide bite" club.

>> Now wrap your nondominant, or support, hand around the grip from the other side. The balls of your thumbs should meet, and place your support-hand fingers on top of your strong hand's fingers. Don't interlace your fingers or anything like that.

REMEMBER

More importantly, don't place your support hand *under* the grip, which is known as "teacupping" the gun. Both of your hands should be parallel to each other on the grip.

Once again, your proximal, or second, knuckles should point toward your target, and your trigger finger should still be outside the triggerguard.

>> For semi-auto pistols, keep your thumbs together and pointing forward, toward your target, along one side of the gun. This position limits the gun's ability to twist in your hands. So if you're right-handed, your thumbs will be on the left side of the gun, as shown in Figure 13-2. At the same time, you once again have to make sure that your thumbs don't interfere with the slide.

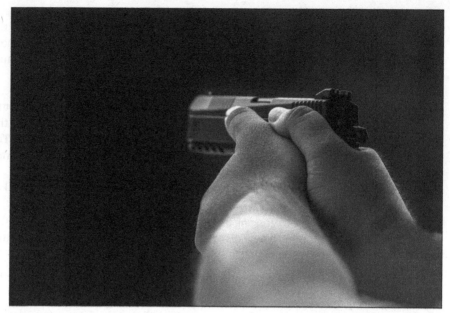

Courtesy of Supermop/Shutterstock

FIGURE 13-2:
Your thumbs
should point
forward without
touching
the slide.

» For revolvers, you grasp the gun's grip the same way, but your thumbs should cross over each other, forming an "X" well behind the hammer.

If you grip a revolver with both thumbs forward, as you would with a semi-auto pistol, your thumbs will be too close to the rear of the cylinder, where they'll be exposed to the blast that comes with firing a shot. This can cause another painful cut, so be careful.

» Regardless of your handgun's style, in terms of positioning, you should be able to reach and use the controls, including the trigger, magazine or cylinder release, or any manual safeties, without having to shift the gun in your hands. However, when it's time to reload or rack the slide, for example, it is your support hand that comes off the grip for those manipulations. Your strong hand should remain locked on the grip as long as you're handling the gun.

» After both of your hands are properly positioned, clamp down on the grip as hard as you can to limit the gun's recoil, which will be significant, especially with larger calibers, so you must be prepared. But you also shouldn't grip the gun so hard that it starts to wobble in your hands or causes your fingertips to throb.

Finding the right balance takes practice. Just remember that with a semi-auto pistol, a weak grip will cause the gun to malfunction after you fire the first shot. Maintain a firm grip as long as you're holding the gun for optimum reliability and control.

Holding onto a rifle or shotgun

Rifles and shotguns are a little different from handguns because they require three points of contact — both of your hands as well as your shoulder:

>> Your strong hand will grasp the gun's grip just as it would with a pistol or revolver, but your support hand needs to cradle the rifle or shotgun's forend for stability. Positioning your support hand as far forward as you can reach, and that the forend provides room for, while still maintaining a comfortable grip will help you manage the gun's recoil.

>> Secure the *buttstock,* or rear of the gun, in your shoulder pocket — the fleshy area just between your shoulder and the far edge of your pectoral muscle — on your right side if you're right-handed or your left side if you're left-handed.

   In this position, the butt of the gun shouldn't touch your collarbone, or any bones for that matter, to prevent injury.

>> As with handguns, if you need to reload or run the bolt, for example, it is your support hand that comes off the forend to do those tasks. Your strong hand should keep the buttstock of the gun snug against your shoulder and the barrel pointed downrange.

>> To aim, tilt your head to rest your cheek against the *comb,* or upper edge, of the stock. You should be able to comfortably look down the sights, or through a scope, without having to lift your head off of the gun.

   Adjustable stocks are very popular these days because they allow you to raise or lower the comb, or adjust the *length of pull* — the distance from the trigger to the end of the buttstock — for a better fit.

Figure 13-3 shows the proper way to hold a shotgun.

Getting into position

If you traveled back in time hundreds of years and happened to stumble upon a shooting match — what luck! — you'd see every competitor turn sideways, extend their blackpowder pistol toward the target with one hand, and tuck their other arm behind their back before pulling the trigger.

Although you can choose to shoot this way at the range nowadays, I want you to actually hit the target. So you'll need a more modern shooting stance.

Courtesy of CrispyPork/Shutterstock

FIGURE 13-3:
This shooter is
holding his
shotgun properly.

Shooting while standing

You essentially have two major stances to choose from if you're shooting a hand-gun from a standing position. I'll take you through them from the ground up, assuming you're already (safely) holding your gun.

>> **The modified Weaver stance** involves planting your feet shoulder-width apart with your knees bent and your support-side leg slightly forward. If you're right-handed, that means your left foot will be a few inches ahead of your right one. This will angle or "blade" your torso toward the target.

This is how you'd stand if you were about to throw a punch.

Lean forward. Then, maintaining a solid grip on your handgun, extend your strong arm straight out toward the target. Your arm, wrist, and gun should all form a straight line. Think of your strong arm as driving the gun toward the target.

Now, add your support hand to the gun's grip and pull the gun back toward your chest, against the tension of your strong arm. I know this will feel really awkward at first, but with practice, this push/pull tension (shown in Figure 13-4) can lock the gun in place to counter the recoil and muzzle rise of shooting.

>> **The isosceles stance** starts similarly. Plant your feet shoulder-width apart. Your feet can be even, but like me, you might feel more comfortable with your support-side foot slightly forward. Again, bend your knees and lean forward.

FIGURE 13-4:
This shooter's left
arm drives the
gun toward the
target while her
right arm pulls
back on it.

Courtesy of guruXOX/Shutterstock

The big difference between this and the modified Weaver stance is that both of your arms push the gun forward equally, with the gun centered straight in front of you. Roll your shoulders forward and bend your elbows just enough so that they aren't completely locked.

If you were to look straight down at yourself in this position, you'd see that your arms create an isosceles triangle with the gun as the top "point," as shown in Figure 13-5.

Which stance works best? If only it were so easy. Gun enthusiasts have been arguing about shooting stances for decades.

Because I value your time, I'll just say that both stances have their pros and cons. The modified Weaver stance can help you control your gun's recoil better — after you master the push/pull grip — and the footing feels more stable. However, with this stance, it's harder to move and rotate to hit targets that are to your left or right downrange.

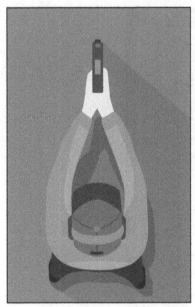

Courtesy of BNP Design Studio/Shutterstock

Conversely, the isosceles stance feels a bit more natural when it comes to gripping and pointing your gun, and you can move and rotate more easily to hit different targets, which is why competitors (like the one shown in Figure 13-6) overwhelmingly choose this stance. However, your footing doesn't provide as much front-to-back stability.

I personally learned to shoot with the modified Weaver and eventually grew into a version of the isosceles stance in which my feet are slightly offset. It just feels better for me now. And that's the key: Find the stance that works for you and feels the most comfortable, and you'll see your accuracy improve.

What about rifles and shotguns? Shooting a long gun from an unsupported, standing position should only be reserved for short-range shots because the weight of the gun makes it difficult to hold the gun on target for any real length of time.

However, if it's the only option available to you, spread your feet shoulder-width apart and angle your support side toward the target so that your nondominant foot is farther forward.

Your support hand grips the gun's forend with that elbow pointing downward. Your strong hand holds onto the grip, and that elbow points outward — but not too dramatically, or you'll be "chicken winging," as it's known — and keep the buttstock snug against your shoulder.

FIGURE 13-6:
This competitor is shooting on the move using an isosceles stance. Also note his thumbs-forward grip.

TIP

A two-point sling can help you stabilize a rifle for standing or kneeling shots. If you're right-handed, hold the gun out in front of you so that the sling hangs below the rifle. Slip your left arm between the rifle and sling, and then bend your elbow so that the sling catches behind the back of your left upper arm and loops around your forearm. (If you're left-handed, do the same thing with your right arm.) Now shoulder the rifle again, and the sling's tension should make it easier to hold the gun on target.

Turn to Chapter 10 to learn more about slings and other helpful accessories like shooting sticks and bipods.

Shooting while kneeling

Taking a knee — or two — can give you a bit more stability, and thus aid your accuracy, but you have to be certain that your muzzle is pointed safely downrange and your finger is nowhere near the trigger as you get into position. If you're already standing:

>> Dropping onto one knee is the fastest and easiest option. Simply step forward with your support-side leg as if you're lunging and lower yourself down onto the knee of your strong leg. Both knees should really create 90-degree angles at this point, but if you have trouble aiming over your gun, lean back and lower yourself onto your strong leg.

The best part of shooting a handgun or rifle from one knee is that you can rest the elbow of your support arm on your support-side knee for even greater stability. Again, you might have to drop back onto your strong knee, as shown in Figure 13-7.

To stand up from a single knee, reverse the process. Keep your gun pointing forward as you rise up and step backward with your support-side leg.

>> Though doing so is really only practical with a handgun, you can also drop down onto both knees. If you're limber enough, lower yourself down onto both knees from a standing position. You can also take one knee and then shift your other knee out from under you.

The benefit of a double-kneeling position is that you can tilt left or right if needed, which might be helpful around corners or barricades.

To stand again, either rise up off of both knees simultaneously or shift back into a single kneeling position before going upright.

FIGURE 13-7:
Note how this Olympic shooter has her support arm braced on her knee.

Shooting while prone

It's hard to keep a gun completely still while you hold it on target because of things like your pulse, your breathing, and muscle tension. Welcome to being alive! For the utmost stability with a rifle, however, you have to take as much of yourself out of the equation as possible. That means lying flat on the ground behind the rifle.

Getting into this position takes time, however, and you need to set the rifle on the ground *before* you lie down. Don't try to get down onto the ground with the rifle in hand. And you'll need a bipod or shooting bag to support the front end of the rile. (For more on those accessories, check out Chapter 10.)

When you're on the ground, lie as flat as possible and position the gun so that it's parallel with your spine, though it'll be lined up with your left or right shoulder depending on your handedness.

Now snug the rifle against your shoulder so that you can comfortably look through your rifle's scope without having to strain your neck. This technique is called attaining a *natural point of aim*. Spread your elbows out wide and plant them firmly into the ground.

REMEMBER

Your scope is designed to help you aim at and hit a target. Never use it to scan terrain in search of a target, because you'll be breaking the second rule of gun safety and letting your muzzle sweep things you don't intend to shoot. That's why you should keep a pair of binoculars handy.

TIP

As I mention in Chapter 10, if your rifle is stabilized with a bipod or shooting bag, your support arm doesn't need to hold onto the forend. Instead, use your support hand to push the stock back into your shoulder pocket. So if you're right-handed, keep your right hand on the grip as usual, and then curl your left hand back under the rifle and apply pressure to the bottom front edge of the buttstock. There might even be a hook or groove there for that purpose.

REMEMBER

Spread your legs out wide and flatten your feet, as shown in Figure 13-8. It'll feel awkward at first, but this position will remove any accuracy-robbing tension from your leg muscles.

Finally, to get out of the prone position safely, make sure to stand up first and *then* pick up your rifle. Don't try to stand up while holding onto the gun.

Sighting in

Aiming is a critical aspect of accurate shooting, but before I can dive into everything that entails, you need to know which of your eyes is dominant. Yes, your brain subconsciously favors one eye over the other.

Courtesy of Guy J. Sagi/Shutterstock

FIGURE 13-8:
For the best results while shooting from prone, flatten your feet.

If you don't know, I have two methods to help you figure out which eye is the dominant one:

>> Make a thumbs up and extend that arm out in front of you. Then pick out a distant object and cover it with your thumb.

Close your left eye. If your thumb is still covering the object, your right eye is the dominant one. If not, you are officially left-eye dominant.

>> For the second method, extend your arms straight out in front of you so your palms face forward. Now put your hands together to create a little opening between your thumbs and index fingers.

Pick out a distant object and, keeping both eyes open, center it within the opening in your hands.

Now close your left eye. If the object is still centered, your right eye is the dominant one. If the object isn't framed by your hands, your left eye is officially dominant.

TIP

Are you left-handed and right-eye dominant, or vice versa? This is called *cross-eye dominance*, which requires a little extra help. But don't worry, I've got you covered later in this chapter.

After you know which eye is dominant, you can learn to aim using *iron sights*. These are the front and rear sights built into the tops of every handgun as well as many shotguns and rifles. (Some shotguns have only front sights, and rifles might not even come with sights because the manufacturer expects you to add a scope or reflex sight, as I discuss in Chapter 10.)

Put very simply, you have to align three points using your eye: the gun's rear sight, the front sight, and whichever part of the target you want to hit. (I suggest the center, or bullseye, to start!) This alignment is known as your *sight picture*.

>> The first step is to examine your target and surroundings. Remember the fourth rule of gun safety: Be sure of your target and what is behind it. Can you see what's behind the target? Is it safe to shoot?

>> Next, bring the gun up to your eye level, which should be easy if you've practiced your grip and stance. Don't lower your head or body to find the gun's sights.

>> With the firearm out in front of you, find the rear sight with your eyes. Specifically, look for the aiming notch, or channel, cut into the top-center portion of the sight. It might be U- or V-shaped, or squared off. The designs vary between models.

>> Close your nondominant eye.

>> Align the sights so that the front blade is centered within the rear sight's notch, with equal amounts of space, or light, on both sides of the front sight. Aligning the sights ensures that your gun has the correct horizontal orientation, or *windage*.

You also want the top edge of the front sight to line up with the top edge of the rear sight, as shown in Figure 13-9. (If your sights have aiming dots, ignore them for now.) Doing so ensures that your gun has the correct vertical orientation, or *elevation*.

>> Here's the most important part: Focus on the front sight. You might try focusing on the target, but doing so makes it harder for you to notice if the gun is wobbling, tilted, or off target. Focusing on the middle point, the front sight, makes it easier to balance all three points.

The trick is to hold the sights in perfect alignment with the target as you pull the trigger. But you should practice aiming and establishing a good sight picture with an unloaded weapon, without pulling the trigger, again and again until it becomes second nature.

Then try aligning the sights with both eyes open. Again, doing so will be awkward at first, and you might experience some double vision, but your dominant eye is still in control. In return, you'll be a bit more relaxed — great for accuracy — and have a better field of view so that you can see what's going on downrange. Anything that increases your situational awareness is a good thing.

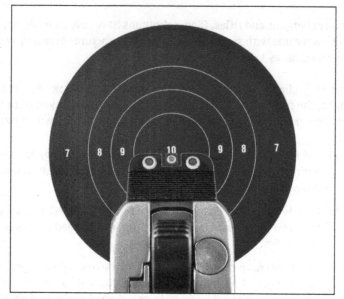

FIGURE 13-9:
Line up the top
edges of the front
and rear sights,
and focus on the
front sight.

Courtesy of kochmun/Shutterstock

**TECHNICAL
STUFF**

Although the lines and dots on some iron sights are primarily designed to help you "pick up" the sights quickly in an emergency, some companies also use them — not the tops of the sights — for alignment. This is why it's important to read your gun's user manual, or contact the company if you aren't sure.

If you're using a shotgun with only a front sight to hit paper targets at the range, the top of the receiver will serve as your rear sight. However, if you're using such a shotgun for sporting purposes, like bird hunting or clay shooting, the front sight is there only to let you know where the barrel is pointing in your peripheral vision because you'll be shooting ahead of your target.

**TECHNICAL
STUFF**

What if you have a reflex sight or scope? As I lay out in Chapter 10, these devices drastically simplify the aiming process because you no longer have to align two points with the target. Instead, after your reflex sight or scope is properly *zeroed* — meaning it's calibrated so that the *reticle*, or aiming point, matches where the bullet will hit at a specific distance — you just have to place the reticle on the target and pull the trigger.

If the target is closer or farther away, your zero point is off, and thus you either need to adjust your scope to reposition the reticle, or you can aim higher or lower, for example. This is why today's reticles are much more complicated than the crosshairs shown in action movies. Many look like elaborate Christmas trees with every line on the Y-axis telling you where to aim for various distances, and lines on the X-axis help you compensate for wind.

Breathing for better accuracy

Speaking of action movies, you might be tempted to hold your breath while you're shooting in the hopes of helping your concentration or reducing your body's movement while aiming. Others will say that you should pull the trigger in the "respiratory pause" between exhaling and inhaling.

I say this: Keep breathing. You need that oxygen to survive. I want you to be comfortable (count how many times I've used that word in this chapter!), and instead of trying to time your shots for a specific window, think about how your body moves when you breathe in and out. Your chest and shoulders rise when you breathe in; they drop when you breathe out. Obviously, this movement can impact your sight alignment, especially if you're breathing hard.

I find the most success when I simply slow my breathing down and breathe using my stomach more than my chest. Also, I only take my shots when my sights are properly aligned. Find what works for you. Let that oxygen flow.

Controlling the trigger

You have a tight grip on your gun. Your stance is textbook perfect. Your sights are on target, your breathing calm. The only thing left (when it's safe to do so) is to place your finger on the trigger and pull it, which is easier said than done.

First off, you aren't really *pulling* the trigger. You're *squeezing* it to the rear against spring tension, and after it travels a certain distance, the trigger will trip the sear inside the gun, causing a round to fire. The trigger then has to move forward again, or reset, before you can start all over again.

In simple terms, good trigger control means squeezing the trigger without disrupting your sight picture.

Mastering this process begins with proper finger placement. (Again, please practice this with an unloaded gun and the barrel pointed in a safe direction.) You want the first pad of your index finger to contact the trigger, though some people find they have more leverage if they use the first joint instead.

Either way, squeeze the trigger straight back as slowly as you can at first so that the *click* (or *bang* when you're ready to practice with live rounds) almost surprises you. Don't jerk the trigger, yank it back, or anything like that. Slow, deliberate movement straight back.

HOW ACCURACY RELATES TO SAFETY

I know that firing guns at the range can be a fun, exhilarating experience. But when I see shooters popping off as many shots as they can and spraying a target — choosing speed over accuracy — I get a little worried. Then, if I see that they also can't hit the broad side of a barn when they slow down, I ask if they want some help because, to me, an inaccurate shooter is a dangerous shooter, and I want to correct those bad habits.

Every bullet that you fire has a destination, a Point B. That shot will end up somewhere, and it's your job to know where it'll go way before you even consider squeezing the trigger. Otherwise, you're putting others at risk.

So if you don't have the skills to make an accurate shot, or you know that a target is simply too far away for you, for example, don't fire. Work on your mechanics, seek training, practice regularly, and above all, know your limits. And when you go to the range, go with some intentionality. Know that every shot is a chance for you to perfect your shooting skills.

The first two segments of your index finger should be the only parts of your hand moving, and any deviation here can throw your shots, as I discuss in the pages ahead. Then, after you fire, slowly let the trigger return forward to reset. Don't just disengage from the trigger.

Practicing Your Shooting Skills Safely

I know that trying to juggle every single mechanic of accurate shooting all at one time can be a bit daunting. But you don't have to be a perfect shot the first time you hit the range or even the 1,000th time, and you can work on each facet of your skills with every trigger squeeze.

To help you along the way, I have some tips and drills for you.

Maximizing your range time

Before you load any ammo into your firearm at the range, you should practice your grip, stance, sight alignment, and breathing. You can even perfect your trigger control with an unloaded gun.

TIP

I also recommend using paper targets with easy-to-see scoring rings that allow you to earn points with every shot. Then you can keep score as you go along and track your progress.

The dime drill

After you ensure that there aren't any rounds in your weapon, take a penny or dime and balance it on top of your gun's front sight, or just behind it on the barrel or slide. If you're at the range with a buddy, they can help you place the object on your gun while you hold the weapon steady.

Establish a firm grip on the gun, point it toward the target, and squeeze the trigger slowly. Do your best to "break the shot," so to speak — listen for that *click* — without letting the coin fall off the gun.

If it falls, that's okay. Practice makes perfect. Just make sure to keep your gun's muzzle pointed in a safe direction as your friend picks up the coin, or set the gun down entirely.

Practice this "dime drill," as it's known, dozens of times until you master your trigger control without tilting the gun or losing your sight picture.

The 5-5-5 drill

When you're ready for live ammo on the range, position a paper target 5 yards out from the firing line. Now load your weapon while you keep the gun pointed in a safe direction and your finger off the trigger. (If you need help loading and reloading your firearm, turn to Chapter 14.)

When it's safe and you're clear to fire, pick a point on the target (maybe the center to start?), get into position, grasp the gun firmly, align your sights on that point of the target, and when you're ready, squeeze off the first shot. Don't be afraid of the recoil. Maintain your grip and contact with the trigger. Ease the trigger forward so that it resets.

Reestablish your sight picture (that is, get back on target) and fire another round when you're ready.

When you've fired five shots at 5 yards, retract your target if you're at an indoor range, or if you're at an outdoor range, go examine your target downrange — *after* the range safety officer has given you the green light, of course. Don't ever walk downrange until it is safe to do so and you're told it's okay.

Look over the five bullet holes in your target. Are they near where you aimed? Spread out? If the holes are far apart, you have to diagnose the problem, as I discuss in a moment. If the holes are all within an inch or two of each other, you can move your target back to 7 yards, 10 yards, or another distance, or add a time constraint. Try shooting five shots into a tight group at 5 yards in five seconds. This is known as the "5-5-5" drill.

The dummy-round drill

This drill requires that you purchase "snap caps" or dummy rounds — inert plastic cartridge replicas — of the correct caliber for your firearm. You also need a friend at the range to load your gun's magazine with a mix of real ammunition and dummy rounds.

With your ammunition mixed, you won't know what's coming next when you try to fire at a paper target: a real round with all the ensuing smoke and recoil, or a lifeless dummy round. And if you're flinching before shots, or jerking the trigger, it'll become painfully obvious when you try to fire the latter.

After you encounter the dummy round, you need to remove it from your gun's chamber. Be careful as you remove the magazine, and then lock the slide or bolt back.

Diagnosing your results

You can't really assess your shooting skills if you don't look over your targets between strings of fire. In fact, evaluating your shots is why you should always learn to shoot with paper targets versus, say, steel targets at an outdoor range. Steel targets make it difficult to see your impacts unless you just painted the steel.

TIP

Before you look over your targets, ensure that your gun is completely empty, and lock the bolt or slide back. Also engage the safety if your gun has one.

Don't be ashamed when you look over the bullet holes on your target. Think of this as a learning moment.

If your shots are trending a certain direction around the point you intended to hit on the target — in other words, if your *points of impact* don't match your *point of aim* — look over Figure 13-10, which details some of the most common shooting maladies for right-handed shooters. (Sorry, lefties, you'll have to reverse everything in Figure 13-10.)

FIGURE 13-10: This chart shows common accuracy mistakes for right-handed shooters.

Breaking wrist upward or misaligned sights

Anticipating recoil (pushing)

Anticipating recoil (heeling)

Poor trigger finger positioning

On target

Too much thumb pressure

Jerking the trigger

Breaking wrist downward or drooping your head

Tightening grip while pulling the trigger

» If your shots are high, you probably aren't aligning your sights properly, or you aren't locking your wrists as you fire.

» If your shots are going high left or right, you're probably anticipating the recoil and flinching, which is causing you to tilt the gun before you fire.

» Shots to the left mean that your index finger isn't contacting the trigger properly, and shots to the right mean that you're applying too much thumb pressure to the side of the gun.

» A lot of new shooters hit low, which could be because you aren't locking your wrists, you're dropping your head, you're tightening your grip as you pull the trigger (in anticipation of recoil), or you're jerking the trigger — yanking it back too quickly at the last second.

Admittedly, the chart shown in Figure 13-10 can be a bit too prescriptive. Maybe you aren't taking your time between shots, or your stance is hurting your ability to hold your sights on target as you squeeze the trigger.

At the end of the day, practice will get you far, but you can't beat a good trainer's one-on-one instruction when it comes to increasing your accuracy.

Overcoming Cross-Eye Dominance

If you happen to be one of those unlucky individuals who is right-handed but left-eye dominant, or vice versa, as I mention earlier in this chapter, a few tricks can help you zero in on your target without getting double vision.

» If you're shooting a handgun, the first and easiest method is simply to raise and orient the firearm so that your dominant eye is forced to take precedence over your nondominant eye. In other words, if you're right-handed but left-eye dominant, instead of bringing your gun up to eye level centered in front of your body, shift it to the left slightly so that your left eye can take over.

» You can also turn your head slightly to achieve the same effect, bringing your dominant eye forward so that it can align the sights and focus on the firearm's front sight.

» If you're shooting a rifle or shotgun — or a handgun from a modified Weaver stance — you can tilt your head sideways so that your dominant eye is on top and better aligned with your sights. This technique might not work with your gun's stock, however, and you don't want to strain your neck.

» Another option is to place a piece of tape on your shooting glasses to block your dominant eye. I know this is awkward as all get-out, but the tape will force your brain to use your nondominant eye.

» Instead of switching eyes or shifting their positions, some gun owners learn to handle and shoot weapons from their nondominant sides. As you can imagine, this ability takes a good deal of practice.

» Finally, reflex sights drastically simplify the aiming process — especially for those with cross-eye dominance — because you only have to superimpose the reticle over the target and squeeze the trigger instead of having to align two independent iron sights.

RANGE TIPS FOR PEOPLE WITH DISABILITIES

Shooting a firearm can be physically challenging, but living with certain disabilities doesn't necessarily mean that you can't hit the range and have some fun like everyone else.

The most important step is finding a gun that fits you and your needs. I would never recommend a gun that is too powerful for someone to manage, or too heavy, or has a slide that is too difficult to operate. So, if you're sensitive to recoil or live in chronic pain, for example, stick with smaller calibers. (Which reminds me: Don't operate guns under the influence of heavy medications.)

You might also be able to add accessories to the weapon to make your life easier, such as a bipod to support the front end of a rifle, a reflex sight for easier aiming, or a hook that can help you rack the slide. A magazine loader is a godsend, too, as I mention in Chapters 10 and 12.

If you have trouble with mobility, consider finding a shooting range that has *benchrests* — wooden or concrete seats for shooting positions — or other supportive fixtures, and you might be able to shoot from a wheelchair as well.

Just remember: Shooting doesn't have to be a solo adventure, so bring friends and get to know your range safety officer.

Chapter **14**

Reloading and Clearing Malfunctions

When I'm on the firing line at my local range with someone brand new to guns, I do most of the work. They'll do the shooting; I'm on the hook for loading the gun, charging it, reloading it, and dealing with malfunctions between safety reminders and pointers to improve their accuracy.

In short, I take care of most of the gun handling, like a trainer, butler, and handyman rolled into one, until I can teach the novice those other operations.

You aren't quite so lucky, but I can give you a strong start. In this chapter, I offer tips and techniques to help you safely reload, unload, and clear malfunctions that might arise with semi-automatic pistols — the most popular guns today. You can apply a lot of this knowledge to other weapons as well, especially those that accept detachable magazines, but pistols are the focus here because no one wants this book to be a thousand pages long. I also assume that you're on a range with spare magazines at the ready.

WARNING

Nothing in this book is a substitute for quality training. Only a certified firearms trainer can teach you the material discussed in the pages ahead in a safe, controlled environment. Do not practice, or even attempt, any of these maneuvers with a loaded gun unless you are on a supervised shooting range.

Dissecting the Anatomy of a Detachable Magazine

Say you've read your gun's user manual — and Chapter 3! — and can discern every major component of your firearm. You know that the *magazine* is what holds the ammunition, the *magazine well* is the opening where the magazine is inserted (that is, the bottom of the grip on most semi-auto pistols), and the *magazine release* is a button or lever that, when depressed, releases the magazine from the gun. Make sense?

Your gun's user manual should also detail one method for reloading it as well. I have a few more options for you in the pages ahead, but before I get to that, it might help for you to understand the basic components of detachable magazines. As you'll see, these are rather simple designs, and yet they play a major role in keeping your firearm cycling reliably. Here's the lowdown on detachable magazines:

>> **Magazine body:** The body is the exterior of the magazine. This aluminum, steel, or polymer outer shell protects the loaded cartridges and holds them all in a vertical "stack" within.

>> **Baseplate:** This is the bottom piece. Most magazines these days have removable baseplates so that you can take the magazines apart and clean them inside and out, but there are exceptions, including models designed for states that restrict your magazine capacity to 10 rounds.

>> **Magazine spring:** The baseplate holds this spring, which pushes the follower — and thus the cartridges — upward, toward the firearm's chamber.

Over time, the magazine spring can lose tension and eventually wear out, so it won't push rounds into the chamber as well as it used to. That said, this loss of tension isn't really a problem unless you plan on firing tens of thousands of rounds at the range.

>> **Follower:** Shown in Figure 14-1, this is the moving component inside the magazine that the ammunition rests upon. It literally *follows* the ammo toward the chamber.

Most magazines today have polymer "anti-tilt" followers that keep cartridges level for proper feeding into your firearm's chamber, and they're usually produced in bright colors so that you can see when the magazine is empty through your gun's ejection port.

>> **Feed lips:** Feed lips help guide the ammunition into the firearm, ensuring that only one round enters the chamber at a time. Feed lips are common wear points — along with the magazine spring and follower — after enough time or rough handling.

>> **Witness holes:** Many magazines also have little cutouts called *witness holes* running down one side that can help you see how many cartridges are loaded within. Some magazine manufacturers also use translucent plastic bodies to accomplish the same thing.

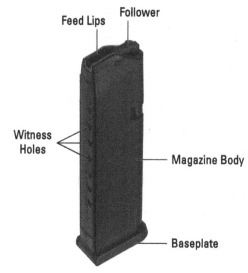

Feed Lips · Follower · Witness Holes · Magazine Body · Baseplate

Courtesy of SolidMaks/Getty Images

FIGURE 14-1:
When a magazine is empty, the follower is visible at the top.

Reloading a Pistol Three Different Ways

Over the years, firearms experts and instructors have developed a few tried-and-true methods for reloading firearms. Some work better than others depending on the situation at hand. I have three to share for you here, but before I get to that, I want to establish some ground rules to follow regardless of technique.

REMEMBER

For example, whenever it's time to top off your weapon — even if you're at the range or out hunting — you need to be aware of where you're pointing your gun and keep your fingers away from the trigger the entire time. Once again, the four safety rules *always* apply. I can't say that enough. (Turn to Chapter 1 if you need a refresher on those.)

Following the safety rules is important because many firearms today can still fire even if their magazines have been removed. Some guns have wonderful features called *magazine disconnects* that prevent them from being fired if a magazine isn't fully installed. So if someone tries to snatch a police officer's gun, for example, the officer can simply jettison the magazine to render the gun inoperable. But no mechanical safety is a substitute for safe gun handling.

You'll naturally want to look down at your weapon when you first learn to reload it with a fresh magazine. But as you get better at reloading over time, get in the habit of keeping your eyes downrange, looking at what's in front of you, while you manipulate your gun just below eye level. This way, you can reload while still maintaining situational awareness.

The empty reload

This reloading technique is also known as an *emergency* or *slide-lock reload* because you initiate it when your firearm is completely empty. With a properly functioning semi-auto pistol, the slide should lock back after you fire the last round. Occasionally, however, the slide returns forward on its own.

TECHNICAL STUFF

The slide is considered "in battery" when it's in the forward position, and "out of battery" when it's locked rearward. The same goes for bolts in rifles and shotguns. Forget what slides and bolts are? Turn back to Chapter 3.

To reload your gun when it's completely empty:

1. **Take your finger off the trigger and keep it outside of the triggerguard.**

2. **Bring the gun back toward your chest and angle it slightly in your dominant, or strong, hand so that the magazine well is easier to access.**

   Keep it just below eye level.

3. **Hit your gun's magazine release button.**

   If you're right-handed, you'll use your right thumb for this. Or, if you're left-handed and the pistol doesn't come with an ambidextrous or reversible magazine release, you'll use your left index or middle finger.

4. **Let the empty magazine fall out of the gun.**

   If it's stuck, you might need to tug on the magazine's baseplate to free it.

5. **Grab a fresh magazine with your nondominant, or support, hand, placing your index finger along the front side of the magazine as you do so.**

   Retrieving a magazine like this (as shown in Figure 14-2) is called "indexing the magazine," and it'll help you line everything up.

6. **Insert the fresh magazine.**

   To make your life easier, make sure that the back of the magazine contacts the rear of the magazine well before you slide the magazine upward into the gun. As you do so, pivot your support hand so that index finger is no longer in the way and your palm can help drive the magazine home.

   That said, don't slam the magazine in too hard. A hard impact can make the slide return forward on its own without putting a round in the chamber.

7. **Rack the slide (or hit the slide release if it's large enough and easy enough to activate).**

   This will chamber a fresh round so that you can fire again if needed — after you assess the situation, get back on target, and so on. See the sidebar "The best way to rack your pistol's slide" for more details.

FIGURE 14-2: Note how this shooter has "indexed" his next magazine in his left hand.

Courtesy of sirtravelalot/Shutterstock

THE BEST WAY TO RACK YOUR PISTOL'S SLIDE

Racking the slide means pulling it back and releasing it so that it can travel forward. The best technique in this regard is the *overhand method,* which begins with holding the gun's grip tightly in your strong hand and ensuring that the gun is pointed safely down-range and your fingers are nowhere near the trigger. Now curl your support hand over the top-rear portion of the slide, as though you're grabbing a handlebar, with four fingers on one side and your palm on the other. Your thumb should be closest to you, and the slide will have grooves or serrations on both sides for traction. Just make sure that your fingers and palm aren't near the ejection port or the frame.

Now pinch the slide with your support hand and pull it toward you a few inches as your strong hand holds the gun in place, as shown in the following figure. Pulling the slide toward you might be difficult because you're fighting stiff spring tension.

Courtesy of Reed Means/Shutterstock

Next, let the slide go. Don't "ride the slide," as they say, or try to push the slide forward. Simply release it and let the recoil spring do what it's supposed to do. As the slide goes forward, it'll strip a fresh round off the top of the new magazine and chamber it.

Another technique, the *slingshot method,* entails using your thumb and forefinger to pinch the slide and retract it, much like you're pulling back on a slingshot's rubber band (see the following figure). The downside with this option is that it doesn't provide much torque and requires more forearm strength.

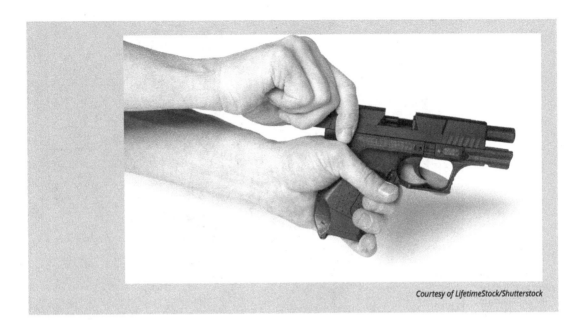

The speed reload

If you know that your gun is running low on ammo but isn't completely empty —
perhaps you've been counting your shots or have a good guess — you can initiate
a speed reload. This technique is very similar to the previous one because you're
going to drop your current magazine and replace it with a fresh one. But you
don't have to rack the slide because a round is already in the chamber, making it
absolutely critical that you follow Step 1 in the following steps:

1. Take your finger off the trigger and keep it out of the triggerguard.

2. Bring the gun back toward you and angle it slightly.

3. Hit the magazine release button.

4. Let the empty magazine fall out of the gun.

5. Retrieve a fresh magazine with your support hand.

6. Insert the magazine into your gun, as shown in Figure 14-3.

That's it. Your gun now has more ammo on tap. Of course, you've also sacrificed
whatever rounds were left in that last magazine, so this technique is really best
relegated to range practice and shooting matches.

FIGURE 14-3: Use your nondominant palm to drive the fresh magazine into the pistol.

The retention reload

The defining characteristic of this technique — also known as a *tactical reload* — is that you hold onto the last magazine after you remove it from your gun. But it's also the most advanced of the three methods because it requires that you clutch two magazines with one hand.

It also takes time, so you should never try it in an emergency. Follow these steps to use the retention reload technique:

1. **Take your finger off the trigger and keep it out of the triggerguard.**

2. **Bring the gun back toward you and angle it slightly so that you can access the magazine well.**

3. **Retrieve a fresh magazine with your support hand.**

   The trick here is to place it between your index and middle fingers. I know it's awkward as all get-out, but it'll become second nature with practice.

4. **Bring your support hand up to the gun and place your thumb on the side of the grip.**

5. **Hit the magazine release and pull the old magazine downward, out of the gun, using your thumb and forefinger.**

   Now you should have two magazines in your support hand.

6. **Line the new magazine up with your gun's magazine well and insert it into the pistol with your support hand.**

7. **Place the old magazine in a pocket. That way, you'll still have it if you need more ammunition later.**

WARNING

Do not place the old magazine in a magazine carrier on your gun belt. You don't want to confuse it with a fully loaded magazine.

Now you can reacquire a solid two-handed hold on your pistol, get back on target if you need to, and so on.

Safely Unloading a Gun

To be a safe, responsible gun owner, you need to know how to safely unload a firearm. Maybe you're done shooting at the range, or someone (who obviously hasn't read this book) hands you a gun that is still loaded. What do you do?

Again, every gun is different, but these steps can help you unload pistols, rifles, and shotguns that accept detachable magazines:

1. **Keep your finger off the trigger and make sure the barrel is pointing in a safe direction.**

   Here a safe direction might mean downrange or toward the ground.

2. **If the firearm has a manual safety that still allows you to unload the gun or manipulate the slide/bolt with the safety in the "on" position, go ahead and engage the safety now.**

3. **Hit the magazine release and remove the magazine.**

4. **Open the action by locking back the slide on a pistol or the bolt on a rifle or shotgun.**

   Do not let the slide or bolt return forward.

5. **Check to make sure there isn't any ammunition in the chamber or magazine well. Now check again.**

6. **If the gun has a manual safety that could not be used earlier, engage it now.**

WARNING

The order of operations here is crucial. Skipping a step or doing something out of order can lead to disaster. For example, if you rack your pistol's slide instead of locking it completely to the rear *and then* remove the magazine, you've just chambered a round — a round that can injure or kill someone who mistakenly believes that the chamber is empty. So be careful.

Troubleshooting Common Pistol Malfunctions

Regardless of how much money you spent on your handgun, it'll eventually malfunction at some point. You can't escape it. Stuff happens. Your gun might jam because it has gotten too dirty, or the magazine spring has given out, or the cartridge in the chamber is a dud.

WARNING

The first step in dealing with a malfunction is to stop what you're doing, take a breath, and figure out what's wrong. You need to slow down and be extra careful in these situations. Continuing on and attempting to fire again could be extremely dangerous. And, once again, keep your gun pointed downrange and take your finger off the trigger.

I cover some of the most common failures in the pages ahead, but a reputable firearms trainer can also take you through these steps in a safe, controlled environment using plastic dummy rounds, for example, before you progress to live ammunition. Range safety officers will also be happy to help in these situations as well, so don't feel like you're alone.

Clearing a failure to eject

A *failure to eject* is the easiest malfunction to spot. It occurs when a spent casing doesn't fully clear the pistol's ejection port as the slide returns forward after firing. It might happen if your gun's extractor is having issues or you aren't holding the gun firmly enough while shooting.

This situation is commonly called a *stovepipe* because the casing sort of resembles one, as you can see in Figure 14-4. You can't fire the next round if the slide is unable to return all the way forward.

You have two options for clearing this type of malfunction. The first is to simply swipe your hand along the top of the slide to knock the casing out of the ejection port.

If that approach doesn't work, your second option is an immediate-action drill, otherwise known as the "tap, rack, reassess" method:

1. *Tap* **the base of the magazine with your palm to make sure that it's properly seated in the magazine well.**

   You might also want to roll the gun to the right because the ejection port is the largest on the right side, and gravity can help the case fall out.

2. *Rack* **the slide firmly with the overhand method I describe earlier in this chapter in the sidebar "The best way to rack your pistol's slide."**

   This action will hopefully force the spent casing out of the gun and chamber a fresh round.

3. *Reassess* **the situation, reacquire your target, and prepare to resume shooting if it is safe to do so.**

FIGURE 14-4: A "stovepipe" malfunction occurs when a spent casing gets caught in the slide.

WARNING

You might hear this drill called the "tap, rack, bang," but that nickname is problematic because it implies that you're supposed to pull the trigger again as soon as you've racked the slide and removed the stuck casing. Some shooters even train themselves to always fire as soon as the casing is removed. But doing so simply isn't safe. You need to reexamine your circumstances to see whether you should fire again. This is the kind of decision-making that should come before every single trigger pull.

Fixing a failure to feed

In this scenario, the next round fails to feed into the chamber correctly from the magazine, preventing the slide from returning forward.

This malfunction typically occurs if the magazine isn't seated properly, but if it keeps happening, it's time to check your ammunition and the magazine itself because the spring, follower, or feed lips could be worn out.

The easiest fix is once again the "tap, rack, reassess" drill, but if that doesn't work, remove the magazine completely, rack the slide a few times, and consider switching to a different magazine or ammunition.

Dealing with double feeds

Ah, yes, the dreaded *double feed*. As you might have guessed, this malfunction occurs when two rounds try to feed into the chamber at the same time, creating a logjam inside your pistol. This might be another magazine-related issue, too.

The fix here can be time consuming, but don't skip a step or get the order wrong:

1. **Keep your barrel pointed safely downrange and take your finger off the trigger.**

2. **Lock the slide back.**

3. **Hit the magazine release.**

   The magazine might not drop out of the magazine well on its own, so be prepared to wriggle its baseplate as you pull downward.

4. **Shake the gun a little if the rounds that caused the double feed haven't fallen out by now, as they should have.**

5. **Check the chamber to make sure that it's empty.**

6. **Reinsert the magazine (or install a new one).**

7. **Rack the slide.**

Now your gun should be operational again.

Diagnosing ammo-related problems

The previous malfunctions are relatively easy to notice because your pistol's slide won't go back into battery, or return fully forward. However, if faulty ammunition is to blame — and no ammo type functions perfectly 100 percent of the time — you might not see anything wrong with the gun, which makes these situations that much more dangerous.

TIP

Need a refresher on ammunition and its various components? Turn back to Chapter 9.

There are three basic ammo-related malfunctions, or *failures to fire*:

>> **Misfire:** A misfire is one result if you pull the trigger but get a *click* instead of a *bang*. There could be an issue with the cartridge's primer or powder, so rack the slide and discard that specific round. Don't try to shoot it again.

>> **Hangfire:** A hangfire will also give you a *click* instead of a *bang* when you pull the trigger. But this time, there's a delay between your gun's hammer hitting the cartridge in the chamber and the propellant inside the case igniting and launching the bullet. You can see why this is dangerous.

Admittedly, hangfires are rare, but there is only one method for dealing with a hangfire safely: Keep the gun pointed downrange and take your finger off the trigger. Now wait an entire minute to see whether the round fires.

If nothing happens after a full 60 seconds, rack the slide and dispose of the faulty round.

>> **Squib load:** A squib load is a cartridge that doesn't have enough powder to fully propel the bullet toward the target, so it gets stuck in the barrel.

This situation is extremely dangerous because if you don't notice the softer *poof* sound that comes with a squib load instead of the usual *bang,* and you pull the trigger again, the second bullet will impact the stuck one, which could cause your barrel to explode and lead to serious injuries.

If you notice the sound difference, lock your pistol's slide back and remove the magazine. Now try to look down the barrel from the rear (good lighting will help) to see if a bullet is obstructing the barrel. You might need to field strip the gun, as I discuss in Chapter 8, after letting it cool down as well.

WARNING

Do not ever try to examine the barrel from the muzzle end.

If a bullet or fragment is stuck in the barrel, you'll have to dislodge it. The best tool for that will be a brass bore rod — the same kind you use to clean the barrel. If that doesn't work, it's time to call a gunsmith.

4

Think Carefully before You Shoot

Prepare for your first hunting trip with information about federal and state regulations, how to hunt ethically, proven techniques, and the equipment you'll need for success.

Get the most from shooting competitions in your area.

Protect your home from the outside and inside without a firearm, and find out more about the Castle Doctrine.

Create a plan to keep your family safe in case of an emergency.

Chapter **15**

Hunting and Sport Shooting

What's your game? Ask a hunter or competitive shooter and that question can mean two drastically different things.

Humans have been hunting animals, or *game,* for meat, trophies, and recreation since, well, the very beginning. Shooting matches, on the other hand, are a bit newer in the grand scheme of things, but these games can be a ton of fun while helping you practice your shooting skills.

You know what both of these pursuits (hunting pun!) have in common, aside from guns? Both are popular because you get to spend time with your friends and family taking part in a shared experience, away from the daily grind, with a common goal. They're also great ways to hone your decision-making skills. You have to identify your targets carefully and find the perfect moment to shoot. Just as importantly, you'll learn when *not* to shoot as well.

In this chapter, I get you a few steps closer to hunting and competing in a shooting match. It's okay if hunting isn't your bag, either. I get it. It involves killing animals, after all. There's no way to sugar coat that. But when it's done the right way, hunting can actually help control animal populations and raise funds that go back to conversation efforts. That said, if you still have reservations, skip to the second half of this chapter on competition.

Preparing to Hunt with a Firearm

If you're interested in hunting, the first thing you should do is find out if any of your friends or family members hunt and would like to take you along on one of their excursions. If you're lucky, they might be able to help you out with the gear, permitting process, and a few more barriers to entry.

You can also hire an outfitter — a professional hunter — to take you into the backwoods for essentially a guided hunt, or you can plan a solo excursion.

Regardless of whether you tag along with others or go it alone, the next step is looking up the wildlife agency in whatever state you plan to hunt in.

Getting to know your state's wildlife agency

Every state has a different wildlife agency that governs hunting and land conservation. In Texas, that's the Parks and Wildlife Department. In Georgia, you're looking at the Department of Natural Resources. Florida has the Fish and Wildlife Conservation Commission. You get the idea.

The websites for each of these agencies will point you in the right direction for your first hunt. They offer lots of helpful information, such as:

>> **The start and end dates for hunting seasons,** which might change depending on the type of game you're after; your choice of weapon, be it a conventional firearm, muzzleloader, bow and arrow, crossbow, or high-power air rifle (yep, that's a thing!); and the land you'll be hunting on.

For example, the public wildlife management area (WMA) near where I live allows deer hunting with archery equipment from September 11 through October 15, and firearms can be used from October 16 through November 1.

Outside those dates, deer hunting is illegal. The idea is to protect the deer population — and other species with hunting seasons — while they grow the rest of the year.

>> **Rules and regulations** defining where you can and can't legally hunt; how many animals you can hunt; age requirements; and how much blaze orange you have to wear so that other hunters can spot you in dense brush, to name just a few examples.

Your state's wildlife agency will also tell you which firearms and ammunition types are acceptable for hunting, whether there are any magazine limits, and much, much more.

It's important to learn the rules and regulations like the back of your hand, so bookmark the rules page of the wildlife agency's website and check back for updates every year. You can't claim ignorance if you break the rules, which can lead to fines, misdemeanors, and other penalties.

>> **Maps of public hunting land,** including state and federal locations, and pertinent information for navigating these areas. The wildlife agency should list any closures and location-specific alerts as well.

>> **Permit or license requirements.** In most states, you'll need a general hunting license as well as additional licenses, permits, stamps, or "tags," for specific game. You might also need to buy a permit to gain access to public land.

I know the fees sound excessive, but the proceeds go back to land and wildlife conservation efforts.

>> **A recordkeeping portal or printout** so that you can log important information about the game that you successfully hunted. For example, you might have to tell the wildlife agency a deer's weight, sex, and number of antler points as well as your personal information. This data helps land managers, conservation officers, and biologists keep tabs on the population figures for various species in different parts of your state.

>> **Access to hunter education courses,** which brings me to . . .

Attending a hunter education course

You need to take a hunter education or safety course to obtain your hunting license. Think of it like driver's ed. Depending on your state's regulations, these classes are available either online or in person, cost anywhere from $20 to $40, and can last a few days. (If you've read other parts of this book, you already know I'm going to recommend in-person courses!)

Your state's wildlife agency should make it easy for you to find an online or in-person hunter education course, and the International Hunter Education Association (IHEA) also has a "find a course" feature on its website. Visit www. ihea-usa.org to learn more.

These courses cover several topics, including:

>> How to hunt responsibly and ethically, which I discuss shortly

>> Land and wildlife conservation

>> State hunting rules and regulations

- >> Firearms and archery safety

- >> Shooting fundamentals

- >> Helpful information about various game

As you can see, these courses cover a ton of material — enough to fill another *For Dummies* book! (Eh, editors?) But the most important aspect is keeping you and your hunting buddies safe. Indeed, you're all carrying guns, and you might have to crawl or climb into positions with a little finesse to make sure that your barrel doesn't sweep yourself or anyone else, for example.

The instructors will remind you about the four rules of gun safety that I cover in Chapter 1, and they might even ask you to demonstrate proper gun handling at a live-fire range.

REMEMBER

As always, you must keep your firearm pointed in a safe direction. Because others might walk in front of you when you're searching for prey, you should point your gun's barrel down toward the ground or straight up toward the sky until you find your target animal. You also shouldn't disengage your firearm's safety or place your index finger on the trigger until you're on target *and* have established what's beyond it. You don't want to shoot another hunter or an off-limits animal.

Finally, when your instructor begins teaching you about all the different animals you can hunt in your state, pay attention. Not only will these miniature biology lessons help you understand your prey better, and give you a leg up when it comes to tracking them in the field, but you also might gain a greater respect for the animals, which is part of being an ethical hunter.

Becoming an ethical hunter

There's a right way and a wrong way to hunt. Your state wildlife agency — not to mention all the hunters who have come before you — would prefer that you abide by a certain code of conduct so that the hunters who come *after* you can continue to enjoy the pursuit in the Great Outdoors. If, for example, you leave trash all over the land you're hunting on, its owner or manager might close it off to future hunters. But there's more to it.

Although I could offer you a long list of dos and don'ts, I think it all comes down to respect. As a good, ethical hunter, you should:

- >> **Respect your quarry.** To start, this means subscribing to the concept of *fair chase,* which means that you hunt in such a way that gives the animal a chance of escaping. So you won't pursue the game with an ATV or use high-tech gear that can help you pinpoint its exact location from miles away. Got it?

REMEMBER

You must also kill the animal as quickly and painlessly as possible. If you're using a firearm or bow, your goal is to only have to shoot once. And if you do end up needing to shoot again or deliver a *coup de grace,* make it quick.

So you have to be accurate with your weapon, know the limits of your shooting skills and your ammunition, and understand exactly where your bullet needs to land on the animal.

In other words, if you're using a .308 Winchester rifle and spot a deer 400 yards away, you need to get a lot closer before you take your shot. Not only will wind and gravity make it much harder to be accurate from that far away, but a .308 Winchester bullet will slow down to the point where it will only wound the animal and provide a slow, painful death.

These are topics a hunter education course can teach you, but it also requires a good deal of practice at the shooting range beforehand. And get as close to the animal as you can without spooking it!

TIP

Respecting the prey also means making the most of its body. So get it out of the woods and to a processor as quickly as you can to salvage as much of the meat as possible. Eat whatever you can (not in one sitting — get a freezer!) and donate the rest to friends, family members, or a local food bank. That way, you're helping your community.

>> **Respect the land.** Just like hikers and campers, you pack out what you pack in. In other words, take your trash with you, and try not to disturb the terrain. Leave the land as it was before you showed up.

In this way, you're ensuring that the habitat can continue to support other animals, and if you're on private land, you're showing the owner or manager that you respect their time and efforts — and that they can continue allowing hunters to grace their property.

REMEMBER

Before you hunt on private land, make sure that you get the owner or manager's permission in writing. Not only is this a good practice, but most state wildlife agencies require it.

>> **Respect the rules and regulations.** Again, you're not really hunting for yourself. You're taking part in a grand tradition and representing out-doorspeople everywhere, which means that you must abide by every law along the way.

As an ethical hunter, if you have two deer tags, you'll harvest only two deer. Exceeding the limit is illegal. Hunting protected animals is illegal. Hunting before or after the official hunting season? Illegal.

- >> **Respect yourself.** Take your safety seriously; pack enough food, clothing, and equipment — including a few first-aid essentials — so that you're comfortable outdoors for long periods of time; and please, please don't touch a firearm after drinking or using a controlled substance.

- >> **Respect other hunters.** If someone else finds your favorite hunting spot or locates an animal before you do, let them have it. Be courteous. Another animal will come along.

  Remember, hunters have guns, and the last thing anybody wants is for a fight to break out among armed individuals.

- >> **Respect nonhunters.** As this list should make clear, I don't want you to set a bad example for anyone, but especially those who aren't familiar with hunting or who might be intimidated by firearms.

  Do your best to keep your gun secure and out of sight until you're actually out in the field, and if your hunt is successful, try to transport the animal's carcass to a local processor discreetly. Doing so shows respect to your prey as well.

Breaking down various types of hunting

According to the 2016 National Survey of Fishing, Hunting, and Wildlife-Associated Recreation, the most popular game species in the U.S. are deer, turkeys, and squirrels.

Thanks to conservation efforts, however, North America has a lot more game to choose from, which I'll sort into categories for you.

- >> **Big game:** Deer, elk, moose, bears, boars, and bison
- >> **Predators:** Coyotes, wolves, and mountain lions
- >> **Furbearers:** Foxes, bobcats, and beavers
- >> **Small game:** Squirrels, rabbits, skunks, and raccoons
- >> **Upland game:** Quails, pheasants, and grouse
- >> **Waterfowl:** Ducks and geese

Of course, these animals live in different places, and hunting them requires different equipment and techniques, too.

Regarding that last part: There are dozens of hunting techniques or methods that you might combine in pursuit of game. For a successful deer hunt, for example, you'll probably want to *scout*, or gather intel about the deer in your area, ahead of time. Scouting usually involves hanging trail cameras along popular deer paths and reviewing the footage that's been captured.

After you know some locations where deer like to frequent, you have a few options. When the hunting season starts, you can grab your gear, don some warm camouflage clothes as well as a blaze-orange vest and cap, and hit the woods, where you might:

>> Position yourself inside a *blind* — essentially a tent to hide in (as shown in Figure 15-1) — and wait for deer to pass by your location.

>> Climb into a *tree stand,* a platform some distance up a tree (*not* the device you use to prop up a Christmas tree in your living room), and once again wait for deer to pass underneath you.

WARNING

Getting into and out of a tree stand can be dangerous, especially with a firearm. The first step is to unload the gun completely and tie a rope or cord around the stock. Slip the free end of the line into your belt and climb into the tree stand. It's also a good idea to secure yourself to the tree with a safety belt or harness so you don't fall and suffer a serious injury. Then, when you're in position, hoist the gun up to you, as shown in Figure 15-2.

>> *Still hunt,* or move slowly and quietly into the woods on foot, pausing every few moments to listen and look for deer.

FIGURE 15-1:
Can you spot the hunting blind in this photo?

Courtesy of ThunderValleyHC/Getty Images

>> *Stalk* your prey, which is very similar to still hunting, except you're actively following deer signs — tracks in snow, scrapes on the ground, or trees where a buck has rubbed his antlers — until you get close enough to take a shot.

Courtesy of Design Pics Inc/Iamy Images

FIGURE 15-2:
After you're safely secured in the tree stand, hoist your gun up to your position.

Each of these methods has its strengths and weaknesses. Blinds and tree stands make for good concealment, but you also have to be ready to sit in place for hours on end — a tough task for the restless. With still hunting and stalking, you're at least moving, albeit slowly, and you're taking part in some of the oldest hunting techniques. You just have to make sure not to make much noise or end up downwind of the deer.

Of course, other methods exist. Some hunters use baits, decoys, or calls to attract their prey; some prefer to drive their prey toward other hunters, or have dogs chase the animals out of cover. Your state decides which methods are considered legal and acceptable for each species.

WARNING

No matter the technique, you must fully identify your prey — and what's behind it — before you take aim or consider shooting. What sounded like an animal might actually be another hunter.

Gathering helpful hunting gear

Hunting can be a little difficult to get into because of all the required gear. Ask any serious hunter and they'll tell you how much money they've poured into the sport. It's not for the faint of heart. However, those same hunters will probably tell you how worthwhile it's all been, too.

You don't have to go big at first, however. Along with a reliable firearm powerful enough to kill your game in one shot — but not so powerful to ruin any chances of harvesting meat — you should start with the following:

>> **Layers of clothing:** You're at the mercy of the elements while you're hunting, so you need to dress appropriately. In cold weather, you need a good thermal base layer, a mid-layer that includes pants and a sweater, and warm, water-proof outer garments. Some of the higher-end clothing companies combine these layers into slimmer attire and include a camouflage pattern to help you blend into the environment.

You'll also need a blaze-orange vest, hat, or both so that other hunters can identify you; thick socks; hand warmers in truly cold conditions; and gloves that don't inhibit your ability to handle or use a firearm.

>> **The best boots you can afford:** Honestly, these will make or break your hunt. You need high-quality boots that are comfortable, sturdy, and water-proof. The boots should have some flex, or give, while providing good traction and ankle support.

If they're new, I recommend breaking the boots in for at least a month before your big hunt. Wear them around the house, run errands in them, test them outside, and maybe even jog in them. If you try to hunt in brand-spanking-new boots, you're in for a world of pain.

>> **A sturdy backpack:** The first consideration is finding a pack that's the right size for your journey. If you're only hunting for a day, your backpack needs to hold just one or two extra layers of clothing, water, food and snacks, ammo, a knife, and whatever else you might need to find your prey and get back to your vehicle in one piece.

If you're camping and hunting for days on end, you'll need a larger pack that can support more gear — and you might want to consider one that'll help you carry an animal's carcass after a successful hunt. Many hunting packs also have holders or straps for bows and long guns as well.

Look for a backpack that's the right length for your torso, and that has an adjustable belt and shoulder straps. You'll want to keep them snug when everything's loaded onto your back.

>> **Binoculars:** You need these to help you spot game from a distance. Ensure that they have a comfortable neck strap or can be easily stowed.

You might be tempted to search for prey with the magnified scope on your rifle, but this technique is dangerous because it breaks the second rule of gun safety — pointing your gun at things you don't intend to shoot. You might also get lost in the scope's limited field of view. Binoculars are better for scanning large tracts of land.

>> **A rangefinder:** After you spot a deer or whatever else you're after, this little device will show you how far away it is — usually to within a few yards — and take the guesswork out of the equation.

You want to be certain about the distance to the animal. As I mention earlier in the chapter, ethical hunting involves respecting your prey and trying to kill it with one shot, which in turn requires gauging the distance accurately. Most of the time, the rangefinder reading will tell you to get closer to the animal, but it might also indicate that you need to aim a little higher to account for the bullet's drop as gravity pulls it downward.

>> **Game calls:** You use these devices to attract the animals you're after. You might feel like an idiot — and your partner might call you one — while you practice your duck, elk, or coyote calls around the house before your big hunt, but these noisemakers will give you an advantage in the field.

>> **Scent-control spray.** Not that you smell (you might; how would I know?), but I've heard that whitetail deer can smell human scents better than blood-hounds. If you're hunting game that have powerful olfactory senses, you should consider a scent-blocking or -reducing spray that you can apply to your boots and outerwear. Then, even if you end up downwind of the prey, there's still a chance you won't alert them.

The trick is to pair the spray with good habits back home, too. Don't put on any cologne or body spray before you go hunting, or use heavily scented soap. (Who are you trying to impress?) I wouldn't even wear clothes that have been washed in scented detergent for fear of giving away my position if the wind isn't in my favor.

Again, this list of gear is just a starting point. If you're hunting with a friend or an outfitter, they'll probably have a few more recommendations for you depending on the game, the terrain, and other variables. Good luck!

Going for Gold at Shooting Matches

If I had to guess, I'd say the world's first shooting match probably occurred just a few minutes after the first firearm was invented. Humans are competitive by nature, and who doesn't want to best their friends at the range by being faster or more accurate with a rifle, shotgun, or handgun?

Competition can be a useful tool for building your skills with firearms, and competence breeds confidence. Getting into the shooting sports, as they're known, requires a little preparation, but I'll lay the foundation for you.

Learning popular shooting disciplines

Since that first shooting match, whenever it was, dozens of different competition styles have sprung up around the globe and even joined the ranks of the Olympics. There are way too many shooting disciplines to name here, but I can group the most popular disciplines into some basic categories:

>> **Precision matches** are what most people think of when they hear "shooting competition." These are traditional events in which competitors get into a position, whether it's standing on the firing line, lying prone on the ground, or sitting at a benchrest (essentially a shooting table), and shoot for the centers, or *bullseyes*, of targets set at various distances with rifles or handguns. They might have to do it on the clock, too.

There are even "Bullseye" matches in which you fire three different types of handguns at 25 and 50 yards at various paces, earning a maximum of 10 points for every shot that lands in the center ring of the target. The more points you get, the better.

Other types of matches might have you shooting rifles at targets hundreds of yards away.

TECHNICAL STUFF

Although these are known as *precision* matches, they're really all about *accuracy*. If you don't know the difference between those terms, turn to Chapter 18.

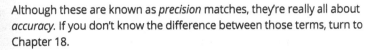

A few different organizations host accuracy-focused matches with different rules, distances, and weapons, but the most popular might be the Civilian Marksmanship Program (CMP), which promotes firearm safety and marksmanship with a special focus on youth participation. To learn more and find a match near you, visit www.thecmp.org.

>> **Action shooting matches** force competitors to move and shoot at multiple targets while being timed. These competitions can be very challenging because they test your accuracy and speed.

Every action shooting match has multiple *stages*, or courses of fire, where you have to run around obstacles and shoot targets in order as you encounter them while avoiding "no shoot" targets placed near those you're authorized to hit. In this way, you're honing your accuracy and decision-making skills.

Your speed factors into your total score, as do hits. If you miss a target or hit a "no shoot" target, points are deducted from your score.

To really test your skills, look for a "multi-gun" match that involves courses of fire for handguns, shotguns, and rifles. Of course, these matches also require the most gear, as I discuss in a moment.

WARNING

Moving with a firearm can be dangerous. You'll see competitors stepping quickly but deliberately as they get into position and shoot before moving on to the next target. The best thing you can do is learn from their movements and practice the same routes without a gun.

If you trip with your firearm in hand, try to keep your fingers out of the triggerguard, and if you drop the gun, let it go. Don't fumble for it or you might accidentally hit the trigger.

>> **Cowboy action shooting (CAS) matches** — which I briefly mention in Chapter 3 — are, in a word, hilarious. Each competitor dresses up like a cowboy or cowgirl from the late 1800s, assumes a faux gunslinger's alias, and shoots paper or steel targets with reproduction firearms modeled after those used in the Old West. That description really doesn't do these matches justice, but you get the idea.

WARNING

If you attend a CAS match, have fun with the cosplay, but the firearms are very real, so the safety rules still apply, okay?

You might also want to check out a Cowboy Mounted Shooting Association (CMSA) match in which skilled athletes — there's no other way to describe them! — race through courses of fire on horseback. To keep everyone safe, the targets are balloons on stands, and the contestants fire specially prepared blanks instead of live ammunition.

>> **Clay shooting** involves using a shotgun to disintegrate little orange discs, or *clay pigeons,* as they fly through the air. The sport is really meant to help you practice your bird-hunting skills.

This category has three major disciplines:

- **Trap shooting** involves hitting clay pigeons launched into the air in front of you from a single "house," or machine, as shown in Figure 15-3. You rotate among five different positions, or stations.

FIGURE 15-3: This trap shooter successfully hit a clay pigeon with his over/under shotgun.

Courtesy of visualspace/Getty Images

- **Skeet shooting** involves two houses 40 meters apart launching clays that crisscross in front of you. You shoot from positions marked on a large semicircle on the ground, and the houses can launch either single clays or two in sequence.

- **Sporting clays** is probably the closest to actual hunting because you walk along a path and shoot at various clays launched from machines along the way. You can see why competitors call this "golf for shotguns."

Most shotguns are acceptable for these three disciplines, but over/under models are the most popular among competitors. To learn more about these double-barreled shotguns and other firearms, turn to Chapter 3.

>> **The Olympics** are the final category in my book because, to me, they represent the pinnacle of shooting skills.

Every four years, the world's top shooters compete in over a dozen shooting events at the Summer Olympics with pistols, traditional rifles, air rifles, and shotguns. The pistol and rifle events are essentially precision matches with wild-looking firearms built specifically for Olympic-level accuracy, and the shotgun events are trap and skeet matches.

Also, I can't forget the Winter Olympics, which hosts the biathlon. Here, athletes have to race against the clock as they cross-country ski to a firing line, and then stand still or lie down to fire .22-caliber rifles at targets. I know it sounds crazy, and it combines two drastically different sports that don't pair well — the skiing is aerobic and makes you breathe hard, which can hurt your shooting accuracy — but the biathlon traces its roots back to Scandinavian hunters who mastered skiing while searching for game. The more you know!

Collecting helpful competition gear

As with hunting, I think one of the greatest barriers to entry for competitive shooting is just how much *stuff* you have to bring along. Each discipline requires a good deal of equipment, but once again, I'm here to help you get started on the right foot.

In Chapter 10, I detail some of the best accessories you should consider for range outings, including a range bag, eye protection, electronic hearing protection, spare magazines, magazine loaders, an armorer's kit in case your gun needs to be repaired onsite, and a cleaning kit.

I'd also wear a hat, weather-appropriate clothing that wicks away sweat and won't snag your firearm or equipment, rugged shoes, and a towel for wiping off your hands.

You need a gun that fits within the match parameters, so it has to be the right type, size, and caliber, and if you're competing in a "stock" event, it can't have any aftermarket parts or modifications. This restriction is a way to level the playing field and ensure that everyone is testing their skills and *not* their guns. That said, plenty of disciplines allow "race guns" with all the bells and whistles to give competitors the edge in terms of speed and accuracy.

TIP

My advice is to make friends with a competitor who can show you the ropes or check out the host organization's website to learn the match rules beforehand.

Ammunition is the next big requirement, and you'll need a lot of it. The match rules might specify certain loads, but I also recommend asking other competitors what rounds they prefer, and buy some in bulk if you can. You'll want to practice with the same ammo when you're not competing.

The rest of the gear depends on the discipline at hand. For precision rifle matches, start with these items:

>> A bipod to support the front end of your rifle

>> Shooting bags to support the front or rear of the rifle

>> A shooting mat to lie down on

>> A high-power scope that you know how to use and adjust

>> A ballistic app on your smartphone that can help you make all the calculations required to hit steel targets hundreds of yards away

>> A rangefinder if you'll be shooting targets at unknown distances

For action shooting matches, I suggest these items:

>> A sturdy gun belt

>> A Kydex pistol holster designed for competition

>> A sling if you'll be using a rifle or shotgun

>> Pouches to hold spare magazines on your belt

>> A timer to practice with

>> Chalk to keep your hands dry between stages

>> A caddy to hold all your gear if you're competing in a multi-gun event

With that last item in the list, please don't show up to the range with a bright-red Radio Flyer or the wagon you use to cart your stuff from the car to the beach.

For Cowboy Action Shooting matches, consider bringing these things:

>> Clothes and a big ol' hat to make you look and feel like someone living on the frontier in the 1800s

>> CHAPS!

>> A replica or reproduction firearm based on one from the Old West and ammunition that fits within the match parameters

>> A period-correct leather holster and gun belt

>> A good sense of humor

Finally, for clay shooting, I recommend these items:

>> A quality double-barreled shotgun

>> A belt-mounted pouch with compartments to hold fresh shotgun shells as well as empty hulls. You'll see some shooters wearing full vests or aprons with pockets for the same purposes.

As you go along, you'll learn what you need to add to your range bag, and if you ever find yourself missing a critical tool, just ask another competitor. There's a good chance they'll lend you an extra shell pouch or gun belt — all while offering valuable tips.

Attending your first match

Wouldn't it be great if I could tell you some amazing tricks to help you win your first ever shooting match? I'd love that, too.

Sadly, the only real way to win is to learn the proper mechanics of the shooting discipline you're interested in and practice them over and over again. The best competitors have mastered their techniques so well that they don't have to think about them. They can tell you that they missed a shot — and *why* they missed — before they ever check their targets downrange.

TIP

Competing for the first time can be intimidating. Instead, you'll probably get more from your first shooting match if you simply *watch* what everyone else is doing and take mental notes. Pay attention to how people position themselves on the firing line and hold their weapons. Note their hands, elbows, shoulders, knees, and feet.

For action shooting matches, keep an eye on the competitors and watch as they move and transition from one target to the next. In that discipline, one common mistake is thinking about the *next* target too much and missing the one right in front of you. Each shooter must slow down, even for a split second, to solve the problem at hand.

Even if you're shy, try to strike up conversations with the other participants. Learn from them. And when you actually compete in the next match, ask a seasoned competitor if they'll watch you tackle a course of fire and offer notes afterward. I can't think of a better way to grow as a shooter in this arena.

Chapter **16**

Firearms and Self-Defense

A 2017 Pew Research poll showed that 67 percent of current gun owners claimed "protection" as the biggest reason for owning a firearm. That's millions of people across the U.S., and you might be one of them.

The most important thing you can learn in this regard is that you should only ever use a gun to defend yourself or your loved ones as a *last resort.* You should never go looking for a fight or escalate a heated situation. Instead, you must find ways to prevent an altercation or remove yourself and your family from any dangerous circumstances that arise.

This "last resort" concept is such a critical idea that I want to print it on billboards all across the country. I don't have that kind of money, though, so I repeat the message throughout this book, and many times in this chapter alone. I really want you to *get it* and live by it.

Although this chapter is dedicated to the heavy topic of self-defense with a firearm — and all the legal and moral aspects surrounding it — I also detail indoor and outdoor security measures that you can implement to make your home safer. This chapter also helps you create an emergency plan that you can share with every member of your family to keep everyone safe and limit your chances of needing to use a gun in the first place.

Before You Reach for a Gun . . .

Benjamin Franklin coined the phrase "an ounce of prevention is worth a pound of cure" to encourage Philadelphians to stay vigilant about house fires, but I think it can apply to burglaries and home invasions, too.

The idea is simple: Implement enough security measures ahead of time and you might just avoid a break-in or limit the collateral damage — and hopefully reduce your chances of needing to use a gun to protect your family.

Of course, everyone's living situation is different. If you live in a gated community, your security needs will look different from someone who lives in an apartment building, for example. So take the time-proven tips in the pages ahead and see if they can work for you. I want you to be prepared without being paranoid.

Protecting your home from the outside

To start "hardening your home," or making it less vulnerable to a burglar or intruder, you need to think about all those things *outside* your home that can serve as security measures:

>> **Learn more about the police in your area.** This information gathering includes Googling where all the police departments and precincts are in your part of the city or county, for example, and learning how many officers are on staff.

Perhaps the most important piece of information to learn is your local law enforcement agency's average response time, or how long it takes for a police officer to arrive at the scene after you dial 911. A number of factors affect this response time, like the type of emergency, how many cops are on duty at the time, and their proximity, but active home invasions and burglaries are considered high priority.

If you live in a major city with a large police force, the response times are generally lower — less than 10 minutes — than you'd experience in rural areas where fewer officers have to cover a lot more territory. In those locales, an officer might not arrive on the scene for an hour.

I give you this information not to scare you but to help you plan accordingly. Think of your home security measures as ways to buy yourself some time.

Your local law enforcement agency might offer this information publicly, or at least provide it to media outlets. As an example, New York City publishes its average response times for emergency services every week, as it has done since 2013. Your city might not provide such granular data, but try to get a better picture.

>> **Upgrade your doors, locks, and windows.** Take a good look at every possible entry point into your home. Could someone kick in your front door, or break a window to reach a lock? Are there any exposed hinges or easy-to-pry surfaces?

Be honest, and if you have doubts, go ahead and invest in a sturdier door with steel hardware, for example, or deadbolts instead of simple door chains that are easy to bypass. You might also want to consider security windows with thicker glass and reinforced frames.

REMEMBER

Make it a habit to lock your doors and windows! According to the FBI, of the 1.1 million burglaries reported in 2019, 55.7 percent involved burglars who successfully forced their way into homes while 6.5 percent were failed attempts. However, burglars were able to gain entry through *unlocked* doors or windows in 37.8 percent of those cases.

Which reminds me: Consider locking the interior door to your garage on a regular basis as well as the garage door itself if you're leaving your home for a few days. These are both vulnerable points of entry.

>> **Invest in an alarm system, cameras, and motion-sensor lighting.** No security setup is 100-percent foolproof, but a monitored alarm system will give you — and the police — a heads up if someone breaks into your home. I also recommend putting up signs and decals alerting others to your home's alarm system.

At the same time, those increasingly popular doorbell cameras (as shown in Figure 16-1) can notify you if someone steps up to your door in the dead of night while recording invaluable evidence.

I also recommend outdoor lights that turn on when they sense motion so that a burglar can't operate under the cover of darkness.

>> **Put up fences.** I know you love thy neighbor and all that, but the idea is to create more barriers for people with bad intentions. No, I don't think you need some 12-foot-tall fence covered in razor wire that blocks all visibility, but I would recommend something that is a little harder to climb or cut through than, say, a two-foot-tall chain-link fence.

>> **Consider your property's landscaping.** If your home has a yard, you'll want to get rid of any flora that could provide a hiding spot for an intruder. So those tall hedges and evergreens near your windows probably need to go. Otherwise, if a burglar can get behind them, they'll have all the time in the world to break in without a neighbor seeing.

You also don't want any trees or trellises that could provide easy access to a balcony or second-story window.

TIP

However, the right greenery can create an effective natural barrier. I'm talking cacti, holly bushes, and thorny plants that'll ward off those looking for easy access points.

FIGURE 16-1:
Doorbell cameras
are great
preventative
measures
because of their
recording
capabilities.

Courtesy of BrandonKleinPhoto/Shutterstock

Protecting your home from the inside

Outdoor security measures are only half the battle. There are more steps you can take inside your home to prevent a burglary in the first place, or slow one down if it does occur, giving you and your family more time to get to a safe place while you wait for the police to arrive. With enough preparation, you won't have to reenact any scenes from *Home Alone*, either.

>> **Be careful on social media.** You might be uber-friendly and tell everyone everything on Facebook — what you ate today, how you're feeling, where you're going. But if you advertise that you're leaving your home for several days, someone might take advantage and use that as an opportunity to break in.

No, I'm not asking you to all of a sudden become an antisocial recluse, but discretion can be a lifesaver. And, honestly, many of us could do with a little less social media in our lives (I say as I check Twitter one more time).

I also don't believe responsible gun owners should broadcast any information about their firearms on social media. Guns are serious; they aren't "cool" or symbols of power. You don't want to intimidate others or advertise that you have something worth stealing to potential burglars.

>> **Install timers for your indoor lights** or set up a "smart home" system allowing you to turn lights on when you aren't home. Either way, it'll be harder for a would-be intruder to figure out that you're gone for the night, thus making your home less of a target.

This is why some people leave TVs on or music playing when they leave for hours on end.

>> **How about a dog?** I've met several self-defense instructors who insist that dogs are better defenses against intruders than guns, and I couldn't agree more. Dogs are lovable, loyal, and tenacious when they need to be. They're also fantastic preventative measures, even if you don't hang up those "beware of dog" signs.

You also don't need to spend thousands of dollars adopting a big, burly German shepherd to protect your family, like the dog shown in Figure 16-2. If your four-legged family member is more of a fluffball, you'll at least have an early warning (or barking) system to alert you if someone comes too close to your home.

(If you work for the U.S. Postal Service, I'm truly sorry.)

>> **Create a safe room.** Designate a room or closet with limited access — so upstairs or in the back of your house with only one door — as a safe space for you and your family to hide in while the police make their way to your home.

You should be able to lock the door and barricade it with a large piece of furniture or a steel bar, and you might also want to keep a phone in the safe room so that you can gather your partner and kids and head to the room without having to first search for your cell phone. This is part of creating a home-defense plan, as I discuss in the pages ahead.

>> **Install a safe in your (aptly named) safe room.** Not only will a sturdy, steel safe protect jewelry and other valuable items like passports and deeds from burglars, but it'll also help you secure your firearm when you aren't using it and keep it out of the hands of unauthorized users — a foundation of responsible gun ownership.

REMEMBER

To learn more about gun safes and how to choose the right one for your needs, make sure to read Chapter 6.

FIGURE 16-2:
A dog's keen
hearing and
protective
instincts can save
your life.

Courtesy of Aneta Jungerova/Shutterstock

Understanding the Castle Doctrine

What if an attacker gets past all of the defenses I discuss in the previous section and threatens your life, or a family member's life, in your home? Are you justified in using your gun?

WARNING

To form the best answer to this question, the first thing you should do is read up on your state's laws regarding self-defense. I'm not a lawyer, and nothing in this chapter should be taken as legal advice. If you have questions or concerns about self-defense and other aspects of owning a firearm, I recommend that you talk to a lawyer in your area.

REMEMBER

I also want to remind you of the fact that guns do not offer second chances. As a responsible gun owner, you should never seek trouble or look for a reason to use your gun. It is only ever a *last resort* if your life is threatened.

Got it? Now, to understand the modern laws surrounding self-defense in the United States, you have to look at English common law from hundreds of years ago, which dictated that if someone tried to attack you, you first had a *duty to retreat* — or try to escape if you can — before you could defend yourself with deadly force, or act in such a way that could seriously injure or kill the other party.

The only exception arrived in the 1600s, when an English court held that people didn't have to retreat inside their homes because "a man's home is his castle." (Look up "Seymane's Case" if you're a history buff.) This exception became known as the *castle doctrine*.

Interpreting the castle doctrine today

Generally speaking, in modern usage, the castle doctrine says that if a violent stranger breaks into your home and threatens to kill or gravely injure you or your family members, you may be justified in using deadly force (such as a firearm) to stop the threat.

A jury will also look at the totality of the circumstances and try to assess whether you acted reasonably — in other words, if you acted as any other reasonable, hypothetical person would have acted in the same situation.

Of course, the specifics of these laws are different in every state, which is why it's so important for you to learn your state's laws regarding self-defense in the home. Some state laws apply only to the home whereas others include your front and back yard, for example, or your vehicle.

California's castle doctrine statute (Penal Code 198.5) holds that you can only use deadly force if an intruder unlawfully and forcibly enters your home and threatens you, your family, or a member of the household with "death or great bodily injury." Notice how this law only applies to intruders, and not guests you've welcomed inside? It also does *not* apply if someone trespasses onto your property outside your home. See the distinction?

Other states, like Florida and Texas, expand the territory for which you can use deadly force. But there are restrictions.

Knowing the limits of the law

WARNING

The castle doctrine isn't absolute, and you should never consider it a free pass to use deadly force in your home, or, depending on your state's laws, your vehicle, workplace, or another location.

Police will investigate the incident, and you might have to prove that you acted reasonably given the circumstances.

I also want to provide you with some examples of when the castle doctrine does *not* apply:

>> If you let someone into your home and then attack them, you're the aggressor, not a defender. You could be charged with assault or murder.

>> If the evidence shows that a person could in no way have threatened your life in your home and you killed them anyway, you'll be charged with murder.

>> And if the attacker realizes their mistake and tries to flee, and you shoot them in the back in your front yard, you've crossed into assault/murder territory.

I'm sorry for being a bit gruesome there. But as I'm trying to make abundantly clear, you should only ever consider using deadly force in very specific instances, and even if you think you're within your rights to use your gun, a prosecutor might see things differently.

I know you're a responsible gun owner. You can spot the difference between some kid trying to steal your TV — which doesn't warrant a deadly response, no matter how much you love that TV — and another person who's bent on hurting you and your family. As a responsible gun owner, you also wouldn't dare answer the door while you're armed, for example, or take your firearm out of the safe if you've had a few drinks.

REMEMBER

Ultimately, you are responsible for responding properly — *reasonably* — to the circumstances as they present themselves. A good firearms trainer can teach you more about self-defense and when your gun is warranted. For tips on finding the right course for you, read Chapter 12.

WARNING

Finally, I must warn you that when police arrive, they might mistake you as the bad guy if you're armed. Think about it from their perspective. They don't know what they're walking into, and they'll want to protect themselves. So if you need to use your gun for any reason, get away from it by the time the police show up.

Creating an Emergency Plan

I'm going to assume that you've run through a fire drill at some point in your life, maybe when you were in school, or if you've ever worked in a large building. Turns out, these aren't just excuses to enjoy the fresh air outside or see whether teachers can remember every student in their classes.

No, these drills provide a way for everyone to learn what to do in such an emergency situation. So if a fire does break out, there'll be less panicking in the hallways, and everyone can hopefully get to safety in an orderly fashion.

Similarly, you should create a plan for your family in case an intruder breaks into your home. Having a plan will help you look after every member of your family without letting your adrenaline get the best of you, and you won't be as quick to use a firearm when it isn't warranted.

REMEMBER

For any of your plans to work, though, you have to designate a safe room, as I describe earlier in this chapter, and do everything you can to not leave it after you're barricaded inside. You're essentially holding a defensive position.

>> If you live alone, your plan is simple: Get to the safe room, barricade the door, and call the police. (That's why I recommend keeping a phone in the safe room, but you might already have your cell phone on you.) Then unlock your safe in the event that you absolutely need to use your firearm.

If the intruder makes it to your safe room, announce that you've called the police and that you're armed. Hopefully that'll be the end of it. If not, they will still need to make it through the barricaded door.

TIP

While you're on the phone with the dispatcher, tell them where you are in the house so that they can notify the police officers before they arrive on the scene. This information will help ensure that the cops don't mistake you for the bad guy.

>> If you live with a partner or other adults, they need to know the plan as well. So if you tell them to run to the safe room, or use a code word, they'll know where to go and what to do.

Communication is key here. Talk through things and make sure everyone is on the same page before there's an emergency, and then practice the plan.

Don't be afraid to assign tasks, either. Another adult can help you barricade the door, or if they get to the safe room before you, they can dial 911.

>> If you have kids, your plan becomes a little more complicated. You and any other adults need to ensure that your children make it to the safe room. To do this, you have to practice ahead of time — just as you would practice a fire drill.

If you tell your kids to get to the safe room, or use a code word, they need to know which room to run to and where to hide once inside. They should also know to call 911 if they're the first to get to the room.

Take care when you practice any safe room drill with your kids. There's a good chance they've already run "active shooter" drills at school, which studies have shown to be traumatizing. You have to walk a fine line: Prepare them, be honest with them, but try not to scare them.

Understanding Self-Defense with a Firearm Outside the Home

Now this is a tricky subject! Before I dive in, I want to once again remind you to learn and live by the gun safety rules outlined in Chapter 1. Those rules need to be so engrained in your mind that they become instinctual and won't evaporate the moment you encounter a stressful situation. You must also follow your state's self-defense laws to a T, and I recommend taking a self-defense or firearms training course (or a few!), as I discuss in Chapter 12, to learn more. I can only scratch the surface here.

Broadly speaking, every state recognizes that you may have to defend yourself when you're out in public *in very specific circumstances.*

You can only use deadly force in a situation in which it's objectively reasonable to believe that such force is necessary to prevent imminent death or serious bodily harm to yourself or another person. A number of states also hold that if someone attacks you, you have a duty to retreat — escape if you can safely do so — before you can fight back with deadly force.

The exception is the castle doctrine. You don't have to retreat in your home.

However, a majority of states have also passed controversial *stand your ground* laws that effectively eliminate the need to retreat before you defend yourself outside the home. Florida was the first state to pass such a law in 2005, and many other states have followed suit. These laws vary between states, but most hold that as long as you're allowed to be in the location where the confrontation occurs and you're legally armed, you do not have to retreat before using deadly force.

These laws are also known as "shoot first" laws because they can embolden armed individuals and encourage what would otherwise be avoidable violence, as some high-profile cases have shown in recent years. Instead of retreating, some people decide to push forward, on the offensive, to use deadly force — and feel legally justified in doing so.

Here are some facts:

>> A 2016 study published in *JAMA Internal Medicine* showed that Florida's stand-your-ground law led to a 32-percent increase in monthly firearm homicide rates in that state.

>> A more recent 2021 study showed that these laws have led to 700 additional homicides each year.

>> Another study examining FBI homicide reports from 2014 to 2018 showed that in states with stand-your-ground laws, cases in which White shooters kill Black victims are deemed justifiable five times more frequently than when the situation is reversed.

You can see the trouble with these laws.

As a responsible gun owner, you should seriously question whether you need to carry a firearm in public, or keep one in your car, in the first place — something I discuss in greater detail in Chapter 11. If you're being honest with yourself, you might find that you don't need to have a weapon on you or within easy reach, so you can keep it locked up at home.

I'm reminded of the expression "If all you have is a hammer, everything looks like a nail." If you're armed, you might think your gun is the only way out of a confrontation. But you have other tools at your disposal, like your ability to escape or de-escalate the situation. With the latter, training courses can teach you how to change your stance and lower your voice to take some of the fire out of a conflict, for example.

I also recommend living your life with the duty to retreat as a guiding principle, even if you reside in a state that doesn't have such a requirement for self-defense. If you find yourself in a truly dangerous situation, try to escape if you can before you resort to other means.

Remember, it's self-defense. Never offense.

5
The Part of Tens

Gain the knowledge to debunk ten common myths about firearms.

Speak the language of guns fluently without mixing up terms and phrases.

Breathe new life into a vintage firearm in just ten steps.

Chapter **17**

Ten Common Myths about Firearms

From a physical or mechanical perspective, guns aren't that complex. As I describe in Chapter 3, and really this whole book, firearms are simple machines. You can take them apart to see how they tick.

But guns are quite complicated when you look at them from pretty much any other angle — historical, political, sociological, you name it.

In an effort to peel back some of those layers, I dedicate this chapter to ten of the most common myths and controversies surrounding gun ownership in the United States today. In this way, I hope to move past both the politics and the rhetoric to give you a better sense of the responsibility required for safely owning and securing a firearm.

WARNING

I talk about some heavy topics in this chapter, like gun violence and mass shootings, so please take care as you read on.

You might not agree with everything you encounter in the pages ahead, and that is totally fine. We can still be friends. Just know that I've done my best to include only objective, peer-reviewed research here.

REMEMBER

Although this chapter is full of research and statistics, the Everytown for Gun Safety Support Fund (www.everytownresearch.org) is a fantastic resource for continuing your education when it comes to gun violence, proven prevention methods, and much more.

Myth: "The Wild West Was Full of Gunplay"

You've probably heard of Wyatt Earp and the shootout at the OK Corral on October 26, 1881, in Tombstone, Arizona Territory. But did you know that it started because a few cowboys refused to follow the law and disarm on their way into town?

The law was simple: Town residents had to leave their guns at home while visitors had to check their guns at a hotel or the sheriff's office, and just like a coat check, they'd receive a token to hold onto until they were ready to retrieve their gun and leave town.

Many frontier towns had similarly strict gun laws, including Abilene, Deadwood, and Dodge City, based on those that first originated in the South in the early 1800s to prohibit citizens from carrying knives and firearms either openly or hidden on one's person.

Gun ownership was widespread back then, but according to historians, those towns that restricted weapons saw relatively few murders in a given year. Keeping the peace was good for business in an established settlement, in stark contrast to the mining and rail boomtowns that lacked law enforcement. So the Wild West wasn't quite as wild as what has been depicted in TV shows and movies for well over a hundred years.

Myth: "A Gun Will Make Me Safer"

I know the idea that guns make you safer might *feel* right. But statistically speaking, a gun will not necessarily make you safer. For example:

» According to a 2014 study published in the *Annals of Internal Medicine,* having access to a firearm doubles your chances of dying by homicide and triples your chances of dying by suicide.

>> A 2003 study published in the *American Journal of Public Health* shows that access to a gun in a domestic violence situation makes it five times more likely that the woman will be killed.

>> The unintentional shooting death rate in the U.S. is four times higher than the rate in other high-income countries, according to a 2019 study published in *Preventative Medicine*.

Now, I'm not here to make you regret purchasing a gun. Instead, you need to be clear-eyed about the risks and do everything you can to be a safe, responsible gun owner. Think of your family and community.

That's why I wrote this book. Memorize and follow the safety rules (as I discuss in Chapter 1), teach them to your family members (Chapter 5), invest in a sturdy safe (Chapter 6), take a training course (Chapter 12), follow all the other recommendations in this book, and don't be afraid to call out others for being irresponsible with their guns. Lives are too precious.

Myth: "Guns Don't Kill People; People Kill People"

There are a few problems with this myth, but the biggest is probably the fact that it diminishes the pain and suffering of so many people who have been injured or lost loved ones due to gun violence.

The goal of some, I think, is to say that guns are just tools — no better or worse than the people who use them. But guns are the only tools designed specifically to kill. That's why we don't have heated debates about hammers or screwdrivers.

I also want to point out that, although it's rare, guns can malfunction and discharge unintentionally. Google "gun recalls" and you'll see just how often manufacturers have to fix guns that can fire on their own. So in the most basic sense, yes, guns as inanimate objects can still injure and kill people.

Finally, people with access to guns kill more people than those who do not have access to guns. According to a 2019 study conducted by University of San Francisco and Harvard professors, the U.S. gun homicide rate is 24.9 times higher than that of other high-income countries. Everyone should see that as a big problem.

Myth: "Polymer Guns Won't Set off Metal Detectors"

In 1990's *Die Hard* 2, terrorists take control of an airport after smuggling guns through a security checkpoint. After one of the movie's many shootouts, Bruce Willis delivers my favorite speech: "That punk pulled a Glock 7 on me. You know what that is? It's a porcelain gun made in Germany. It doesn't show up on your airport X-ray machines here, and it costs more than what you make in a month!"

I always crack up at the number of inaccuracies. There is no Glock 7. Bruce's character is actually referring to the 9mm Glock 17, which was made in Austria (not Germany) with a polymer, or plastic, frame (not ceramic). And although it was indeed expensive at $550 in 1990 — or $1,183 in today's dollars — it will most certainly set off a metal detector.

The Glock 17 caused a bit of a panic when it hit our shores in 1986. (It didn't help that the former dictator of Libya made news when he purchased one that same year.) Though it wasn't the first gun to use a polymer frame, some were concerned that it could pass through a metal detector without setting off any alarms. The hubbub even led Congress to pass the Undetectable Firearms Act of 1988, which banned the sale or possession of any firearm that didn't contain at least 3.7 ounces of easily detected steel.

Congress settled on that seemingly random number after a series of compromises. But I can safely say that Glock pistols (and every other factory-made firearm, for that matter) contain a lot more steel than that thanks to their heavy-duty barrels and slides.

REMEMBER

These guns will absolutely set off alarms at airport security checkpoints, and they frequently do. In 2021 alone, TSA agents found 5,972 guns in passengers' carry-on luggage. That's 5,972 people who should read this book.

The one caveat is that 3D printing has indeed made it possible to create all-plastic, small-caliber, single-shot pistols that might remain undetected — if a TSA agent doesn't recognize the shape of the firearm as it passes through the X-ray machine. This possibility is obviously concerning, but if it's any consolation, these guns will typically shatter after firing a few shots.

Myth: "The Only Thing That Can Stop a Bad Guy with a Gun Is a Good Guy with a Gun"

This myth first appeared in response to a truly despicable mass shooting, so I have to discuss it in that context.

Statistically, police officers are really the only "good guys with guns" that stop "bad guys with guns," or active shooters, as they are known. It's extremely rare that armed civilians intervene and save the day.

In 2014, the FBI released a report studying mass shootings that occurred from 2000 to 2013. Of the 160 that the bureau identified, only 5 (3.1 percent) ended after an armed citizen in each case exchanged gunfire with the shooters. And of those five citizens, four were armed security guards.

Notably, 21 incidents (13.1 percent) ended when *unarmed* citizens successfully restrained the shooter. With the rest, police intervened, or the shooter decided to flee, surrender, or die by suicide. Which brings me to a related myth . . .

Myth: "Millions of People Defend Themselves with Guns Every Year"

This claim has been plaguing researchers for decades. In 1995, two criminologists published a report estimating that people use guns to defend themselves between 2.1 and 2.5 million times per year.

Other researchers question these figures, despite how often they're repeated. For example, that same study claims 200,000 respondents had to shoot their aggressors, and yet those numbers are not reflected in hospital records.

At the same time, it's incredibly difficult to measure "defensive gun uses" because of their subjective nature. One person might think they're defending themselves in an encounter when, in reality, they're escalating the situation by brandishing their weapon. So one person's defensive gun use could actually be aggravated assault or worse. Who's to say?

I also wonder how many "defenders" end up injuring or killing innocent bystanders by mistake.

A more recent Harvard study that examined data from the National Crime Victimization Survey found that people defended themselves with a gun in roughly 0.9 percent of crimes committed from 2007 to 2011. The research also showed that for every person who uses a gun in self-defense, nearly six people use a gun to commit a crime.

Myth: "Guns Can Blow You Away"

Thanks to movies and TV shows, some people believe that when a person is shot, they'll fly backward a certain distance. You might even see a bad guy fly across a room or through a big glass window in campier films.

The real world is still bound by the laws of physics, however.

Bullets travel at very high speeds and concentrate all their kinetic energy into a very small area, creating a lot of pressure. In most cases, this means bullets will penetrate a surface upon impact (or ricochet in some instances). Yet, because of their small size compared to humans, bullets don't have much momentum, and certainly not enough to knock someone back or "blow them away."

The reality is that if someone is shot, they might jolt or take a step or two backward, but this occurs from surprise or pain, not the force of the bullet. Remember that the next time you sit down to watch a cheesy action flick.

Myth: "Every Gun Sale Already Requires a Background Check"

False. Currently, federal law requires that licensed gun dealers conduct background checks whenever an unlicensed individual attempts to purchase a firearm. The goal is to ensure that the buyer is not legally prohibited from owning a gun for past criminal history, substance abuse, or a dishonorable discharge from the military, to name just a few examples.

But federally, no background check is required for guns sold by unlicensed individuals. So if Person A sells a gun to Person B at, say, a gun show or online, there is no mechanism to determine whether Person B is legally allowed to own firearms or to prevent the sale from going forward. And right now, this type of sale is totally legal on the federal level as long as Person A is not "in the business" of selling guns, which can be a little complicated to determine.

You can see how this situation would create an opening for gun trafficking — just like leaving your firearm unsecured at home. Thankfully, more than a dozen states have corrected this problem by requiring background checks for every single gun sale, regardless of location or who's selling the weapon.

REMEMBER

To learn more about the background check process, including holds and wait times, turn back to Chapter 4.

Myth: "Blame Video Games, Not Guns"

It's easy and quite common for people to blame video games after a teenage boy commits an act of gun violence, such as a mass shooting. But researchers have never been able to prove that violent video games make people violent. According to a 2004 report from the U.S. Secret Service and Department of Education, out of dozens of school attacks, only 12 percent of perpetrators showed an interest in violent video games. Instead, violent video games should be considered in the larger context of a threat assessment.

More recently, in 2017, the American Psychological Association warned against correlating an act of real-world violence to the perpetrator's exposure to violent media, concluding that there wasn't enough evidence to support such claims.

People also play the same video games around the world, yet the levels of gun violence are disproportionate. For example, in Japan, people spend much more money on video games per year than Americans, but the country rarely experiences more than 10 gun deaths per year, whereas the U.S. experienced 39,707 and 45,222 gun deaths in 2019 and 2020, according to the Centers for Disease Control and Prevention. Easy access to guns is the most obvious culprit, not violent media.

Myth: "I Love Guns — They Make Me Who I Am"

Here in the South, I see my fair share of "2A" and rifle bumper stickers on a daily basis. I've met people who have gun images tattooed on their bodies.

I'm not here to judge. The Second Amendment means different things to different people. But you don't have to let guns define your personality.

If you get only one thing out of this book, I hope it's the notion that gun owner-ship should never be taken lightly. Firearms demand respect because of what they can do.

However, the countless people whose lives have been affected by gun violence deserve even greater respect. Statistically, your chances of running into someone who has had a traumatic experience involving a firearm in the U.S. are pretty high. They could pass you on the sidewalk, share an elevator with you, or drive next to you on the road, and you might never know. So be considerate. Think twice about broadcasting your passion for firearms, or devoting your life to them. It's not a harmless hobby.

REMEMBER

As I mention in Chapter 5, if you're truly serious about protecting your family and home, you shouldn't advertise the fact that you own guns. Otherwise, you're just asking for trouble from criminals. And you should also think twice about carrying a gun in public, as I discuss in Chapter 16.

Chapter **18**

Ten (or More) Gun Terms You're Using Incorrectly

While vacationing in Mexico a few years ago, I tried to order hot dogs using what fragments of Spanish I remembered from classes in high school. I asked for "*dos perros caliente, por favor,*" and the cook immediately burst out laughing before telling me to say "*salchichas*" instead. Apparently, I had ordered two warm canines.

The gun world has its own language barrier. There are so many different words and phrases to describe all the various firearm types, components, and uses. *Some* words are interchangeable in a given context, but others should never be confused. Trying to figure out all the jargon can be daunting, if not headache inducing.

Worse yet, some gun enthusiasts treat the terminology as a way to "gatekeep" others. Use a certain word or phrase incorrectly and you're immediately labeled as someone who can't possibly understand guns — even if they generally knew what you were trying to say in the first place.

Well, whether you're new to firearms or could use a refresher, I'm here to make your life easier. In this chapter, I explain some of the most common mistakes I hear when people talk about guns in an effort to elevate the conversation and make sure everyone's on the same page.

Saying "Clip" Instead of "Magazine"

This one tops the list because it drives gun enthusiasts absolutely nuts. Although I get the irritation, I also understand what people are describing when they say "clip." (So maybe take it easy, gun folks?)

A *magazine* is simply the part of a firearm that holds ammunition. Many older weapons had integral or fixed magazines that you had to push rounds down into to load. To speed up that process, inventors created the *clip*, which holds several rounds so that it's easier to load into an integral magazine all at once. Classic military rifles like the M1 Garand of World War II use clips.

But the 20th century also saw the dawn of detachable magazines for even faster reloading, and this is what most semi-auto firearms use today. (For a little more backstory, check out Chapter 3.) Figure 18-1 shows both a clip and a magazine.

FIGURE 18-1:
A clip (left) and a detachable magazine (right).

Courtesy of asbtkb/Adobe Stock

Bullets, Cartridges, and More

Speaking of ammunition (or "ammo" if you're in a hurry), it might be helpful to break down some of the more common terms that get confused.

In the simplest terms, the *cartridge* is what you load into the gun. It encompasses the casing, primer, gunpowder, and bullet. When you fire the gun, the primer ignites the gunpowder in the casing, which propels the *bullet,* the projectile that exits the muzzle of the gun (see Figure 18-2).

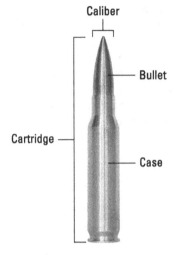

Caliber

Bullet

Cartridge

Case

FIGURE 18-2:
The bullet is the projectile loaded into the case.

Cartridge, *round,* and *load* are interchangeable. But you can see why the term *bullet* is not. So, although saying that a gun or magazine "holds X number of bullets" is technically correct, your best bet is to stick with "cartridges" or "rounds." Otherwise, gun enthusiasts might look at you sideways.

Finally, in the strictest sense, *caliber* means the diameter of the bullet in inches. For example, a .45-caliber bullet is approximately 0.45 inches in diameter. Europeans prefer to use millimeters to express the same measurement, so a 9mm bullet is 9 millimeters in diameter, but saying "9mm caliber" in a sentence would be technically incorrect because you're not using inches.

In a broader sense, however, it's totally fine to include millimeters when talking about various calibers collectively. If someone asks what caliber your gun is, for example, just say it's a 9mm. You'll be branded a weirdo if you refer to your 9mm as a ".355."

To learn more about various types of ammunition, flip back to Chapter 9.

Accuracy versus Precision

In the firearms world, it's common to hear the terms "accuracy" and "precision" used interchangeably, but they don't mean the same thing. *Accuracy* refers to how close your shot is to the desired point of impact. So if you aim for the bullseye of a target and hit the bullseye, you are accurate.

Precision refers to how close your shots are to each other. If all your hits on the target are next to each other, you're precise. But if you're aiming for the bullseye and can seem only to cluster hits in the bottom-left corner, you're precise but not accurate. The goal is to be both, as shown in Figure 18-3.

| Not accurate or precise | Precise but not accurate | Accurate but not precise | Accurate and precise |

Courtesy of Casper1774Studio/Getty Images

The Two Meanings of Pistol

This one might seem a little odd. A pistol is a pistol, right? Well, not always.

To some people, a *pistol* means *any handgun* — and a few dictionaries support this definition, stating that the term applies to any firearm designed to be operated with one hand. This meaning is a bit antiquated, however.

On the other hand (pun absolutely intended), most gun enthusiasts will tell you that *pistol* applies only to *semi-automatic handguns.* This meaning creates two distinct categories among handguns — pistols and revolvers — making it easier to wade through all the options out there.

In the end, use the latter definition if you want to sound young, hip, and well informed. And don't worry about the fact that most starter pistols used to begin track and field competitions are actually revolvers.

Semi-Automatic versus Automatic

If you've ever seen a reenactor load and fire a flintlock musket, you know just how slow and labor intensive the process could be. But as I discuss in Chapter 3, over time, inventors found ways of essentially automating some of the steps involved to increase a weapon's rate of fire.

A *semi-automatic* weapon allows you to fire one shot per trigger pull, and as long as the magazine still has ammunition, the gun will load the next round into the chamber for you. To fire again, you have to pull the trigger again. In other words, if loading and firing are the two main steps involved, a semi-auto will do the loading, or half of the work, for you. Hence the "semi" part.

An *automatic* weapon, or machine gun, will continue loading and firing as long as you depress the trigger and the gun has ammunition. This is also known as "fully automatic" or "full-auto" fire.

Lastly, a *select-fire* weapon — like most military rifles — allows you to toggle between semi- and fully automatic firing modes.

REMEMBER

In the United States, the National Firearms Act (NFA) of 1934 was the first federal regulation to restrict the ownership of weapons capable of fully automatic fire, and the Firearms Owners Protection Act (FOPA) of 1986 banned civilians from owning machine guns manufactured after May 19, 1986. To learn more about these federal regulations, turn back to Chapter 2.

Assault Rifles and Assault Weapons

A lot of people on both sides of the political spectrum mix up these two terms, which is absolutely understandable. (If you hear someone make this same mistake, maybe suggest they buy this book at full price?)

Assault rifle is a military term used to describe a select-fire weapon that uses intermediate cartridges and detachable magazines, allowing a soldier to assault an enemy position with a high volume of fire. The term quite literally arrived with the German *Sturmgewehr 44* (or "assault rifle" of 1944 in English) of World War II, and "intermediate cartridges" are rifle rounds that fit between pistol rounds and large, high-caliber rifle rounds in terms of size and performance.

Assault weapon is a policy term that varies depending on what law you're looking at. The federal assault weapons ban that lasted from 1994 to 2004 — which serves as the basis for a few states' current bans — explicitly outlawed several military-style weapons by name and further defined assault weapons as semi-automatic pistols, rifles, and shotguns that 1) use detachable magazines holding 10 or more rounds and 2) have a few features derived from military weapons, such as collapsible stocks, pistol grips, and flash hiders.

To use the most obvious example that captures headlines, the U.S. military's select-fire M16 is an *assault rifle.* And because the semi-automatic version of the M16 designed for the civilian market, the AR-15, has many of the same features, it is currently considered an *assault weapon* in states like California and Maryland, and it was banned from 1994 to 2004 on the federal level.

Why Suppressors Aren't Quite Silencers

A *sound suppressor* is a device that reduces a gun's sound signature, or report, when it's fired. Traditional suppressors are tubes that you attach to the muzzle of a firearm, but they come in all shapes and sizes today, and some are even seamlessly integrated into barrels.

Note that I say "reduces" and not "eliminates." Although you could call a sound suppressor a *silencer* — as Hiram Percy Maxim, the man who invented the first one, did back in 1909 — they do not completely silence or mute gunshots, despite their whisper-quiet depictions in action movies and spy thrillers.

In reality, although sound suppressors virtually eliminate a host weapon's muzzle flash, making it very difficult to figure out where a shot came from, they merely muffle the sound of gunfire, much as a muffler does for a car engine. (Maxim went on to design those, too, by the way.) You still need to wear hearing protection with suppressed firearms.

In the end, *silencer* and *suppressor* are completely interchangeable. The latter is just a tad more accurate (or precise?) than the other. Sticklers may get a case of the vapors if you say "silencer," but federal laws actually use that language, as do a few of the companies that make and sell them.

Standard and High Capacity

How much ammo does your gun hold? What a *loaded* question!

As I mentioned, almost every firearm today uses detachable magazines. A 9mm Glock 17 pistol typically leaves the factory, or "comes standard," with 17-round magazines. Thus, its *standard capacity* is 17 rounds, which is kind of the benchmark for most full-sized, striker-fired 9mm pistols today. The slightly smaller Glock 19 comes standard with 15-round magazines.

Are these *high-capacity* magazines? According to several states, including California, Hawaii, New York, and Maryland — not to mention the now-expired federal assault weapons ban — yes. These jurisdictions have outlawed high-capacity or large-capacity magazines (LCMs), which they define as detachable magazines that hold more than ten rounds.

Politically, the ten-round limit is contentious. But looking at things objectively, or historically, anything over ten rounds *is* pretty high. For hundreds of years, firearms were single-shot weapons. In the 1800s, revolvers raised the onboard capacity to five or six rounds (roughly two-thirds less than a Glock 17), and the Civil War prompted the development of lever-action rifles that held more ammunition. In the 20th century, the world wars brought about higher-capacity weapons that later made their way into the hands of civilians — like the Browning *Hi-Power* pistol, which was named that because it held 13 rounds.

Clearly, wars and later 20th century developments led to higher capacities. But thankfully, most of us don't live on battlefields.

Grip and Handle Defined

In the gun world, *grip* can denote 1) the part of the firearm that you grasp and hold onto, or 2) how you hold onto the gun. You hold the pistol's grip, for example, and you also want a firm grip when you fire.

The gun's grip might look like a handle and act like a handle, but you call it the grip because *handle* specifically refers to controlling and manipulating the firearm. You have to be careful when you handle a gun, and firearms instructors teach gun-handling skills to their students.

If you're a good gun handler, you know how to establish a solid grip on the gun's grip. Can you handle that?

Chapter **19**

Ten Steps to Restore a Classic Gun

irearms are durable goods. Because of their materials and construction, they can last hundreds of years, especially if you take care of them. But you might also inherit vintage guns that were *not* properly maintained.

You could send the antique to a reputable restoration company and spend a small fortune getting it back into pristine shape, but if you're moderately handy and have the right tools, you might be able to tackle the job yourself.

In this chapter, I take you through the process of restoring an antique gun in ten easy steps. By the end, your great-great-grandpa's gun might not look "factory new," but you'll be the proud owner of a piece of history.

WARNING

However, if you're hesitant about your abilities, please leave the work to a professional. I don't want you to ruin an old gun because you got bitten by the DIY bug! I'm also assuming the gun is so old that a warranty no longer applies, and thus you won't lose coverage for altering the firearm.

Unload and Inspect the Firearm

The first thing you should do with a vintage gun — or any firearm that isn't being used — is make sure it's unloaded. If the gun has a detachable magazine, go ahead and remove it. Lock open the action and ensure that there isn't a round in the chamber. Retract the slide (for semi-auto pistols) or bolt (for rifles and shotguns), or open the cylinder (for revolvers). If the gun uses an integral magazine, you need to empty it as well.

If you can't figure out how to release the magazine, lock the action open, or engage the safety (if there is one) at this point, try to learn more about the gun through some online sleuthing, as I describe in the next section.

WARNING

Until you can unload the weapon and ensure that it's safe, stay away from the trigger. Always follow the four rules of gun safety outlined in Chapter 1.

After you've verified that the gun is unloaded, take a closer look. Jot down any markings or serial numbers you come across; these might help you identify the gun's caliber, manufacturer, point of origin, and production date.

Also keep an eye out for areas that are broken, missing parts, or need a little extra TLC, like the barrel's rifling. If you can already tell that the gun needs serious work, start an inventory of what needs to be repaired or replaced.

Research the Make and Model

Hopefully, at this point you've at least figured out the gun's manufacturer and model. I know that can be a tall order for some weapons built for World War I and II, when several manufacturers pitched in to produce the same models, including companies that had nothing to do with guns before the wars broke out — like the Singer Sewing Machine Company, which made a few hundred 1911-style pistols for American soldiers.

Now it's time to learn more about the gun. The internet has some great information as well as a ton of misleading information, so be careful. Wikipedia can give you a broad overview of the weapon, but check the footnotes for original sources, including books, articles, and videos. YouTube might also host a few videos of experts discussing the gun in question. If you can find research from historians, museums, and auction houses, you're on the right track.

As you learn more about the gun, try to answer these questions:

>> How does the gun operate, and what ammunition does it use?

>> What does a mint-condition version of this particular gun look like?

>> Are any parts or components missing?

>> How rare or valuable is this make and model? Who used it?

>> What is the gun made out of? Are the metal components mostly steel or aluminum? If the gun has some wooden components, what kind of wood? Does it have any special or unique materials that might need special care?

Decide What You Want to Do with It

After you've made yourself into an amateur historian in one very specific area — I'm still waiting for someone to bring up the Smith & Wesson Model 1-1/2 in casual conversation — you have a big question to answer: What do you want to do with the gun?

Do you want to hold onto the gun and pass it down to your children? Or maybe you learned how rare and valuable the gun is during your research and are now interested in selling it to a collector.

TIP

Regarding that last point: If the gun is super rare, most collectors would probably prefer that you *don't* attempt to restore it, or at least leave it to a professional, because if you mess up the gun's finish or another aspect of it, it'll lose its value.

WARNING

You might be tempted to get the gun back into "shooting shape" and hit the range with it, but doing so could be dangerous. You have to consider several factors here, including the gun's age, condition, and whether you can find new, low-pressure ammo for it. (Avoid vintage or high-pressure rounds, which could cause the gun to crack or explode.) You need to have a professional gunsmith inspect the gun to see whether it can be safely operated after it's restored. But even then, you might still run into trouble, so be careful.

Carefully Disassemble and Clean It

A good cleaning can help you get a better idea of the gun's condition, so you'll need to take gun the gun apart and break out your dedicated cleaning kit. (Need help with that? Turn to Chapter 8.)

Hopefully your research has given you some idea of how to take the firearm apart and, more importantly, put it back together again. You'll want to detail strip the gun all the way down to the nuts and bolts. Take your time. You might need screwdrivers and punches.

TIP

I also recommend that you take pictures of every step of the disassembly process so that you have something to reference when it's time to reinstall small pieces like pins and springs. Old guns can be very complicated.

After you've carefully taken the gun apart, wipe every component down with a dry toothbrush or rag to remove whatever films and residues have accumulated over the years. Then scrub the metal components with a cleaning solvent. For wood — like stocks, grip panels, and forends — use a slightly damp rag to remove any dirt or buildup.

The barrel requires a bit more attention; I outline that process in Chapter 8.

Remove Light Rust from Metal Surfaces

I've restored a few old guns covered in rust because they were left in hot, humid environments for years. (Attics are terrible places to keep guns, by the way.) Heavy rust will eat into metal and create little dimples called pitting.

Even if you can't remove all the rust, the goal is to limit the spread and ensure that the metal isn't damaged any further. I guide you through these three steps in Chapter 8, but the trick is to start by cleaning the area with solvent or CLP, which should remove some of the surface rust. Then you should try wiping the affected area with Flitz metal polish. If there's still rusting and pitting, it's time to gently scrub the area with the finest steel wool and lubricant. See Chapter 8 for more details.

When you're done, be sure to wipe away any lubricant you've used with a rag and inspect the area. If you still see some rusting or pitting, that's totally okay, as I discuss in the following pages.

Replace Any Missing or Damaged Parts

A friend of mine owns a Japanese Type 99 rifle that his grandfather brought back home after World War II, but somewhere along the way, the entire bolt went missing. So to restore that gun, he'd have to find a replacement bolt. But where do you begin?

Several online retailers offer replacement parts for classic weapons, especially those of the military-surplus variety. Look for reputable dealers, and if you want the gun to retain its value, make sure the component is authentic, meaning it was produced by the gun's original manufacturer around the same time. I do not recommend purchasing a newly manufactured part that merely looks like an old part unless you can't find an original.

REMEMBER

Because of how guns were made in the past, the replacement part might require special fitting — essentially meticulous filing — so that it can be installed properly. This task might also require a gunsmith.

Refinish the Metal — or Not

Say you've cleaned the gun to the best of your abilities and removed as much of the surface rust as possible. Do you need to go any further in restoring the metal? That depends.

Some people, myself included, prefer that vintage guns look worn and weathered. In my mind, it adds to their appeal and speaks to their age. Many collectors prefer that rarer guns retain their original finishes, too.

On the other hand, if you want the gun to look "factory new," especially if it's a common model, you have two options:

>> If your gun's metal parts were originally blued, or finished with a black oxide coating that actually looks blue in color, a "cold bluing" kit will allow you to restore that finish at home. The quality of the bluing depends on how well you polish and degrease the parts beforehand.

I don't recommend this option for novices because these kits use toxic chemicals, and it's difficult to apply the finish evenly. If you go this route, follow the kit's instructions carefully and obey state and EPA regulations when it comes to using and disposing of the chemicals.

>> The second option is to contact a professional restoration service. Obviously, this is a more expensive option, but the best gun restorers can handle more complicated finishes, like nitre bluing and color casehardening, and make truly old guns look brand new.

Restore the Wood

There's nothing quite like the feel of old wooden stocks on classic guns. They tell a story just like the metal components. So it's up to you whether you want to go any further than simply wiping away any dirt or grime with a damp rag.

Everyone seems to have a different technique for refinishing wood, and I'll defer to the carpenters out there, but the following steps offer the best method I've seen for guns.

WARNING

Just make sure you're working in a well-ventilated area and dispose of used rags immediately. Don't leave them in a pile, or throw them in the trash without first soaking them in water or letting them dry thoroughly because they can combust!

1. **Carefully remove all the hardware from the wood, like screws and sling loops, and brush off any small particles or debris.**

2. **Scrub the wood with a rag soaked in lacquer thinner.**

   This removes the old finish, and you can touch up rough spots with a wire brush, but don't get too enthusiastic and start sanding the wood down. There's history in those nicks and grooves, and if you alter the wood's shape or edges, you might impact the gun's operation when it's reassembled.

3. **Let the wood dry.**

4. **When the wood's completely dry, apply a thin coat of linseed oil.** (Tung oil is another popular option for gun stocks.) If you want the wood to be dark, you can add in a bit of oil-based walnut stain.

5. **Wipe away any excess oil and let the wood dry again.** It should darken over time. Do not leave the wood untreated because it can swell or warp over time and cause problems with the gun's functioning.

Clean, Lubricate, and Reassemble It

After you have the metal and wood pieces in good shape again, it's time to clean them one more time, add some lubricant, and put the gun back together again. If you need help with that last step, look over the pictures you took during the disassembly process.

Then, depending on the gun, rack the slide, run the bolt, or spin the cylinder to ensure that everything's back in its correct position. Also test the safety mechanisms and release buttons to ensure that they function properly. If not, you've got to work backward until you find the mistake.

Have a Gunsmith Back Up your Work

This final step might seem like overkill, but you have so much to gain from having a professional gunsmith inspect the firearm when you're done with it. As I mention earlier in this chapter, they can examine the major components and assess whether the gun is safe to shoot again. You can't spend too much on peace of mind.

You don't want to end up in the ER because you thought everything about the gun was "fine" and didn't consult an expert.

On top of that, if you're intent on selling the gun, there's a good chance the gunsmith will know a collector or reenactor who might be interested in it.

But even if the gun is just for you and your family, it never hurts to have another person who loves classic guns and their history appreciate all the time and energy you've put into this project.

Index

H

"hammerless" model, 58

handguards, 47

handguns
about, 56
ammunition for, 41, 128–129
bullets for, 134–136
establishing firm grips on, 204–206
revolvers, 56–58
semi-automatic, 58–63
statistics on deaths by, 22

handle, 286

handloaded ammunition, 110

hangfire, 237

Hawaii, 27–28, 73, 76, 184, 285

head, 129

headstamp, 129, 140

high capacity, 285

history
of firearms, 36–41
as a reason for gun ownership, 9–10

holds, for purchases, 75–76

holsters
about, 146–148
for training courses, 189

"Home Firearms Safety" course, 186

homes
about, 81–82
dangers of overpenetration, 87–89
protection from the inside, 260–262
protection from the outside, 258–260
talking with people outside the family, 86–87
talking with the family, 82–85
upgrades to, 159–161

humidity, firearms and, 104

hunter education course, 243–244

hunting and sport shooting
about, 241
attending your first match, 256
competition gear, 254–256
competition in, 251–256
ethical hunters, 244–246
hunter education courses, 243–244
hunting gear, 249–250
preparing for, 242–250
as a reason for gun ownership, 9
respecting other hunters, 246
shooting disciplines, 251–254
state wildlife agencies, 242–243
types of hunting, 246–248

hybrid casings, 129

I

icons, explained, 2–3

identifying common wear points, 120–121

IHEA (International Hunter Education Association), 243

Illinois, 73, 76

indoor lights, timers for, 261

Industrial Revolution, 39

inside-the-waistband (IWB) carry, 147, 176

inside-the-waistband (IWB) holsters, 147

inspecting classic guns, 288

instructors, for training courses, 192–193

integral suppressors, 158

interior inspections, 118

intermediate cartridges, 283

internal ballistics, 132

internal magazines, checking guns with, 18

International Hunter Education Association (IHEA), 243

Internet resources
besmartforkids.org, 104
Cheat Sheet, 3
Civilian Marksmanship Program (CMP), 251
Everytown Gun Law Navigator, 30
Everytown Gun Law Rankings, 30
for gun regulations, 30–31
International Hunter Education Association (IHEA), 243
"Personal Firearms Record," 112
"Resources for Victims and Survivors of Gun Violence," 85

investment, as a purchase consideration, 69

iron sights, 150–151, 159, 216

isosceles stance, 208–209, 210

IWB (inside-the-waistband) carry, 147, 176

IWB (inside-the-waistband) holsters, 147

J

jacketed hollow points (JHPs), 135

JAMA Internal Medicine, 267

JHPs (jacketed hollow points), 135

K

Kalashnikov, Mikhail, 47

Kennedy, Robert F., 23

keypad locks, 100–101

kneeling, shooting while, 211–212

kneepads, for training courses, 190

L

land, respecting the, 245

landscaping, 259

N

naming conventions, 36–37

National Firearms Act (1934), 21–23, 162, 283

National Instant Criminal Background Check System (NICS), 24, 75

National Survey of Fishing, Hunting, and Wildlife-Associated Recreation, 246

Nebraska, 73

neighbors, notifying of gun ownership, 86–87

New Jersey, 27–28, 73, 76

New York, 27–28, 73, 285

New Zealand, 33

NICS (National Instant Criminal Background Check System), 24, 75

9mm bullet, 131

"noise reduction rating" (NRR), 198

nonhunters, respecting, 246

normal wear and tear, 119–122

North Carolina, 73

NRR ("noise reduction rating"), 198

O

off-body options, 148, 178

off-limit locations, 174–175

Olympics, 253–254

open carry, 175–176, 178–179

open holsters, drawing from, 178–179

open-tip match (OTM) bullets, 137, 138

optics, 150–153

Oregon, 29, 92

Oswald, Lee Harvey, 23

OTM (open-tip match) bullets, 137, 138

O/U (over/under) models, 52

outside-the-waistband (OWB) carry, 146, 176–177

overall length, specifications for, 69

overcoming cross-eye dominance, 222–223

overpenetration, dangers of, 87–89

over/under (O/U) models, 52

OWB (outside-the-waistband) carry, 146, 176–177

P

"+P" rounds, 111

"+P+" rounds, 111

paddle holsters, 147

Parkerizing, 120

Parks and Wildlife Department, 242

passive earmuffs, 198

pellets, 51

Penal Code 198.5, 263

"permitless carry," 174

"Personal Firearms Record," 112

Picatinny rails, 49, 150–151

"Pistol 101" course, 186

pistols
    about, 282
    reloading, 227–233

piston, 47

plastic casings, 129

PLCAA (Protection of Lawful Commerce in Arms Act, 2005), 25, 106

"plug and lay" parts, 122

pocket carry, 147, 177

pocket holsters, 147

point of aim (POA), 159, 220

point of impact (POI), 159, 220

police
    about, 258
    notifying of gun ownership, 86
    stops by, 169

polymer guns, 274

polymer-tipped bullets, 137, 138, 139

position, for shooting, 207–213

precision, compared with accuracy, 282

precision matches, 251, 255–256

predator hunting, 246

primer, 41, 130, 141

projectiles, 141

prone, shooting while, 212–213

Protection of Lawful Commerce in Arms Act (PLCAA, 2005), 25, 106

publications
    American Journal of Public Health, 173
    JAMA Internal Medicine, 267

pump-action shotguns, 54–55

purchases
    about, 65
    first trip to gun store, 66–70
    gun shows, 77
    new *vs.* used, 71
    requirements for, 72–76
    trying before, 69–70

purpose, as a purchase consideration, 67–68

push/pull grip, 209

Q

quarry, respecting the, 244–245

R

racking the slide, 230–231

range bag, 163

rangefinder, for hunting, 250

reassembling, of classic guns, 293

recalls, 95

receivers, 49

recoil shields, 163

recoil spring, 47–48, 120

recordkeeping, importance of, 112

recreational shooting, as a reason for gun ownership, 9

About the Author

Greg Lickenbrock is a senior firearms analyst and technical advisor for Everytown for Gun Safety, the largest non-profit organization in the United States dedicated to reducing gun violence. Before that, he served as an editor and writer for several outdoor and firearm-related magazines, including *Combat Handguns* and *Guns of the Old West*, giving him the opportunity to attend training courses and test hundreds of firearms. He was also a teacher and earned a Master of Fine Arts in creative writing from the University of Montana and a Bachelor of Arts in English from the University of Florida.

Author's Acknowledgments

I would like to thank several people for making this book a reality, including my executive editor, Steve Hayes, for guiding the book's development; my wonderful project editor, Susan Christophersen, who showed me the ropes and polished my writing; Ryan Busse, the best technical editor I could've asked for; and Wiley's exceptional production staff.

I'd also like to thank my colleagues at Everytown for their support, for working tirelessly to make our streets safer, as well as my friends and family for their love and dedication. It takes a village, and I couldn't have done it without you all — especially my parents, who always fostered my creativity.

Finally, thank you, Sarah, the love of my life, for always inspiring me. You make every day better than the last.

Publisher's Acknowledgments

Executive Editor: Steven Hayes

Project and Copy Editor: Susan Christophersen

Technical Editor: Ryan Busse

Production Editor: Pradesh Kumar

Cover Image: